Interpreting
Consumer Choice

Routledge Interpretive Marketing Research

EDITED BY STEPHEN BROWN AND BARBARA B. STERN, *University of Ulster, Northern Ireland and Rutgers, the State University of New Jersey, USA*

Recent years have witnessed an 'interpretative turn' in marketing and consumer research. Methodologists from the humanities are taking their place alongside those drawn from the traditional social sciences.

Qualitative and literary modes of marketing discourse are growing in popularity. Art and aesthetics are increasingly firing the marketing imagination.

This series brings together the most innovative work in the burgeoning interpretative marketing research tradition. It ranges across the methodological spectrum from grounded theory to personal introspection, covers all aspects of the postmodern marketing 'mix', from advertising to product development, and embraces marketing's principal sub-disciplines.

1. The Why of Consumption
Edited by S. Ratneshwar, Glen Mick and Cynthia Huffman

2. Imagining Marketing
Art, Aesthetics and the Avant-garde
Edited by Stephen Brown and Anthony Patterson.

3. Marketing and Social Construction
Exploring the Rhetorics of Managed Consumption
Chris Hackley

4. Visual Consumption
Jonathan Schroeder

5. Consuming Books
The Marketing and Consumption of Literature
Edited by Stephen Brown

6. The Undermining of Beliefs in the Autonomy and Rationality of Consumers
John O'Shaugnessy and Nicholas Jackson O'Shaugnessy

7. Marketing Discourse
A Critical Perspective
Per Skålén, Markus Fellesson and Martin Fougère

8. Explorations in Consumer Culture Theory
Edited by John F. Sherry Jr. and Eileen Fisher

9. Interpretation in Social Life, Social Science, and Marketing
John O'Shaugnessy

10. Interpreting Consumer Choice
The Behavioral Perspective Model
Gordon R. Foxall

Also available in Routledge Interpretive Marketing Research series:

Representing Consumers
Voices, views and visions
Edited by Barbara B. Stern

Romancing the Market
Edited by Stephen Brown, Anne Marie Doherty and Bill Clarke

Consumer Value
A framework for analysis and research
Edited by Morris B. Holbrook

Marketing and Feminism
Current issues and research
Edited by Miriam Catterall, Pauline
Maclaran and Lorna Stevens

Interpreting Consumer Choice

The Behavioral Perspective Model

Gordon R. Foxall

Routledge
Taylor & Francis Group
New York   London

First published 2010
by Routledge
270 Madison Ave, New York, NY 10016

Simultaneously published in the UK
by Routledge
2 Park Square, Milton Park, Abingdon, Oxon OX14 4RN

Routledge is an imprint of the Taylor & Francis Group, an informa business

Library of Congress Cataloging in Publication Data
Foxall, G. R.
    Interpreting consumer choice : the behavioral perspective model / Gordon R. Foxall.
       p. cm. — (Routledge interpretive marketing research ; 10)
    Includes bibliographical references and index.
    1. Consumer behavior.   2. Consumers' preferences.   3. Consumers—Attitudes.
    I. Title.
    HF5415.32.F686 2010
    658.8'342—dc22
    2009017565

Material incorporated in this book has previously been published in Foxall, G. R. "'Science and interpretation in consumer research: a radical behaviourist perspective," which
appeared in the *European Journal of Marketing*, 29(9), 1995, 3—99. This has been
augmented by material from the *Journal of Marketing Management*, *Journal of Economic Psychology*, and *Advances in Consumer Research*.

ISBN10: 0-415-47760-3 (hbk)
ISBN10: 0-203-86689-4 (ebk)

ISBN13: 978-0-415-47760-4 (hbk)
ISBN13: 978-0-203-86689-4 (ebk)

Contents

List of Figures		ix
List of Tables		xi
List of Boxes		xiii
1	Overview of the BPM	1
2	The Story So Far	13
3	Ways of Wondering	38
4	The Meaning of Consumer Behavior	64
5	A Model of Interpretation	91
6	Interpreting Consumer Choice	113
7	The Nature of the Interpretation	148
	Afterword	161
Bibliography		163
Index		181

Figures

1.1   Summative Behavioral Perspective Model.   9

1.2   The BPM Contingency Matrix.   10

1.3   Operant classes of consumer behavior.   11

6.1   BPM interpretation of saving and financial asset
       management.   127

6.2   Adopter categories as defined by Rogers and the BPM.   130

Tables

5.1   Three Levels of Interpretive Analysis   96

6.1   Ecological Adaptation of Consumer Operants to
       Marketing Environments   135

Boxes

3.1   The essence of operant behaviorism.   51

3.2   Epistemological basis of radical behaviorism: ontology.   53

3.3   Epistemological basis of radical behaviorism: methodology.   54

4.1   Comparison of the treatment of behavior settings in eco-behavioral science.   71

4.2   Schedules and patterns of reinforcement.   73

4.3   Recent developments in the study of "hedonic consumption."   81

1 Overview of the BPM

> Obviously we cannot predict or control human behavior in daily life with the precision obtained in the laboratory, but we can nevertheless use results from the laboratory to interpret behavior elsewhere. Such an interpretation of human behavior in daily life has been criticized as metascience, but all the sciences resort to something much like it . . . [T]he principles of genetics are used to interpret the facts of evolution, as the behavior of substances under high pressures and temperatures are used to interpret geological events in the history of the earth. What is happening in interstellar space, where control is out of the question, is largely a matter of interpretation in this sense . . . In much the same way principles emerging from an experimental analysis of behavior have been applied in the design of education, psychotherapy, incentive systems in industry, penology, and in many other fields.
>
> —B. F. Skinner (1974, pp. 228–229)

The impetus for a program of consumer research that takes radical behaviorism as its initial foundation lies in the prevailing success not of that paradigm but of that of the cognitive psychology that in some respects has superseded it. Consumer research in the context of contemporary marketing-oriented economies has been, since its inception in the 1960s, overwhelmingly cognitive. Since cognitivism was also the dominant framework of conceptualization and analysis in psychology at that time, many of its underlying assumptions and methodological tenets were taken for granted in the earliest stages of the development of modern consumer psychology. The governing paradigm in any subject area is scarcely subjected to criticism with the same intellectual rigor as those schools of thought that are not in the ascendant, and many of the explanatory conventions that were adopted in the new approach to consumer behavior seemed to go unquestioned even when the empirical (and, sometimes, the logical) basis for their acceptance was shaky. The need for an intellectual agenda that would seek to establish the place and role of cognitive psychology, assuming it deserved to have them, in consumer research led to the investigations that have become known as the Behavioral Perspective Model, or BPM, research program. The choice of radical behaviorism stemmed from its minimal deployment of theoretical terms, its avoidance of cognitive terminology, and its insistence on explaining behavioral responses exclusively by reference to environmental stimuli. In establishing how far one could progress with such a minimalist program, it would be possible to ascertain how far an alternative, cognitive explanation would have to be incorporated into any attempt at understanding consumer choice, and how this might be accomplished. Perhaps there would be no need for a cognitive framework; perhaps the need for such a paradigm would entirely eclipse the behaviorist approach; perhaps some kind of integration of the two would become necessary such that neither was overshadowed by the other but each functioned usefully on its own explanatory level.

The BPM research program has five conceptually distinct but overlapping and continuing phases: (i) *conceptual*: a period of critical analysis of the prevailing cognitive paradigm from the standpoint of an alternative, behaviorist theory (1980–1990); (ii) *theoretical*:the development of the BPM as a means of representing the radical behaviorist methodology in a manner appropriate for the analysis of economic behavior and its use as an interpretive device (1989–2000); (iii) *empirical*:the use of the model to predict consumers' affective responses to purchase and consumption environments (1997–2009); (iv) *behavioral economics*: the development of matching theory and behavioral economics approaches based on the BPM variables (2000–2009); and (v) *philosophical*: the development of post-behaviorist models of behavioral explanation, intentional behaviorism, and superpersonal cognitive psychology (2003–2009). None of these is completed; indeed each is needed in order to stimulate the progress of the others; each has antecedents that predate and projections that postdate the temporal ranges suggested here. The dates are approximate and only indicative; this book is nevertheless concerned with the second, interpretive phase. That is, with the development of a model of consumer behavior based on radical behaviorism and its use to interpret aspects of consumer behavior that had previously fallen predominantly within the domain of consumer psychology. Although this phase, like all the others, continues now, it is important I feel to maintain this account of it within the framework that gave rise to it during the years specified. Only in this way is it possible to maintain the concerns that motivated it and that emerged from it: the tentative character of the whole project is my belief that the model would remain confined to an interpretive stance, that it would not of itself be the source of empirical research in its own cause, that it would serve as a standpoint from which to critique the prevailing orthodoxy, and that radical behaviorism, though useful, was always to be the subject of a critical attitude. I think that it is necessary to preserve this atmosphere of thought and expectation if the subsequent developments within the research program are to be appreciated. I have therefore maintained by and large the text and references as they were generated at the time, updating predominantly by interpreting some of the results through the insights that existed at the time rather than by means of later additions and progressions in theory, philosophy, and empirical work.

The conceptual phase and the earliest part of the theoretical phase are described in *Consumer Psychology in Behavioral Perspective* (Foxall, 1990) and *Consumers in Context: The BPM Research Program* (Foxall, 1996). The initial empirical phase is described in several papers and developed conceptually and theoretically in *Understanding Consumer Choice* (Foxall, 2005), while the behavior economic phase is described and developed in *The Behavioral Economics of Consumer Brand Choice* (Foxall, James, Oliveira-Castro,and Schrezenmaier, 2007), as well as in later papers. The emerging field of consumer behavior analysis is comprehensively mapped out in the three-volume set, *Consumer Behavior Analysis: Critical Perspectives in Business and Management* (Foxall, 2002) The philosophical phase is described in *Context and Cognition: Interpreting Complex Behavior* (Foxall, 2004) and applied to the findings of the empirical programs in *Explaining Consumer Choice* (Foxall, 2007). Two further monographs are in course of preparation: *Reward, Emotion, and Choice: From Neuroeconomics to Neurophilosophy* deals with the role of neuroeconomics in the analysis of consumer choice, while *The Marketing Firm* applies and extends this thinking to the analysis of organizational behavior. In order that the full import of these anticipated works can be appreciated, it is necessary now to reiterate the results of the theoretical/interpretative phase of the research program.

The program has progressed well beyond the phase represented here, but that does not mean that the interpretive approach has been superseded. The philosophical phase has shown that a perspective that includes intentional and cognitive explanation is indeed invaluable to the explanation of consumer behavior, but that the insights and methods gained from the study of economic choice in the context of radical behaviorism are equally integral to this intellectual task. I do not anticipate its findings in this chapter, the purpose of which is to celebrate the significance of the interpretive phase. All inquiry rests upon interpretation; comprehension and appreciation of the results of the most rigorous quantitative study depend on the accuracy of the underlying interpretation that is made of them, their relation to theory, and the ways in which the techniques which led to their generation influenced their production. Some of the tentative suggestions made in this book to the effect that the BPM might amount to no more than an interpretive device have proved overcautious. Nevertheless, without a fundamental qualitative interpretational understanding of what one's model—one's ultimate theoretical position—is all about, it is impossible to make sense of the significance of the testing and appraisal of the model and theory. Moreover, the interpretation fulfills its own part in the quest to understand consumer behavior: it represents a level of analysis that is complete in its own right, whatever wider contribution it may make to the understanding of theoretical and empirical developments. That is what this book is about.

OUTLINE OF THE BEHAVIORAL PERSPECTIVE MODEL

The BPM is derived and justified in later chapters, but before we get to that point there is a lot of necessary description and evaluation of the philosophical basis whose capacity to interpret consumer choice is being appraised in this study. Some preliminary idea of what the model is all about may therefore be useful at this stage. This is not a full exposition: it is an outline of the model that is intended to serve as a reference point during the early exposition.

Some Basics

Purchasing is approach behavior with both reinforcing and punishing consequences—outcomes, that is, that are likely to increase the probability of its being repeated and others that have an inhibiting effect. Buying a well-known brand is reinforced by acquiring the attributes of the product class and the resulting consumption possibilities. It is simultaneously punished by the surrender of money, depriving the buyer of opportunities to acquire other reinforcers, possibly inviting censure or generating dissonance. The sequence comprises the following behavioral contingencies:

$$S^D \rightarrow R \rightarrow S^R \text{ and } S^A$$

where S^D is a discriminative stimulus, an element of the setting in the presence of which the individual emits response, R, the consequences of which are a reinforcing stimulus, S^R, and an aversive or punishing stimulus, S^A. The same S^R and S^A are involved in the control of the corresponding escape behavior, non-purchase (which may result in short- or long-term saving and/or the purchase of an alternative brand or product). The contingencies controlling such escape are

$$S^D \rightarrow R^E \rightarrow S^R \text{ and } S^A$$

where R^E is the escape behavior, S^R the avoidance of/escape from the aversive consequences of purchasing the target brand, and S^A the loss of reinforcers contingent on purchasing. The probability of each of these alternative responses—the approach represented by purchase, and the escape/avoidance represented by non-purchase—is a function of the consumer's history of reinforcement. The strength of approach depends on reinforcer effectiveness, the reinforcement schedule in operation, and the quantity and quality of available reinforcers. That of escape is a function of the amount of money purchasing would require the consumer to surrender, his/her access to alternative reinforcers, and the loss of the exchange value represented by money. The probability of purchasing a specific brand can be depicted as the equilibrium point at the interaction of two functions representing the strengths of approach and escape behaviors.

In the context of animal experiments, the basic elements of the *three-term contingency*—the paradigm's fundamental explanatory mode, consisting of antecedent stimulus, behavior, and consequences—can be readily identified, and the effects of their interrelationships, prescribed by the reinforcement schedule imposed, can be objectively observed. But within the complex situations in which much human social behavior takes place, it is often impossible to isolate the elements and their linkages so unambiguously. However, areas of human behavior that lie beyond the rigorous analysis made possible in laboratory experimentation are open to an interpretation founded on the extension of scientific laws derived from the analysis of the simpler behavior.

Such an interpretation must nevertheless take account of the most recent improvements in understanding human economic behavior in relation to the environment in which it occurs. The BPM therefore recognizes two broad deviations from orthodox behavior theory in positing as its independent variables (i) a continuum of relatively open/relatively closed behavior settings, and (ii) the bifurcation of reinforcement into utilitarian and instrumental consequences of behavior. The following account discusses the nature of these variables after briefly describing the model's dependent variable.

Dependent Variable: Rate of Consumer Response

A response is behavior which can be related to the environmental contingencies that control its rate of occurrence. The BPM account of purchase and consumption conceptualizes behavior at a more molar level than that of the individual response: for instance, by considering the whole sequence of pre-purchase, purchase, and post-purchase activity as a single unit and by noting the generalization of purchase responses from one retail setting to another or the extension of purchasing in one setting from one to many items. A model of consumer behavior based on operant principles must be able to relate the strengthening or elimination of responses consistently to the environmental consequences which reinforce or punish them. In the case of human behavior in the relatively unrestrained environments characteristic of economic purchase and consumption, the schedules of reinforcement can be no more than inferred from the behavior and its consequences. It is a test of the validity of the model that this process of interpretation can be carried out systematically and consistently with the predictions of a behavioral analysis.

Antecedent Variable: The Behavior Setting

Consumer behavior settings are the physical and social surroundings in which purchase decisions are made and acts of purchase and consumption are performed. They comprise the antecedent stimuli that prefigure or signal the reinforcing and punishing consequences of behaving in a particular way. *Relatively closed settings* are those in which the contingencies that shape and maintain consumer behavior can be closely and unambiguously specified and controlled by marketers or researchers. The closure of purchase or consumption settings increases as the number of available reinforcers declines, and as the control of marketers over deprivation and reinforcement expands: for instance, obtaining the services provided by a postal system that is a public monopoly takes place in such a setting. *Relatively open settings* are, by contrast, those from which such control is (largely) absent or where the contingencies that control behavior cannot be unambiguously specified by the researcher; in a supermarket, for instance, although some sources of environmental control (such as the physical deployment of point-of-sale advertising and the prominent placing of leading brands at eye level) are evident, it may be impossible to specify completely and with finality why a consumer chose a given brand by reference to behavioral criteria alone. It is possible, however, to provide an interpretation of the behavior in these terms, as cognitive psychology would provide another based on the analogy of computer-based information processing. In sum, the distinction between closed and open behavior settings is based—as far as experimental analysis is concerned—on the relative ease with which behavior can be brought under contingency control and—in the case of an interpretive analysis—on the extent to which the rate of response can be accurately and objectively attributed to environmental influences. Hence in the interpretive account of consumer behavior provided by the BPM, the criteria for the positioning of a given behavior setting on the open-closed continuum are (a) *availability of and access to reinforcement*, which encompasses three considerations: (i) the number of reinforcers available, (ii) the number of means of obtaining the reinforcers, and (iii) the necessity of performing specific tasks on which the reinforcers are contingent; and (b) *the external control of the consumer situation*, which rests on three more considerations: (i) whether the marketer or other provider of the product/service controls access to the reinforcers, (ii) whether the contingencies are imposed by agents not themselves subject to them, and (iii) whether there are readily accessible alternatives to being in the situation (cf. Schwartz and Lacey, 1988).

Independent Variable: Utilitarian and Informational Reinforcement

The reinforcement of human operant behavior plays a broader role than is the case for animals. Reinforcers for human behavior may act informationally as well as by utilitarian means to strengthen behavior. *Utilitarian* or *functional* reinforcement refers to the strengthening of purchase and consumption behaviors through the generation of fantasies, feelings, fun, amusement, arousal, sensory stimulation, and enjoyment. Utilitarian reinforcers are consequences of behavior that are internal to the individual, feelings of pleasure and satisfaction, positive affect, and other internal states which are produced by and reward overt actions. They correspond to the affective phenomenology ascribed by some authors to the playful aspects of consumption and may be related to intrinsic motivation.

However, human operant experiments indicate that the reinforcers employed may be informational rather than utilitarian: they signal to subjects the accuracy of their performance or that it has been otherwise satisfactory. It is improbable that the points earned by these subjects and the negligible sums of money for which they are typically exchanged act as reinforcers in the way that food pellets strengthen animal behavior. Such rewards possess little if any intrinsic capacity to reinforce affluent well-fed humans. Moreover, the operant performance of adult human subjects is disorderly and variable in the absence of performance-related information. Once adequate information (scores or graphs showing relative achievement) is made available, performances become orderly and behavioral change is sensitive to the schedule in operation and is more rapid. The points or money are not in themselves a motivating factor, and a different kind of reinforcement is apparently operating in these circumstances. The resulting concept, *informational* or *symbolic* reinforcement, does not refer the provision of "information" per se: it is specific informational feedback on the individual's performance or achievement which has implications for the rate at which that performance continues. The essence of informational reinforcement is that it helps consumers solve problems posed by the web of contingencies to which their learning histories have brought them. It does so by providing precise feedback on the correctness and appropriateness of their performances as consumers in terms of not only immediate economic rationality, but also, more particularly, the wider socio-economic ramifications such as status, prestige, and social acceptance. Informational reinforcement is the product of external consequences of behavior, often publicly available and of social significance. It is closely related to the process in which consumers' behavior is governed by rules which they or others have extracted from the contingencies that face them which may suggest a cognitive dimension. This bifurcation of the consequences of behavior extends the range of reinforcing agencies with the intention of providing a more comprehensive behavioral interpretation of purchase and consumption. The reality and independence of utilitarian and informational sources of reinforcement is empirically supported by a large volume of applied behavior analytic studies of human economic behavior. Field experiments incorporating incentives in the form of monetary rewards, competitions and social praise (sources of utilitarian reinforcement), and performance feedback in the form of records of recent consumption levels (informational reinforcement) indicate the powerful influence of these consequential stimuli in reducing such environmentally injurious activities as car exhaust pollution, littering, and excess fuel consumption.

The key independent variable incorporated in the BPM is thus utilitarian and informational reinforcement, usually combined in the concept of the *pattern* of reinforcement. The consumer's unique learning history determines the saliency of the configuration of utilitarian and informational reinforcers made available through purchase and/or consumption of the products and services on offer. Utilitarian and informational reinforcers are conceptualized as exerting, in each case, a relatively high or relatively low level of control over behavior. "High versus low utilitarian reinforcement" denotes the extent to which the consequences of behavior are affective, emotive, or pleasant. "High versus low informational reinforcement" denotes the extent to which the consequences of behavior provide data that regulate (or allow the individual to regulate through conscious calculation and verbal formulation of contingencies) the rate at which the relevant purchase or consumption responses are emitted. "High informational reinforcement" infers a great deal of relevant feedback on performance through which further responses can be adjusted or regulated. "Low informational reinforcement" means a smaller quantity of such information or a lower quality of feedback.

Synthesis: The Consumer Situation

An account of situated consumer behavior must incorporate variables that refer to differences between environments, which can be specified independently of the person, and variables that refer to differences between persons, which can be specified independently of the environment. In the BPM, the extrapersonal variables refer to the settings in which pre-purchase, purchase, and post-purchase activities occur (including the relevant elements of the marketing mix). The personal variables derive from the learning history which summarizes the consumer's previous experience. Hence a situation of purchase and consumption is defined by reference to (i) the relative openness of the settings in which these behaviors take place, (ii) the nature and relative importance of the utilitarian and informational reinforcers that have influenced consumer responses in the past and that are now signaled by the setting stimuli as contingent upon the performance of specific purchase and/or consumption responses, and (iii) the unique personal learning history of the consumer.

Much micro-consumer behavior such as store selection or brand choice is a function of the specific contingencies of reinforcement operating in a given setting plus the individual factors brought to the setting by the consumer—his or her prior experience with brands or stores, for instance, which determine the detailed influence of the situation on his or her behavior. It is the combined effect of the personal and environmental factors, and their interrelationships, summarized in the BPM, that transform the general setting into a situation of immediate personal relevance to the consumer. A situation is more specific than a setting; it is defined and circumscribed not only by the setting variables which signal utilitarian and informational consequences of behavior, but also by the salience of those discriminative stimuli as determined by the consumer's learning history. These consequences are of two kinds: (i) immediate outcomes (finding and acquiring products) of behavior in the current setting (browsing, negotiating, or purchasing in a clothes store) and (ii) subsequent outcomes of post-purchase activities (e.g., wearing the clothes purchased) delivered later, perhaps in another setting (e.g., a restaurant). Figure 1.1 summarizes the BPM account of situated consumer behavior. The consumer situation comprises the current behavior setting and the consumer's history of reinforcement in similar settings. The behavior setting is the set of discriminative stimuli that signal reinforcement contingent on the performance of specified consumer behaviors. Point-of-sale advertising might, for instance, signal the social status that will follow purchase of a particular item or jewelry (informational reinforcement) or the physical well-being that will result from consumption of a course of vitamins (utilitarian reinforcement). The salience of these signals for the consumer depends on his/her learning history: whether these or similar behaviors have been so rewarded in the past. The resulting consumer situation determines the rate at which the consumer now responds, if at all. The resulting utilitarian and/or informational reinforcement (or possibly punishment) modifies his or her learning history and thus alters the probability of performing similar behaviors in the future.

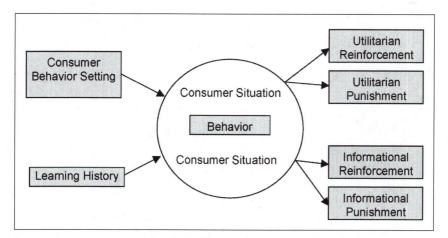

Figure 1.1   Summative Behavioral Perspective Model.

Situational Analysis of Consumer Behavior

An interpretive account of consumer activity should systematically relate known topographies of purchase and consumption to the contingencies on which they are maintained. From the derivation of the BPM described previously, there emerge eight distinct categories of contingencies, combinations of setting and reinforcer variables in terms of which such topographies can be described. These situational categories are shown in the BPM Contingency Matrix (Figure 1.2). Before explicating this in more detail, the following outline first identifies the fundamental classes of consumer behavior and the schedules of reinforcement that apparently control them. It then relates them to the situational categories defined in the Contingency Matrix.

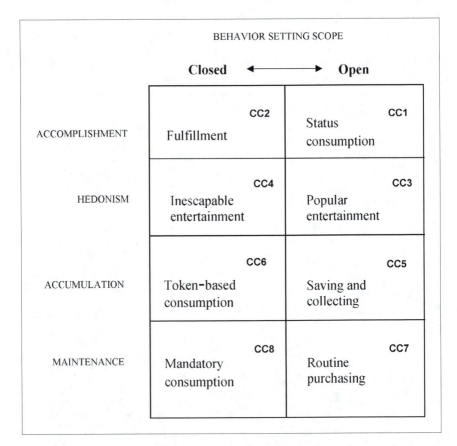

Figure 1.2   The BPM Contingency Matrix. (CC = Contingency Category.)

Major Classes of Consumer Behavior

Like other behaviors, purchase and consumption can be classified according to the nature of their consequences, the pattern of utilitarian and informational reinforcement on which they are maintained. This pattern also involves the schedule of reinforcement in operation, that is, the frequency with which responses are followed by reinforcers. When a response is reinforced every time it occurs, the procedure is known as *continuous reinforcement* (CRF). When less than every response is reinforced, the behavior takes longer to learn but extinguishes slowly. *Fixed interval* (FI) schedules provide reinforcement when a given period of time has elapsed for a response made after that period; on *variable interval* (VI) schedules, the period of time that must elapse before a response is reinforced varies from reinforcement to reinforcement. *Fixed ratio* (FR) schedules provide reinforcement when a specific number of responses has been performed, regardless of the time required, while *variable ratio* (VR) schedules are arranged such that a different number of responses is required to produce reinforcement on each occasion. Ratio schedules maintain a higher rate of responding than interval schedules. Fixed schedules maintain patterns of responding characterized by a pause after each reinforcement, while variable schedules maintain a steady rate of responding.

Shaping and maintenance of complex behavior may reflect several concurrent reinforcement schedules that exert multiple, complex influences, but, for this exposition, consumer behavior can be interpreted in terms of one or other of the familiar schedules. The four classes into which the consequences of consumer behavior are divided are accomplishment, pleasure, accumulation, and maintenance (Figure 1.3).

Accomplishment refers to social and economic achievement and maintains such behaviors as the acquisition and conspicuous consumption of status symbols, and the activities involved in seeking sensation and excitement or personal fulfillment as long as these acts resulted in the accumulation of some measure of attainment (points, products, certificates, rites of passage, etc.) which mark progress. Accomplishment is the pattern of consequences produced by high levels of both utilitarian and informational reinforcement.

	High utilitarian reinforcement	Low utilitarian reinforcement
High informational reinforcement	ACCOMPLISHMENT	ACCUMULATION
Low informational reinforcement	HEDONISM	MAINTENANCE

Figure 1.3 Operant classes of consumer behavior.

Behaviors controlled by accomplishment are apparently maintained on a VR schedule. In the case of the open behavior setting (Contingency Category 1: *Status Consumption*) a typical example is the pre-purchase search for and comparative evaluation of information relating to luxuries or discontinuous innovations; in the case of the closed setting (Contingency Category 2: *Fulfillment*), casino gambling provides a typical instance.

Hedonism is the result of all forms of popular entertainment and of behaviors such as taking medication which are controlled (negatively reinforced) by the alleviation of suffering or displeasure. It is the consequence linked with a high level of utilitarian reinforcement but only a low level of informational reinforcement which, nevertheless, is neither absent nor unimportant. These behaviors occur as if maintained by a VI schedule of reinforcement. In the open behavior setting (Contingency Category 3: *Popular Entertainment*), an example is the TV game show, while in the closed setting (Contingency Category 4: *Inescapable Entertainment*), a typical example would be in-flight consumption of meals or movies.

Accumulation is produced by consumer behaviors involving collecting, saving (notably saving up irregularly to buy something), installment buying, and responses to promotional deals requiring the accumulation of tokens or coupons. It is the consequence that embodies a high level of informational reinforcement but a low level of utilitarian reinforcement, though the latter is neither absent nor, necessarily, unimportant. Such behaviors are apparently maintained on FR schedules. An example of accumulation in an open setting (Contingency Category 5: *Saving and Collecting*) is collecting packet tops to obtain a fairly trivial free gift, while accumulating airmiles as one uses airline services exemplifies the relevant behavior in a closed setting (Contingency Category 6: *Token-based Consumption*). The distinction between open and closed settings derives from the inevitability of the ultimate reward. In the case of trivial free gifts, collecting is not enforced and the consumer has a degree of choice. Automatically given tokens leading to more substantial target rewards such as consumer durable products may engender greater compulsion and, by implication, a more closed setting.

Maintenance is the consequence of the activities involved in survival (e.g., regular food purchasing) and the fulfillment of social and cultural obligations of citizenship (e.g., the consumption of public goods for which taxes are paid at regular intervals). Note that maintenance does not refer simply to physical survival and well-being but includes the outcomes of performing the cultural and economic duties of the society, especially as the consumer makes sense of social being through consumption and consumption-related behaviors. These behaviors are seemingly maintained on FI schedules. The routine weekly purchasing of food items and other fast-moving consumer goods in a supermarket is an example of the behavior in question in an open behavior setting (Contingency Category 7: *Routine Purchasing*), while mandatory consumption of public goods, for which compulsory taxes are levied, exemplifies such behavior in a closed setting (Contingency Category 8: *Mandatory Purchase or Consumption*).

2   The Story So Far

In a sense, of course, all philosophizing is a perversion of reality: for, in a sense, no philosophic theory makes any difference to practice. It has no working by which we can test it. It is an attempt to organize the confused and contradictory world of common sense, and an attempt which invariably meets with partial failure—and with partial success. It invariably involves cramming both feet into one shoe: *almost every philosophy seems to begin as a revolt of common sense against some other theory, and ends—as it becomes itself more developed and approaches completeness—by itself becoming equally preposterous—to everyone but its author.* The theories are certainly, all of them, implicit in the inexact experience of every day, but once extracted they make the world appear as strange as Bottom in his ass's head . . . Of course one cannot avoid metaphysics altogether, because nowhere can a sharp line be drawn—to draw a line between metaphysics and common sense would itself be metaphysics and not common sense. But relativism does I think *suggest* this recommendation: not to pursue any theory to a conclusion, and to avoid complete consistency. Now the world of natural science may be unsatisfying, but after all it is the most satisfactory that we know, so far as it goes. And it is the only one which we must *all* accept.

—T. S. Eliot to Norbert Wiener, January 6, 1915
(in Eliot, 1988, p. 80; emphasis in original)

This book employs and assesses one of the most parsimonious approaches to explanation in psychology, radical behaviorism, in order to ascertain its relevance to the interpretation of consumer behavior. Although some rather obvious observations can be made about the routine nature of much consumer choice in terms of its habitual nature, and while some again rather obvious interpretations of marketing tactics such as those that retailers use can be made in terms of alleged conditioning of consumer behavior, there is a much deeper reason for taking an interest in the relevance of radical behaviorism to marketing phenomena. This is the necessity to *explain* consumer and marketer behavior as a part of social and behavioral science, to *understand* their nature as pervasive elements of human endeavor; this entails determining the usefulness of social scientific paradigms to this task. It is usual to jump in at this point with whatever one's favorite school of social thought or technique of analysis might be and to apply these to some aspect of consumption and management in the hope that something will come out that will advance the quest for theoretical knowledge. The reason I have chosen to use radical behaviorism is that it presents a fundamental approach to the explanation of behavior, one that assumes that when the environmental stimuli that predict and control behavioral phenomena have been discovered, the behavior has been explained. This assumption, though naïve in the better sense of the word, is invaluable because it enables us not only to evaluate the claim that it makes by establishing the degree of usefulness of the paradigm of which it is a part to the explanatory endeavor (perhaps it will prove to have none), but also to use it as a standpoint for the evaluation of other, more elaborate means of explanation. A key question, for example, is at what stage does this most basic approach to behavioral science break down and require the addition of further paradigms if consumer behavior is to be adequately explained? It helps us define at each stage in the research program the nature of explanation and to determine the nature of consumer behavior itself as a social, economic, and biological phenomenon by viewing it through the lenses of competing sources of understanding.

This methodological pluralism has always been a part of the research program that is the concern of this book: from its earliest days, it has sought to employ critically alternative and even mutually incompatible theoretical viewpoints (Foxall, 1981, 1983, 1988a, 1990, 1998a, 1998b), though the starting point has, for the reason mentioned previously, always been radical behaviorism. This attitude reflects an admiration for the achievements of this simple philosophy of psychology, an acknowledgement that it has proved useful for the explanation of some human and animal behaviors in certain types of experimental and natural settings, rather than an ideological devotion to it. Rather, radical behaviorism has always been critically viewed as a system that is unlikely to provide a comprehensive explanation of human behavior but that is a necessary component in the theoretical and empirical quest for a more perfect system that can. The research program has, therefore, always been critical of radical behaviorism while using it (e.g., Foxall, 1990); the extent of the criticism has developed considerably in recent years as, along with the establishment of successful usage of this philosophy to predict and possibly influence consumer choice, broader questions as to the explanation of the results of our empirical program have arisen (e.g., Foxall, 2004, 2005, 2007, 2007d). The result has not been the abandonment of radical behaviorism by any means but rather its contextualization in a broader approach to social scientific explanation. New theories of human behavior have been derived—*intentional behaviorism* and *super-personal cognitive psychology*—which are dependent upon the identification of molar patterns of operant behavior but which transcend the philosophical constraints of radical behaviorism. The emphasis of explanation has developed naturally toward the biological basis of social science while encompassing still the role of a selective environment in the shaping and maintenance of behavior.

The latest developments in this particular direction are the subject of further intended monographs (Foxall, in press, a; in press, b). But this book has a unique mission. Many years were spent in the early part of this research program first critiquing the prevailing cognitive view of consumer research from the standpoint of radical behaviorism, and second ascertaining the extent to which the resulting model of consumer choice, the *Behavioral Perspective Model* (Foxall, 1990), would provide alternative interpretations of consumer behavior. These phases of the program remain extant, but their primary influences were exerted during the period from 1980 to 2000. During this time I was urged by numerous well-meaning marketing professors to move on quickly to the stage of empirical investigation in order to make the model relevant to managerial concerns. I resisted this for the reason that unless the appropriate theoretical groundwork is first accomplished, there is no sure way of evaluating the prescriptions for management that might follow or, for that matter, the contribution of the work to the explanation of human behavior more generally. I even toyed with the idea for some time that the BPM was essentially an interpretive device that would stand proud of empirical investigation, and a collection of papers that are primarily concerned with interpretation and its philosophical and theoretical implications was subsequently published (Foxall, 1996). Nevertheless, empirical work was envisaged in 1990 that would provide some means of evaluating the model by predicting consumers' emotional reactions to the range of situations that derived from it, though the consequent need to encompass more basic work in environmental psychology before this could be meaningfully undertaken delayed even this phase of naturalistic investigation until 1996–1997. This research project has continued to the present day and makes a vital contribution to the incorporation of neuroscience and neuroeconomics into the overall program (Foxall, 2008). Another empirical project has been concerned with the use of behavioral economics to examine hypotheses derived from the BPM. This work began with the observation that patterns of multi-brand purchasing to which Ehrenberg and his colleagues have accorded great attention are similar in general form to the patterns of choice behavior identified in matching experiments by behavior analysts (Foxall, 1999). The ensuing research has proved invaluable not only as a means of extending the range of applicability of the model and thereby offering a critical perspective on work on aggregate patterns of consumer brand choice, but also as an avenue through which a behavioral economic research project could be undertaken within the BPM framework. I have always been fortunate in terms of the colleagues with whom I have been able to work on these empirical projects; doctoral students and visiting scholars have played important roles in various parts of it and I hope that my dedication of *Explaining Consumer Choice* (Foxall, 2007) goes some way toward thanking them. I would like to mention here especially Jorge Oliveira-Castro whose insights into the operationalization of the BPM variables in their application to product and brand choice and collaboration in formulating and testing resting behavioral economic models have been invaluable. The early papers stemming from these projects have now been published together (Foxall, James, Oliveira-Castro, and Schrezenmaier, 2007) and the work continues apace, as do several other applications. I mention this to put on record the general flavor of research on *consumer behavior analysis*, a framework which was the subject of a three-volume set published by Routledge (Foxall, 2002).

This book, however, returns to the value of the BPM as an interpretive device. The significance of this approach is more easily fixed in light of the findings of the research program since the last major appraisal was made (Foxall, 1996). I do not intend to take into consideration the philosophical advances made recently with respect to intentional behaviorism and super-personal cognitive psychology since that is to go beyond the initial project of an interpretation of consumer choice based on extensional behavioral science. It offers an alternative to the cognitive and other interpretations of consumer choice and lays the basis for any subsequent reliance on non-behaviorist reasoning; it provides an understanding of what is possible as a result of depending entirely upon a behavioral interpretation of consumer choice and, as a result, what is not available through exclusive reliance upon its alternatives. As an exercise in pluralistic socio-economic research, it constructs a standpoint form which to critique cognitive and other interpretations, and in ultimately suggesting the inadequacies of a purely extensional approach it indicates not only how a radical behaviorist interpretation must be supplemented or supplanted but also how sufficient the obvious alternative paradigms are likely to be to this task. A concomitant research program has actively involved the use of cognitive variables in the prediction and explanation of consumer behavior (see, e.g., Foxall and James, 2009), and this has contributed also to a deeper appreciation of the capabilities and limitations of this resolutely non-behaviorist methodology. But there are advantages in laying a fundamental, behaviorist foundation for the *interpretation* of consumer behavior, even though this entails rigors of its own.

Interpretation is employed when the use of direct, empirical scientific methodology is inappropriate or impossible. This does not mean, however, that it cannot or should not be conducted in the absence of the usual canons of scientific judgment or that it cannot give rise to empirical testing. The methodology of most qualitative research is preoccupied with establishing criteria by means of which an interpretation can be known and evaluated, and these are for the most part criteria for judgments that have been developed from quantitative scientific practice: assessments of validity and reliability, for instance. The specter of completely unanswerable interpretation has no place in a scientific account, though it may belong legitimately to the realm of literature. Our aim here is to establish means by which a scientifically consistent interpretation of consumer choice is feasible. It is not the intention here, nor is it desirable, that this should purport to be *the* interpretation of consumer choice. We are not dealing here in a world of crucial experiments, ultimately refutable propositions, and certain knowledge. (Nor does science ever, of course, but we must emphasize here that the current enterprise is much further along the continuum than most conventional scientific practice from the ideal position, that is, the scientific practice of popular imagination). A multiplicity of interpretations is necessary, each to be tested where it can be by methods as scientific as can be, but all participating in a debate which aims to produce as complete an avenue to knowledge as is possible.

The quest for a basis for interpretation that meets these requirements is never context-free or lacking in some degree of theory-ladenness, though it is not always easy to specify the nature of the bias inherent within it, nor to articulate its implications for the flavor of interpretation to which it will lead or the peculiarities involved in its evaluation. In the case of the approach pursued here, however, it is comparatively easy to state the epistemological basis and hence to evaluate its results and critique them both against that position and its alternatives.

Although the predominant theoretical position in consumer research has long been and remains cognitive, the possibility that behavior analysis can provide a complementary understanding of some phenomena, especially in the realm of retail management, crops up from time to time. It is rare for the suggestion to be raised that behaviorism might provide an explanation for consumer choice or that consumer researchers might seek to understand consumer behavior in terms derived from it, let alone what the methodological and ontological implications of such an intellectual exploration might be. However, these are serious concerns for any field that seeks methodological multiplicity and the growth of knowledge through the interaction of competing research programs. Hence the research program with which this book is concerned has sought to lay and appraise the contribution that radical behaviorism might make to the understanding of consumer choice, to critically evaluate the resulting account by reference to both the internal standards of behaviorism, and to evaluate the conclusions reached with respect to consumer behavior and the underlying assumptions of the behaviorist approach from the viewpoint of other approaches to social scientific knowledge, principally cognitive psychology. At no time has there been a desire to exclude cognitive accounts, though an emphasis on reordering the balance between cognitive and behavioral theories in consumer research has resulted at times in a concentration on the role of the latter and a sustained critique of the former. The spirit of the research program has always been, however, to test behaviorism to destruction and to introduce alternative sources of explanation as required. We are now at the exciting part of the program where further explanatory power is required, and this book is concerned with the incorporation of intentional and cognitive reasoning within the behavioral model of consumer behavior with which we have been working.

Interpretation is a form of translation, a process of rendering what is observed in terms of another system of plausibility, one that is distinct from the descriptive terms in which the observation is initially recorded. The hermeneutical method, for instance, is a means of establishing the meaning of currently available texts by reconstructing them in the context of the epistemology in which they were originally produced. It is not a way of rendering what one has observed in the descriptive idioms of current everyday discourse. It is, therefore, a highly theoretical undertaking which requires a systematically established foundation of reliable knowledge. Now, hermeneutics is often defined as the process of coming to understand a text (in its extended meaning) not from one's own point of view but form that of the material's originator. *Hermeneutics* derives from the Greek ρμηνεύω (*hermeneuō* meaning "translate" or "interpret"). It involves the use of principles which relate the interpretation systematically to the text. But it is overwhelmingly a methodology that seeks to reconstruct the meaning the text would have had for its utterer.

> In the last two millennia, the scope of hermeneutics has expanded to include the investigation and interpretation not only of oral, textual and artistic works, but of human behavior generally, including language and patterns of speech, social institutions, and ritual behaviors (such as religious ceremonies, political rallies, football matches, rock concerts, etc.). Hermeneutics interprets or inquires into the meaning and import of these phenomena, through understanding the point of view and "inner life" (Dilthey) of an insider, or the first-person perspective of an engaged participant in these phenomena. ("Hermeneutics," 2009, para. 5)

This is not the methodology I adopt in this book. This assumes that there is no reliable means by which a first-person account of behavior can be achieved (though it exists) but that a heterophenomenological account can be given on the basis of scientific knowledge of the environmental and biological factors that cause behavior coupled with the investigator's personal phenomenology (i.e., his subjective experience of his private behavior). Although both claim to provide an account of the personal level of explanation, the hermeneutic approach is unable to present evidence for the validity and reliability of its conclusions, whereas the approach taken in this book can at least point to the scientific evidence on which it is based. Interpretation cannot proceed in isolation from a template in terms of which the interpretation is to take place. This book bases its interpretive foundation on work in the economic psychology of consumer choice that provides a plausible yet evaluable model of how consumer behavior works and how it is related to marketing activity. Whereas some interpretive approaches eschew models (and often for good reason), I argue that the appraisal of an interpretation depends vitally on the existence of an underlying disciplinary framework. This is not to say that interpretation is a matter of testing a model in the usual positivist manner; rather, the outcomes of an interpretive exercise can be assessed, and further building accomplished, only if the interpretation can be traced back to an explicit understanding of how human behavior is motivated and shaped. In the worst possible outcome, neither model nor interpretation may be "correct," but at least it is possible to understand why through a critique of the foundational assumptions of the work of translation that is at the heart of the interpretive imagination.

Interpretive consumer research usually proceeds with a minimum of structure and preconceptions. My aim is to present a more structured approach than is usual but to employ nevertheless minimal assumptions and theories. The book aims to show how a simple framework that embodies the rewards and costs associated with consumer choice can be used to interpret a wide range of consumer behaviors from everyday purchasing and saving, innovative choice, imitation, and "green" consumer behavior, to compulsive behaviors such as addictions (to shopping, to gambling, to alcohol and other drugs, etc.). This requires taking a qualitative approach to interpreting behavior and dealing along the way with the epistemological problems that arise in such research. There will be a particular emphasis on the emotional as well as cognitive aspects of consumption. The main theme is that consumer behavior can be understood with the aid of a very simple model that proposes how the consequences of consumption impact consumers' subsequent choices. The objective is to show that a basic model can be used to interpret consumer behavior in general. The emphasis is not on the quantitative evaluation of such a model but upon its capacity to fulfill the requirements of an acceptable interpretive model—to deal with questions of validity and reliability, generalizability, and so on. Consumer behavior will not be treated, as is often the case, in isolation from the marketing influences that shape it, but will be portrayed as a course of human choice that is dynamically linked with managerial concerns. Unlike much work of a purportedly "interpretive" nature in consumer research, this book is not speculative but is based on a wealth of model development and empirical testing that has gone on for the last twenty-five years and is continuing now. Unlike earlier accounts of this research program, however, it concentrates on the interpretive uses of the model, that is, the ways in which it can elucidate all aspects of consumer choice, from everyday routine consumption through extreme compulsions, using similar explicatory tools. The qualitative approach allows the methodological concerns mentioned previously to be addressed in greater detail than has been the case hitherto, but also to extend them to new areas such as the use of a case-study approach.

This book is part of the sequence of monographs that have traced the development of this research program since Routledge published my *Consumer Psychology in Behavioral Perspective* in 1990. The book is, therefore, unique, and it is difficult to make comparisons, but if I must answer this question I would say that other interpretive approaches lack the underlying model testing and extension that have characterized this program, and that the book differs from others in this series of monographs by concentrating on interpretive consumer research. It differs also from the standard cognitive treatments of consumer decision making by showing how the environment shapes choice. Perhaps more important than any of these, it unites the study of consumer behavior with that of marketing management by bringing together the two aspects of human experience in a single framework, showing for maybe the first time how they intersect to produce the act of choice. This makes it possible to discuss how marketing works, what it does, in relation to our knowledge of what consumers do. The book strives to bring the findings of one of the most active research programs in consumer research to a broader audience of marketing scholars and social scientists by presenting an accessible account of consumption—the very business of life—in affluent, marketing-oriented economies. The approach is verbal and invitational. Each chapter contains notes that link the present account with the theoretical and philosophical concerns of the research program, as well as its empirical findings, for readers who wish to take this aspect of the work further.

BEHAVIOR ANALYSIS

Behavior analysis is "the area of philosophy, research, and application that encompasses the experimental analysis of behavior, applied behavior analysis, operant psychology, operant conditioning, behaviorism, and Skinnerian psychology" (Vaughan, 1989, p. 97). Its metatheory, radical behaviorism, is founded on the view that the objective and empirical methods of the physical sciences can be applied to the analysis of human behavior (Zuriff, 1985). It proposes that a behavior has been explained when the environmental factors which influence the rate at which it is repeated have been identified so that the response can be predicted and, through manipulation of the "contingencies of reinforcement," controlled. Such explanation makes no causal reference to internal states such as moods, or to internal processes such as information storage and retrieval, or to internal events such as attitudes, intentions, or traits of personality which are the stock in trade of cognitive theories (Skinner, 1938, 1950, 1963). Behavior analysis does not ignore private events such as thoughts and feelings but casts them as responses to be explained in their own right, the collateral effects of the same stimuli that occasion publicly available actions (Skinner, 1974). Nor is behavior analysis anti-theoretical, though it rejects theory building that explains observed behavior in terms of entities—neural, mental, or conceptual—posited to exist at some other level than observed behavior. Such theories are said to be *incomplete*, halting investigation by failing to identify the factors that account for the inner events and processes held to be the causes of behavior—in particular, they ignore the environmental precursors of those inner events; *fictional*, inferring the alleged internal causes of behavior from the behaviors they purport to explicate, adding nothing real to observation but simply re-describing it; and *superfluous*, replaceable by simpler, behavioral explanations that identify the environmental factors controlling behavior without resorting to explanatory fictions and offering a more direct route to knowledge (Wessells, 1981).

These tenets of scientific inquiry are valuable in pluralistic consumer research for suggesting an alternative explanation of consumer behavior to that provided by cognitive and other inner-state theories and are thus a source of the counter-inductive hypotheses on which the "active interplay of competing theories," the critical comparative stances required for scientific progress (Feyerabend, 1975), may depend. It is not argued that they be uncritically accepted, only that they form one more standpoint from which to comprehend the prevailing metatheories of consumer research: a behavioral perspective on purchase and consumption cannot be neglected, but it is one among many.

Behavior analysis requires that the stimuli held to control behavior be unambiguously described and accurately related to the rate at which closely specified responses occur. Experimental operant psychologists working with animal subjects can clearly define discriminative and reinforcing stimuli and demonstrate their causal relationship with specific responses. Not only can the elements of the controlling contingencies be readily identified, but the specific effects of their interrelationships as prescribed by the reinforcement schedule(s) imposed can be predicted. The central assumption is that the simple behavior so studied can be explained by reference to its environmental antecedents and consequences. But operant psychology has long ceased to confine itself to the experimental analysis of animal behavior: its extensions include educational and therapeutic interventions and the design of cultures (Skinner, 1953, 1957a, 1957b, 1971). These natural contexts of human social interaction, like those in which most consumer behavior takes place, rarely resemble the closed settings found in the laboratory. Within such complex situations, it is often impossible to isolate the environmental contingencies held to control behavior with the accuracy and certainty required of the experimentalist (Chomsky, 1959). Hence the radical behaviorist account of complex human behavior in social situations, typified by purchase and consumption, takes the form of a conceptual extrapolation of learning principles derived from the study of the operant responses of animals in the constrained setting of the laboratory experiment to the "real world" situations in which such behavior takes place. Skinner (1969) draws a clear distinction between experimental operant analysis which is scientific and which leads to *explanation*, and the extension of principles learned from that analysis to the *interpretation* of more complex cases.

By extrapolating from laboratory to life, an operant analysis is inevitably modified. In the study of complex actions, it is impossible to ascertain the contingencies that control response rate with the accuracy and precision available to the scientist who can assiduously control and monitor both dependent and independent variables. But it is possible to present a "plausible account" of complex actions (Skinner, 1957b, p. 11), "an interpretation, not an explanation . . . merely useful, neither true or false" (Skinner, 1988b, p. 208). All the more complex sciences are ultimately forced to rely on the extrapolation of simple principles gained in experimentation (Skinner, 1973, p. 261). Therefore, while the behaviorist interpretation is unprovable (more importantly, unfalsifiable), it is claimed preferable by its supporters to those which cannot be supported by knowledge of simpler systems gained from carefully executed experiments (Skinner, 1969, p. 100; 1974, pp. 226–232; 1988a, p. 208).

THE BEHAVIORAL PERSPECTIVE MODEL

The BPM offers an approach to the explication of consumer behavior which is not provided by alternative theories. It defines independent variables (discriminative or setting stimuli, and reinforcers) which are held to determine the schedules of reinforcement in operation and relates them to the dependent variable (rate of responding) of known patterns of consumer purchase and consumption activity. As a result of the extension of the fundamental behavior analytic framework by the inclusion of a continuum of settings and the bifurcation of reinforcement, and the recognition of the importance of verbal behavior in humans leading to a recognition of proximate as well as distal causation, the model provides an interpretation of consumer behavior in complex social situations based on a critical evaluation of modern behavior analysis. Of course, no scientific paradigm, taken alone, can provide a comprehensive explanation of so complex a field as consumer behavior. Each perspective presents insights not made available by the others. While recognizing the merits of the prevailing paradigm, still overwhelmingly cognitive, consumer research can benefit from an accurate appreciation of the ontological and methodological concerns of its alternatives. The BPM of purchase and consumption derives from a research program that has sought to fix the scope and limits of the contribution of behavior analysis (Skinner, 1953) to consumer research. Assuming that "the variables of which human behavior is a function lie in the environment" (Skinner, 1977, p. 1), behavior analysis explains the rate at which responses recur by reference to the consequences they have produced in the past. A comprehensive account will eventually incorporate both cognitive and behavioral sources of explanation, but, as a prelude to such synthesis, the BPM explores the implications of a radical environmental perspective on choice (Foxall, 1990).

The BPM contributes to marketing science in two ways. *First, it provides a means of conceptualizing situational influences on consumer behavior.* Cognitive decision models assume purchasing to be the outcome of goal-directed information processing: the consumer sets objectives, plans their achievement, and intentionally deploys resources to secure desired benefits. None of these models omits external influences on consumer choice, but none stresses them either. In the process, such models tend to de-contextualize consumer behavior. In spite of recent interest in the effects of situational variables on consumer choice, no general conceptual framework has yet emerged. The theoretical contribution of the BPM comprises such a framework. *Second, the BPM suggests a new understanding of marketing strategy.* Some consumer researchers have described systems that explain behavior by reference to external stimuli rather than internal states and processes, thereby opening up the possibility of a balanced perspective. But no model of purchase and consumption has emerged that is both based on empirical principles of human behavior and relevant to marketing management. The applied contribution of the BPM is its elucidation of marketer behavior.

The BPM does more than re-describe consumer choice in operant terminology; it organizes well-established and documented patterns of consumer behavior, relating each to unique and appropriate contingencies. The systematic way in which various patterns of consumer behavior have also been related to reinforcement schedules indicates that the BPM interpretation is reliably postulating relationships among its dependent and independent variables. The BPM presents a behavioral interpretation of purchase and consumption which does not seek to eliminate alternative explanations. The inevitability of a plurality of explanatory mechanisms is in fact central to its approach (Foxall, 1990). Further research should proceed toward the synthesis of environmental and intrapersonal sources of motivation, in which quest the isolation of the utilitarian and informational effects of reinforcement suggests a relationship with affective and cognitive theories of consumer behavior which should be pursued. The BPM interpretation also elucidates marketing practice. Its explanatory variables and its categorization of the contingencies influencing consumer behavior are centrally relevant to our understanding of the strategic conduct of customer-oriented marketing. This applied emphasis of the model also gives impetus to the development of a synthesis of cognitive and behavioral accounts of consumer choice. In open societies, consumers are seldom so constrained that they cannot escape or avoid aversive contingencies. Further refinement of the model will include an account of consumers' cognitive interpretations, representations, and manipulations of the contingencies that influence their behavior.

In the concluding chapter of *The Behavior of Organisms*, Skinner used the now famous words, "Let him extrapolate who will" (1938, p. 422). It is time for that challenge to be more generally accepted. Indeed, only by examining critically the implications of extending operant principles gained in the laboratory to the complexities of human social and economic behavior is it possible to understand the nature and ramifications of an interpretation of consumer choice based on behavior analysis. In contrast to earlier attempts to apply behavioral psychology to the analysis of purchase and consumption, this chapter deals comprehensively with the nature of an operant interpretation and its implications for consumer research. It elaborates a behavior analytic model of consumer choice, explores its applicability to sequences of behavior occurring during the life cycle of the individual consumer and over the market life cycle of products and services, and evaluates the model's contribution to the development of consumer psychology. According to this philosophy of psychology, a response has been explained when the environmental factors that account systematically for the rate at which it is emitted have been identified. Operant explanation, therefore, makes no causal reference to internal events and states such as attitudes and emotions, feelings and physiology, though it does not deny their existence and importance: like the public and overt actions which accompany them, these private and covert phenomena are depicted as responses under the control of reinforcing and punishing stimuli. This is far removed from the stimulus-response psychology frequently associated with behaviorism (Lee, 1988). The rate at which a response is currently performed is attributed by behavior analysts to the consequences that have previously followed responses belonging to the same operant class. Prebehavioral stimuli do not *elicit* responses, as they do in classical conditioning; rather, they signal the likely consequences of behaving in a specified manner. Antecedent, or discriminative, stimuli are, like the reinforcing and punishing consequences of the behavior they prefigure, components of the environment rather than the individual. The causal mechanism of behavior analysis can thus be summarized succinctly in terms of its "three-term contingency": a response, the discriminative stimuli in the presence of which it is emitted, and the reinforcing and punishing consequences which it produces (Skinner, 1953, p. 110).

Of all the schools of psychology, operant behaviorism comes closest to the idea of a scientific paradigm as articulated by Kuhn (1962). It is more closely specified in terms of a coherent philosophy of science, defined subject matter, methodological sophistication, and explanatory precision than cognitive or phenomenological psychology. It is somewhat surprising, therefore, that operant behaviorism has not been used in consumer research to provide a description and explanation of purchase and consumption in the context of situational and other environmental influences. It is true that consumer researchers have occasionally mentioned the possibility of a behavior analytic perspective on purchase and consumption; moreover, quasi-operant systems have sometimes been incorporated into general research frameworks. In addition, economic psychologists and behavioral economists have shown that the economic behavior of animals is operant: the bar presses or key pecks emitted by animals in experimental settings, the food pellets they produce, and the rate at which one is translated into the other are analogous to money, commodities, and prices (Allison, 1983; Hursh, 1980, 1984; Lea, 1978).

Models of human economic performance devised by extrapolation from these settings indicate the possibility of describing consumer behavior in operant terms and of formulating alternative theories of choice to those based on utility maximization (Alhadeff, 1982; Herrnstein, 1988). All of these approaches recognize the importance of environmental influence on purchase and consumption. Nevertheless, despite its ad hoc attempts to account for the impact of the physical and social surroundings, the consumer's task orientation, antecedent states, and temporal perspective, consumer psychology has failed to evolve a theoretical perspective which deals comprehensively with the effect of the situation on choice and use. Still less has consumer psychology, dominated by an emphasis on cognitive information processing, come to terms with the explanatory implications of behavior analysis, which attributes the control of behavior to environmental factors, even to the exclusion of organocentric or intrapersonal processes and events (Skinner, 1938, 1953, 1974, 1985). Several factors, which stem from over-simplification of the role of behavior analysis and the nature of consumer behavior, may account for this.

First, the impression is frequently given that behaviorism is *passé*, a paradigm superseded by the cognitive revolution, so ontologically restricted that it provides an inadequate basis for a discipline that has rediscovered mental causation. But it is strange that just as consumer research has begun to emphasize the relative nature of knowledge and the necessity of methodological pluralism, it should consciously exclude any perspective from consideration. In a pluralistic consumer psychology, each paradigm is capable of acting as a philosophical standpoint from which others might be criticized, stimulating the production of empirical data that would otherwise not be generated, and suggesting counter-inductive hypotheses to account for the data produced within alternative theoretical frameworks (Feyerabend, 1975; Foxall, 1990; Valentine, 1992). A further consideration which argues against the premature abandonment of operant behaviorism is the recent upsurge in intellectual activity among behaviorists who have turned to the operant explanation of verbal behavior, including thought and other activities which have for long been the exclusive domain of cognitivists. It is quite inaccurate to present behaviorism as having been superseded given the work of such behavioral scientists as Hayes (1989), Hayes, Barnes-Holmes and Roche (2004) and Rachlin (1994, 2000). Second, psychologists, economists, and marketing scientists have tended to extrapolate somewhat uncritically from the general findings of animal experiments to human marketing activity without considering the vast differences in complexity that separates these realms. In particular, they have given scant consideration to the cognitive complexity of human consumers as compared with non-human animals; in behaviorist terms, they have too frequently assumed that behavior is shaped entirely by contact with the contingencies of reinforcement and punishment and have made no allowance for the rule governance of human performance (Skinner, 1969; cf. Foxall, 1987). The recent use of behavior analysis in the marketing literature, for instance, makes no reference to the possibility of consumers' adoption and creation of rules which describe the contingencies of reinforcement and their acting according to them when they are not in direct contact with the contingencies themselves. Both marketing authors and economic psychologists have assumed an excessive degree of continuity between animal and human behavior, which is not borne out by the empirical analysis of human operant performance under verbal control (Horne and Lowe, 1993). Third, economic psychologists and behavioral economists have ignored the complexities of the marketing system, confining their analyses to the effects of price and its analogs on demand and failing to take into consideration the effects of non-price elements of the marketing mix such as advertising and sales promotion. Yet it would be absurd to suggest that the experimental analysis of animal behavior throws more than superficial light on human behavior in complex social situations such as those of purchase and consumption. Any move away from the analysis of animals' economic behavior to that of human consumers in affluent economies must recognize the fundamental source of discontinuity arising from the vast amount of choice available to consumers who wield high levels of discretionary income, and the impetus given to both the creation and satisfaction of contrived consumer demand by the competitive marketing actions of suppliers (Foxall, 1981, 1984a). Finally, all of these professional groups have avoided examination of the philosophical implications of a behaviorist epistemology for the explanation of consumer behavior and the conduct of research in this field. Marketing authors have deliberately ignored the theoretical and explanatory ramifications of a behavioral analysis of consumer choice in order to concentrate on the ways in which retailers make use of reinforcement schedules to influence the rate of purchasing. Those economists and psychologists who have applied behavior theory to the economic realm have similarly been content with description, albeit usually of an elaborate kind, while omitting consideration of the underlying fact that "[b]ehaviorism is not the science of human behavior; it is the philosophy of that science" (Skinner, 1974, p. 3).

The BPM is concerned with the explanation of consumer behavior in its situational context (Foxall, 1986, 1990). The first objective of the BPM research program is to ascertain the viability of an account of purchase and consumption founded upon a critical understanding of behavior analysis. Whereas marketing and economic psychology have made piecemeal use of behavior analysis, the BPM program is concerned to derive as complete a model of consumer behavior based on this paradigm as is feasible, to determine the extent to which mainstream behavior analysis alone can contribute to the understanding of consumer choice, and to make any necessary modifications or additions to orthodox behavior theory, while remaining true to its underlying principles, in order to render its explanation more convincing. The second objective is to understand the nature of the account so produced: to evaluate the explanation provided and to assess its contribution to the advance of consumer psychology. This entails considerations of the scientific status of the behavioristic account and its capacity to engender novel explanations of consumer behavior and to generate new data. In the pursuit of the first objective, the program has already developed three emphases that are not usually found in mainstream behavior theory, but which seem, nevertheless, consistent with its spirit (Foxall, 1986, 1990). First, the model makes a distinction between relatively closed consumer behavior settings, environments in which the rate of behavior can be fairly unambiguously ascribed to operant conditioning, and relatively open consumer behavior settings, in which the operant account competes more strongly with alternative explanations. Second, the model does not assume that all reinforcement in humans is utilitarian in nature (i.e., confined to pleasurable and utilitarian consequences) but posits that reinforcement may be bifurcated into utilitarian and informational elements. The latter includes feedback on an individual's performance both as a consumer and as a member of a social system, reflecting his or her achieved social status, for instance. Finally, the model ascribes behavior to proximal or internal causes as well as the distal effects of the contingencies of reinforcement. The sources of proximal causation are, first, the verbal discriminative stimuli that consist in covert rules of behavior, and second, feelings and other internal events which may function as discriminative and reinforcing stimuli as well as collateral responses. But, despite the catalytic effects of internal verbal discriminative stimuli, the ultimate determinants of behavior must be sought in the environment. In the pursuit of the second objective, the program emphasizes that behavior analysis is an interpretation as well as a science. It proceeds on the basis of scientific rigor and precision—indeed, as an example of Machian positivism (Smith, 1986) involving the specification of dependent and independent variables and the functional relationships between them—only in the tightly controlled experimental settings of the operant laboratory. Even there, some interpretation is required as the operant scientist attributes behavior to its contingencies of reinforcement rather than to classical conditioning or cognitive processing. In complex settings, marked by multiple sources of behavioral causation, it relies more obviously on interpretation, an account of the complex phenomena in terms derived from the rigorous analysis of simpler systems. The BPM research program therefore asks how far an account of complex purchase and consumption activities can be based on behavior analysis.

Chomsky's (1959) renowned critique of operant behaviorism's application to complex (verbal) behavior maintained that the stimulus and response categories so easily identified and manipulated in the animal laboratory could not be rigorously specified in complex situations. This critique poses key questions, which this chapter seeks to answer. To what extent does the BPM provide a scientific approach to the analysis of consumer behavior, one which proceeds in terms, inductive or deductive, that show an acceptable level of correspondence between theoretical terms and their operational measures? And at what point does this scientific approach break down, making interpretation inevitable? How valid and reliable are interpretations of consumer behavior in the behavior analytical mould, and what is their function in the development of consumer psychology?

AFTER SCIENCE

Interpretative Behavior Analysis

We have seen that Skinner argues that areas of human behavior which lie beyond the rigorous analysis made possible in laboratory experimentation are open to an account based upon the extension of scientific laws derived from the analysis of simpler behavior patterns observed in less complicated situations. But, in the study of complex actions, such as verbal behavior, it may be impossible to ascertain the contingencies that control response rate with the accuracy and precision available to the scientist who can assiduously control and monitor both dependent and independent variables. But it is possible to present a "plausible account" or interpretation of such complex actions (Skinner, 1957b, p. 11; 1988a, p. 364). The behavior analytic interpretation, like those that deal with the evolution of life or the geophysics of the earth's core, is unprovable, but preferable nonetheless to those which cannot be supported by knowledge of simpler systems gained from carefully executed experiments (Skinner, 1969, p. 100; 1974, pp. 226–232; 1988a, p. 208). Skinner wrote, "When phenomena are out of reach in time or space, or too large or small to be directly manipulated, we must talk about them with less than a complete account of relevant conditions. What has been learned under more favorable conditions is then invaluable" (1973, p. 261).

He provides another example. Just as geophysics is founded upon the inductive principle that laws derived from laboratory experimentation indicate that comparable states exist deep within the earth, so "familiar facts about verbal behavior are interpreted with principles derived from the laboratory study of contingencies of reinforcement, even though the contingencies maintained by the verbal environment cannot be precisely ascertained. In both of these examples, principles derived from research conducted under the favorable conditions of the laboratory are used to give a plausible account of facts which are not at the moment under experimental control" (Skinner, 1969, p. 100). In summary, the behavior analytic account of complex human behavior in social situations takes the form of an extension of learning principles derived from the study of the operant responses of human and non-human animals in the constrained setting of the laboratory experiment to the "real world" situations in which such behavior takes place. Operant behaviorists have taken pains to emphasize the distinction between scientific, factual knowledge and the extended accounts derived from it. For instance,

Skinner points out in introducing his programmatic study of verbal response that "[t]he emphasis is upon an orderly arrangement of well-known facts, in accordance with a formulation of behavior derived from an experimental analysis of a more rigorous sort. The present extension to verbal behavior is thus an exercise in interpretation rather than a quantitative extrapolation of rigorous experimental results" (Skinner, 1957b, p. 11).

"Plausibility"

However, in the process of interpreting, the nature of an operant analysis is inescapably altered. Behavior analysis offers, in support of its interpretative account, its "plausibility," a term which is not well defined but which refers presumably to the degree in which the account persuades the reader that the behavior in question has been rendered more intelligible through reference to a sphere of observation (the experimental) where behavior can be shown to be under environmental control. Interpretation in the social sciences sometimes rests upon no more than this: the persuasiveness of the account is held to be its sole recommendation. Skinner's unwillingness to equate interpretation with extrapolation is presumably based on the recognition that some discontinuities exist between the laboratory and life. The appraisal of plausibility in this context rests upon considerations of the necessary relationship of interpretative accounts with empirical evidence and the closeness of the interpretation to the analog on which it is based. The assessment of a model's capacity to describe and delimit is therefore judged on two grounds. The first is the explanatory plausibility of its account of consumer behavior: how far is each of its variables needed in order to account persuasively for empirically demonstrated patterns of consumer behavior? And how far is each required to contribute to the integrity of the model itself? The second is the empirical correspondence of the model, its capacity to derive operational variables which could be used in empirical research.

The analog derived from the laboratory must, nevertheless, be applied to the more complex realm it interprets with sensitivity to the ontological and methodological differences that divide the two. Thus the extent to which an interpretative account accurately relates behavior to elements of the environment cannot be ascertained with certainty. How rigorous an explanation can interpretative behaviorism provide of behaviors whose alleged environmental determinants cannot be observed with the same degree of objectiveness and empiricalness as the operant laboratory affords? Most if not all human social behavior falls into this category precisely because it is verbal. Certainly, the purchase and consumption of nearly all economic goods typify complex interactions of this sort. The criterion we are offered is the plausibility of the account, presumably a function of the degree to which the account is judged to make the behavior in question more intelligible. Skinner offers as the cornerstone of the acceptability of his interpretative operant account the foundation of the interpretation, the experimental evidence for operant conditioning of simple behaviors, whether animal or human matters not at all, in the laboratory. But this is insufficient to judge what purports to be a natural scientific approach to psychology. Criticism of operant interpretations centers on the remoteness from complex human behavior of the analog (animal behavior in experimental settings) in terms of which the account is couched (e.g., Bethlehem, 1987; Mackenzie, 1977; Proctor and Weeks, 1990). Both radical behaviorists and their critics agree that the plausibility of an interpretation depends on the empirical correspondence of its terms with the objectively available data. Yet the critics have repeatedly maintained that the empirical foundation advanced by some behaviorists for the interpretations they have developed is simply too remote from the reality to which operant interpretative accounts refer.

A scientific model is usually expected to accomplish three things. It must first specify its dependent variable and the independent variables in terms of which it proposes an explanation. Secondly, it must specify the relationships among these variables so that empirical testing can occur. Finally, it must propose rules of correspondence, linking its theoretical categories with the operationally measurable empirical entities to which they refer. Yet all sciences are forced to interpret when they can no longer explain. Interpretation often suggests unique routes to investigation and explanation, and is inescapable in the integration and synthesis of a variety of findings. This is nowhere more evident than in the theory of evolution, the most integrative framework in the socio-biological sciences, especially in its human implications (e.g., Betzig, 1989; Dawkins, 1976, 1986; Goldsmith, 1991; Mayr, 1991; Smith, 1986). Furthermore, all scientific explanations interpret to a degree: even the activities of animals in operant chambers and their causes can be attributed to classical conditioning and cognitive mapping of the environment as well as to learning histories and the contingencies of reinforcement. In the case of an operant analysis of complex human behavior, two entirely complementary possibilities arise. The first is continued operant experimentation with human participants, the results of which are open to interpretation but supported, where applicable, by the demonstration of environmental control and by the continuity of behavior analytic principles from the domain of animal experimentation. Such human experiments could now be extended more clearly into the economic realm. The second is an interpretative account founded where possible upon a scientific metaprinciple such as that of "selection by consequences" (Skinner, 1981). To this essentially evolutionary analog we now turn.

The Evolutionary Analog

Behavior analysis seeks to establish the plausibility of its accounts of both animal and human behaviors by employing the evolution of biological species through natural selection as an analog for the procedure in which operant behavior is selected by the environment (Skinner, 1981). Operant conditioning has also been portrayed by its adherents as an evolutionary process in its own right—one whose causal mode is selection through consequences. The essence of evolutionary explanation lies in the inferred action of a selective environment on the continuity of the form, function, and behavior of an organism or organization and the species to which it belongs. Evolutionary biology deals with the selection of organisms that are adapted to living and reproducing in a specific local environment. Such an organism—its form, function, and behavior—constitutes the phenotype which is the result of the organism's genetic composition (genotype) and the action of the environment on that organism during the course of its development (ontogeny). Although the environment acts directly upon the phenotype, of course, the fundamental unit of selection is the gene since it alone is capable of self-replication and of thereby ensuring the continuity of selected features through their manifestation in the inheriting phenotype through successive generations (Dawkins, 1982). Genes contain both genotype and phenotype information. Variation in the phenotype is closely related to variation in the genotype: though phenotypic variation may be modified by the environment, characteristics becoming statistically dominant during this process are not—in the Darwinian account—heritable through sexual reproduction except through mutation of genotype of phenotype information. The action of the environment on the phenotype determines the extent to which the genotype potential is expressed. Variation between individuals means that some are better suited (adapted) to a particular immediate environment than are others, and this has implications for (but is not identical with) their genotypic fitness, that is, their capacity to reproduce successfully. "Survival of the fittest" refers to the selective action of the environment in which more adapted or adaptable individuals are able to survive and reproduce their advantageous characteristics.

The metaprinciple of "selection by consequences" is used by Skinner (1981) to describe and relate natural selection, which is shaped and maintained by "contingencies of survival," and the selection and persistence of instrumental human behavior in operant conditioning, in which behavior is shaped and maintained by "contingencies of reinforcement." A subset of the latter is cultural evolution, in which behaviors that are of utility to the survival and welfare of social groups and organizations are selected and transmitted, according to their consequences, from generation to generation. This is not the place to consider in full the philosophical evidence for and against this stance (see Catania and Harnad, 1988, for an extensive review by numerous scholars). However, it is pertinent to note three sources of support for the proposition. First, the evolutionary biologist Dawkins points out that in natural selection, "the replicators are the genes, and the consequences by which they are selected are their phenotypic effects, that is, mostly their effects on the embryonic development of the body in which they sit." However, in operant conditioning, the replicators are the habits in the animal's repertoire, originally spontaneously produced (the equivalent of mutation). The consequences are reinforcement, positive and negative [and punishment]. The habits can be seen as replicators because their frequency of emergence from the animal's motor system increases, or decreases, as a result of their reinforcement [or punishing] consequences. (Dawkins, 1988, p. 33)

The principal causal agency is the environment which acts to select the consequences of some behaviors but not others and thereby ensures the continuity of that which is selected. Second, the philosopher of social science van Parijs (1981) identifies the evolutionary process, as it occurs in the social and economic spheres, as that of operant conditioning. He designates this mechanism, which relies on behavioral reinforcement, as "R-evolution" in contrast to the "NS-evolution," which characterizes the survival of the fittest that occurs in natural selection. Richelle, who, unlike Dawkins and van Parijs, is a behaviorist and a leading philosopher of radical behaviorism, has also written of the compatibility of natural selection and the environmental selection of behavior:

There is nothing implausible in the idea that one basic process is at work throughout numerous levels of complexity or in a wide variety of living species. The same fundamental mechanism is called upon in evolutionary biology to account for the simplest and for the most complex living forms. The same is true of the basic principles governing the genetic code. One basic principle is acceptable if it provides for structural diversification. This is exactly what the variation-selection process does in biological evolution. But the observed diversity must not hide the basic process that produces it. The same might be true of behavior . . . Viewed in this perspective, operant behavior has little to do with the repetition of stereotyped responses which has become the popular representation of it. It is a highly dynamic process grounded in behavioral variation. Novel and creative behavior, and problem-solving do not raise particular difficulties in this view. (1987, pp. 135–136, p. 134).

Third, evolutionary economics rests on the idea of selection by consequences. Dosi and Orsenigo, for instance, refers to the evolutionary process as that in which "individual and organizational behaviors, to different degrees and through different processes, are selected, penalized or rewarded" (1988, p. 13). In contrast to the presumption of conditions of static equilibrium which pervades neoclassical economics, evolutionary economics emphasizes "discovery, learning, selection, evolution and complexity" (p. 15). The sole mechanism which can account for the selection and transmission of certain behaviors, whose consequences are invention and innovation, is operant conditioning.

CONCLUSION

Human operant experimentation, within the confines of the laboratory, offers evidence for the empirical grounding of behavior analysts' interpretations of complex human affairs. There is no doubt that such scientific testing of behavior analytic propositions will continue. But, as has been noted, even these experiments produce findings that are amenable to alternative interpretations: cognitive, Pavlovian, dispositional. The same is true, perhaps more true, of field experiments in token economies and applied behavior analysis. But, despite this, such work still confirms the possibility of an operant interpretation. And it provides a foundation for the broader interpretation of human behavior in complex social and economic settings with which we are here concerned. But the tentative nature of the interpretation so achieved must be acknowledged, and the possibility that it will give rise to a technology of consumer marketing, a prescriptive basis for managerial control, is remote. The BPM provides a behavior analytic account of managerial as well as consumer behavior, an interpretation of what marketers are doing (Foxall, 1992b): it does not lead to an enhanced armory for marketing practice. This technological limitation of behavior analysis is inherent in the nature of complex social reality, though some behavior analysts have sometimes given an impression to the contrary. Take, for instance, Skinner's criticism of cognitivists and others who, he claims, have deviated from a scientific approach to psychology:

> Those who so triumphantly announce the death of behaviorism are announcing their own escape from the canons of scientific method. Psychology is apparently abandoning all efforts to stay within the dimensional system of natural science. It can no longer define its terms by pointing to referents, much less referents measurable in centimeters, grams, and seconds. It has returned to a hypothetical inner world . . . There is no doubt of the freedom thus enjoyed. A great many things can be talked about when standards are less rigorous. (1983, p. 10)

These words betray a disingenuousness among operant behaviorists who appear to put their interpretative accounts on a similar basis to that of scientific rigor. It is precisely the freedom from rigor to which Skinner alludes that makes interpretation necessary in the operant account of complex behavior as well as elsewhere. Rigor is never deliberately rejected but it is impossible to achieve in these realms, whatever the source of the interpretation. But whereas cognitivism is overtly based on a metaphor, the computer analog, operant behaviorism is ostensibly based on the findings of rigorous experiments which are, it is claimed, extrapolable to areas where further experimentation is denied the researcher. Yet—and this is the brunt of the criticism—the realms to which the interpretations apply, notably human verbal behavior, are so far removed from the sphere of experimentation that the claims for the scientific foundation of the extended account lack plausibility for all but the most ideologically committed. For their part, cognitivists would also point to the large amount of experimental work on which their claims are based, ignored by behaviorists as though only their own interpretations had acceptable experimental foundation. Far more realistic is the guidance provided by Lee:

> In the end, an interpretation is always a plausible guess about the relevant contingencies. We can only gather information and continue to regard our interpretations as fallible and always open to improvement. Of course, the impossibility of a complete and rigorous account of the content of conduct is hard to accept, because we have long presumed that definitive answers are available. We need to face this limitation with equanimity. Certainly, we need to be determined to resist the pressure to present our interpretation as anything other than hypotheses. (1988, p. 138)

In any case, operant behaviorism proposes a simple test of the conceptual adequacy of its ontological and methodological stance and the explicatory framework in which it inheres. Skinner's test of the utility of any concept that lays claim to explanatory power in this context is whether it extends the *technology* of behavior, whether it enhances prediction and control (Skinner, 1945; Stalker and Ziff, 1988, p. 207). The experimental research which takes place within the ordered confines of the operant chamber, which allows the direct, measurable manipulation of the independent variables as well as direct, measurable observations of their effect on response rates, is uniquely geared to, first, the establishment of control and predictability and, thereafter, to their refinement. The scientific purview of operant behaviorism, given its methodological basis, provides therefore an account of the simple, observable behaviors in which it has majored—typically, the bar press of the rat and the peck of the pigeon—in the relatively unambiguous terms of their empirically identifiable determinants. Knowledge gained through interpretation is of a different order. In particular, interpretative accounts of complexity based on the analysis of simpler systems are fundamentally different in their technological implications. No meteorologist can predict or control the weather with accuracy approaching that of the results gained in wind tunnels and other experimental settings. The essence of an interpretation is that it is an *ex post* account, be it of evolutionary processes, geophysical phenomena, or consumer choice. This fundamental difference between science and interpretation bypasses the basic objectives attributed by behaviorists to scientific endeavor, namely, prediction and control. Hence the fervor with which some operant behaviorists have spoken of the technology of behavior appears, in this light, somewhat over-optimistic. In his earlier writings, Skinner appeared to claim that such interpretation transcended mere guided speculation. In *Verbal Behavior*, for instance, he implied that he was providing a more rigorous analysis than his account actually allowed, suggesting that the behavioral technology that was based on operant conditioning in experimental situations would one day, and sooner rather than later, be feasible in more complex environments. So,

> The formulation is inherently practical and suggests *immediate technological applications at almost every step.* Although the emphasis is not upon experimental or statistical facts, the book is not theoretical in the usual sense. It makes no appeal to hypothetical explanatory variables. The ultimate aim is the *prediction and control of verbal behavior* (Skinner, 1957b, p. 12; emphasis added)

Yet, in his more recent writings on the subject, Skinner seems to distance himself from such bold technological aims, from any hint of the same transferability of the experimental rigor that would make immediate technological applications possible in more open settings.

The conceptual attenuation involved in the extension of operant principles of explanation from the laboratory to the complications of the world of human behavior in open settings, shaped by unknowable learning histories, entails a quite different order of explanation from that presented in Skinner's *Behavior of Organisms* (1938), interpretational as that was in itself. Although Lee (1988) calls upon behaviorists to improve constantly their interpretative accounts of complex human conduct, this is likely to come about as the result of further logical criticism and some casual observation than by strictly controlled experimentation. The "plausible account" offered by interpretation amounts to a series of "tentative hypotheses" (Lacey, 1974, p. 40). But how feasible is rigorous experimentation that conforms to the behaviorist requirements of objectiveness and empiricalness (Zuriff, 1985) to substantiate or even improve the interpretation? At no foreseeable time is the interpretative nature of the radical behaviorist account of complex behavior likely to yield to what Skinner himself terms "a rigorous analysis" (presumably one on which a successful technology of behavior, reflecting the scientific goals of prediction and control, could be based). Indeed, it is probable that the essence of the subject matter precludes it, for the required contingencies, whatever their ontological status, are likely to remain indefinitely unavailable for rigorous empirical analysis (Foxall, 1990). Complex situations of human social behavior are precisely those whose consequences are not immediately contingent upon behavior, and where behavior can be learned in the absence of key elements of the three-term contingency (Bandura, 1977). They are, moreover, those in which superstitious interpretative accounts often dominate, albeit unconsciously, the verbal descriptions the actors themselves give of their behavior, accounts which shape and maintain further responding (Foxall, 1987, 1990).

Despite making bold claims for the epistemological status of their explanatory system, behavior analysts have generally been somewhat conservative in undertaking the interpretation of complex human behavior, especially economic behavior. Skinner's account in *Science and Human Behavior* (1953) is no more than a cursory overview. A proper reluctance to overstep the mark in respect of advocating an unjustified extension of behavioral principles to complex settings and situations, even to the point of being unwilling to ascribe inappropriate reinforcement schedules, seems to have inhibited all but the very brave (or foolhardy). Yet the BPM demonstrates that a plausible interpretation of complex behaviors is possible with minimal modification of the basic behavior analytic model and without fundamental deviation from its principles. The interpretation remains true to the tenets of a behavioral analysis by deviating from orthodox radical behaviorism only on the basis of a reasoned logical criticism of the operant stance or on the evidence of proximate operant experimentation. Whether the particular extensions of behavior theory adopted for this account of consumer choice can be employed more widely in the analysis of complex human behavior is an empirical question. Nevertheless, the BPM indicates a tentative solution to the problem with which this chapter has been concerned throughout: how to reconcile the scientific stance of behavior analysis with the imperative toward interpretation in complex situations. The chapter has shown that behavior analysis can contribute both scientifically and interpretatively to consumer psychology. It has been shown that the operational specification of the consumer behavior setting, and of utilitarian and informational reinforcement, is feasible; and the viability of empirical testing is confirmed by the investigation now underway (Foxall, 1994c) based on insights from environmental psychology. Further, the chapter has demonstrated that plausible interpretations of consumer behavior can be generated within a critically derived behavior analytic framework.

It may well be that the pursuit of these twin activities of scientific investigation and interpretation will further support one of the model's key explanatory dimensions. For a scientific approach, involving operational measurement and the falsification of hypotheses may prove to be more easily executed in a relatively closed consumer setting where the relevant reinforcers and punishers can be identified intersubjectively with the least amount of ambiguity. In such circumstance—for instance, the purchase of a TV license, the payment of taxes, or the linking of life assurance with a mortgage—a relevant learning history can be assumed with a high degree of confidence. The more open the consumer behavior setting, however, the more likely is an interpretative stance and the more obvious and convincing are alternative explanations. This is not to imply that operant principles are not at work in those environments, only that it is often more difficult to demonstrate their unique explanatory power. Nor is it to argue for the veracity of alternative explanatory systems, though it recognizes their place in psychological research and the inevitability of their continuing role within the scientific community. The BPM research program is founded on the proposition that human economic behavior, regardless of its setting, can be construed as operant, that the continuity of environmental influence across settings and situations must be a fundamental assumption of a science of behavior. The challenge for the behavior analysis of purchase and consumption is to ensure the continued viability of an operant explanation of consumer choice.

3   Ways of Wondering

> This is a work of unabashed advocacy. I want to argue in favour of a
> particular way of looking at animals and plants, and a particular way
> of wondering why they do the things that they do. What I am advo-
> cating is not a new theory, not a hypothesis which can be verified or
> falsified, not a model which can be judged by its predictions . . . What
> I am advocating is a point of view, a way of looking at familiar facts
> and ideas, and a way of asking new questions about them. Any reader
> who expects a convincing new theory in the conventional sense of the
> word is bound to be left, therefore, with a disappointed "so what?"
> feeling. But I am not trying to convince anyone of the truth of any
> factual propositions. Rather, I am trying to show the reader a way of
> seeing biological facts.
>
> —Richard Dawkins (1982, p. 1)

Critical relativism has been advocated in consumer research as a means
of freeing the discipline from the monism inherent in its almost exclusive
reliance upon the ontology and methodology of the natural sciences. Its
advocates have based their reasoning on the works of such philosophers as
Laudan (1984) and Feyerabend (1975). Laudan contends that the evaluation of theories and research traditions must always occur *within a comparative context,* taking the form of an assessment of "how [a theory's]
effectiveness or progressiveness compares with its competitors" (Laudan,
1977, p. 120). The "epistemological anarchy" of Feyerabend is more far-
reaching in its implications, emphasizing the critical interplay of competing explanations, pursued in a spirit of active proliferation and tenacity,
as essential to the growth of knowledge (Feyerabend, 1975, p. 30, p. 47).
The idea of critical relativism has sparked debate between protagonists for
traditional positivism, on the one hand, and hermeneutical method, on
the other, raising considerations of methodological monism versus methodological pluralism, the incommensurability of competing paradigms,
and the evaluation of explanations. The debate exhibits a similar cycle of
methodological confrontation, epistemological questioning, and search for
rapprochement to that found in other areas of applied inquiry such as organizational analysis.

The debate centering on positivism versus hermeneutics in consumer
research shows three tendencies to which the present inquiry is directed.
First, the objective of methodological pluralism, accepted in some degree by
nearly all parties to the debate, has not been achieved because a particular

source of methodology, terminally labeled "positivistic," has often been denied consideration; as a result, the implications of positivism for the *interpretation* of consumer research (an admittedly ironic ramification of positivism) has been ignored. This chapter seeks to demonstrate that even an extreme form of positivism, the purely descriptive approach derived from Bridgman (1927) and Mach ([1893] 1974), rather than the *logical* positivism of the Vienna Circle which, through its development of logical empiricism, became more accommodating to the epistemological assumptions of even interpretivist consumer researchers (Hunt, 1989, 1990, 1991; cf. Ayer, 1936), has much to offer a genuinely pluralistic consumer research. Since, as is argued, even a social science based deliberately upon Machian positivism must bend considerably toward interpretation when it is applied to complex human behavior, understanding its import for explanation in this context ought to interest those who advocate an interpretivist stance. (It may, incidentally, be instructive also for advocates of a natural science–derived positivism as the sole methodological model for consumer research). Second, the debate has frequently been conducted in abstract terms, preoccupied with the philosophy of science almost as an end in itself, and detached from the epistemological claims and consequences of actual explanatory systems. While it is understandable that advocates of novel approaches to consumer research will initially adduce broad, programmatic arguments and visions, it is necessary at some stage that the implications of their arguments be brought to bear upon actual theoretical frameworks which can guide our investigations and understandings. The following account examines the interrelationship of positivism and interpretation by reference to a specific, established philosophy of behavioral science, radical ("Skinnerian") behaviorism (Skinner, 1938, 1945, 1953, 1974). This system, in which behavior is held to be determined by its environmental consequences rather than by intrapersonal mental events and processes or by human agency and intentionality (Zuriff, 1985), has been evaluated by disparate authors as the most complete paradigm in psychology. Yet, despite its occasional mention in the consumer research and marketing literature, its epistemological import for consumer research has not been explored in depth. Consumer researchers who have referred to radical behaviorism have usually been interested only in the possibility of conditioning consumer choice by means of manipulating promotional stimuli, rather than in the implications for consumer research of recent behaviorist thought and research on rule-governed rather than contingency-shaped behavior (Hayes, 1989; cf. Skinner, 1969). However, such work is of substantive interest in a pluralistic consumer research and provides a concrete vehicle by which to address philosophical issues that currently impact our discipline. Third, the debate appears to have reached something of an impasse. By drawing a sharp distinction between positivism and interpretation, advocates of both a naturalistic approach to consumer research (i.e., the view that the methods of natural science are both appropriate and necessary to progress in social science) and those of interpretation have tended to argue for one or other methodology to predominate to the exclusion of the other. This has led to overly restrictive prescriptions for the nature of social science research and the methodological implications of natural science methods of procedure and exclusion such as hypothetico-deductivism. Both the "positivistic" view that interpretation is non-empirical and non-scientific and that which equates methodological pluralism with post-positivism and, on occasion, postmodernism make compromise impossible. More importantly, these exclusive views of the nature of science and interpretation ignore the subtle interrelationship of positivistic and interpretive inquiry in actual epistemological systems. This chapter is concerned with another "way of wondering," one which is not concerned with the biological realities of plants and non-human animals but with those of the complex social and economic behaviors of animals who are all too human. It takes the form of the construction, refinement, application, and evaluation of a model of consumer behavior derived from a critical appraisal of radical behaviorism (Foxall, 1990). Moreover, in contradistinction to other attempts to apply behaviorism in consumer research, it aims specifically to identify the nature of radical behaviorist *interpretation* (as opposed to its mode of scientific *explanation*), to derive and apply an interpretive framework capable of suggesting an operant account of consumer behavior, and to propose its pragmatic evaluation. This aim is not the simple one of advocating radical behaviorism as an approach to consumer research per se. Rather it is to examine a philosophy of behavioral science which is occasionally and somewhat cursorily mentioned in marketing and consumer research, to establish *in detail* the implications of incorporating it into the canon of consumer theory, and to show its limitations as well as its contributions to understanding consumer behavior.

I argue, first, that the cause of methodological pluralism is hampered by the stress on a research tradition that is uncritically post-positivist: while hermeneutic approaches provide a useful addition to the canon of consumer research methodology, they have noteworthy limitations that can be overcome only by including epistemologies derived from positivistic philosophies of science. Moreover, positivistically inclined systems such as radical behaviorism provide unique insights into the relationship between science and interpretation and increase the overall understanding of consumer behavior by providing additional definitions of the meaning of purchase and consumption. Second, the chapter describes in some depth the ontology and methodology of radical behaviorism, and its ultimate reliance upon interpretive methods in order to give an account of complex human behavior. Third, the chapter draws upon a critique of radical behaviorism to derive a model of consumer behavior based critically on the interpretive powers of this paradigm. Fourth, an interpretive method is introduced which builds upon this critical consideration of radical behaviorist interpretation; four classes of consumer behavior identified by the model are analyzed using this interpretive method: accomplishment, hedonism, accumulation, and maintenance. Finally, the chapter evaluates this approach to consumer and marketing research.

POSITIVISM AND PLURALISM IN CONSUMER RESEARCH

Debate about the relationship of logical empiricism and interpretation, as apparently alternative pathways to explanation and understanding, is endemic even to established scientific disciplines such as biology, physics, and technology (e.g., Sober, 1993; Wolpert, 1992; Ziman, 1978). Yet, among philosophers of natural science, watertight definitions of positivism, realism, and interpretation are elusive, and the alternative methodologies are often described pragmatically in contradistinction to one another rather than in absolute terms.

Boden argues that we may "regard 'an explanation' as any answer to a why question that is accepted by the questioner as making the event in question somehow more intelligible." But, she continues, "a 'scientific explanation' may be defined as an explanation that is justified by reference to publicly observable facts, and which is rationally linked to other, similar explanations in a reasonably systematic manner" (1972, p. 32). Hence, science has usually aimed toward explanatory theory rather than understanding or *Verstehen* (Chalmers, 1982; Phillips, 1987; Rosenberg, 1988). Its ultimate goal, often expressed normatively since its achievement cannot be unequivocally recognized, is theory that is true in the sense of corresponding with the way things really are. This realist stance has been held tenaciously, in spite of the onslaught of relativistic philosophies of science (especially since Kuhn's [1962] model of paradigmatic succession) by scientists themselves to describe what they actually do (Crick, 1988; Polkinghorne, 1984; Wolpert, 1992). Science, in this traditional sense, is associated with a positivistic position that emphasizes methodological monism, empiricism, the formation of descriptive laws based on systematic intersubjective observation, nominalism, the avoidance of unobservables, the eschewal of teleology, and the belief that theory comprises generalized observations rather than a prior guidance of research (O'Shaughnessy, 1992, pp. 233–234; cf. Ehrenberg, 1992).

Of special interest in the context of this chapter is the treatment of science in radical behaviorism. In *Science and Human Behavior*, Skinner emphasized that the scientific attitude entailed direct access to the facts themselves rather than the opinions of non-scientific authorities and drew attention to the central requirement of intellectual honesty among scientists for whom the subject matter must have primary authority. The practice of science consists in "a search for order, for uniformities, for lawful relations among the events in nature. It begins . . . by observing single episodes, but it quickly passes on to the general rule, to scientific law" (1953, p. 13). Such a descriptive science is not anti-theoretical, though its theoretical concentration is on the establishment of empirical regularities rather than on explanations that employ unobservables (such as attitudes, intentions, and traits of personality) which are alleged to exist at some other level than the observed data (Skinner, 1950). The aim of science is ultimately the prediction and control of its subject matter: empirical observation, based on the presumption that nature is orderly and repetitive, is a "search for causal laws, regularities, in behavior that can be generalized." Hence, "science involves a form of investigation in which the legitimacy of generalizations and theories is evaluated against their relations to empirical data, or observed facts" (Schwartz and Lacey, 1982, p. 75). Once causal laws have been established, they can be invoked to explain individual phenomena; specific observations can be made intelligible by being placed into appropriate categories which the law-like generalizations have revealed (Schwartz, 1989, p. 6). Another radical behaviorist, Lee (1988, pp. 17–18), characterizes science as knowledge that is extraordinary and reliable. It is extraordinary in that its search for facts and explanations probes beyond casual observation to reveal an understanding that is beyond everyday knowing. Science, for instance, has revealed an atomic structure not empirically available to the untrained observer. Science is reliable insofar as its results are independent of who the observer is and when they have been shown to be replicable across situations (Zuriff, 1985). Writing in the context of organizational analysis, Lee contrasts positivism, as an approach based on "inferential statistics, hypothesis testing, mathematical analysis, experimental and quasi-experimental design" (1991, p. 342), with interpretive approaches such as ethnography, hermeneutics, phenomenology, and case study. Positivism, he notes, tends toward an objective viewpoint, proceeds via a nomothetic conceptualization and the quantification of data; the investigator is assumed to be outside the subject matter, and thus to produce an etic account. By contrast, interpretivism is subjective, idiographic, qualitative, insider-based, and emic. In short, the difference is that between the methods that have traditionally been assumed to apply in the natural and physical sciences and those deemed more appropriate to the substantially different subject matter which is the domain of social science (Phillips, 1987). Indeed, the main point of contention highlighted in the positivism versus interpretation debate in social science revolves around the so-called doctrine of naturalism to the effect that social science must adopt the methods of traditional scientific inquiry in order to progress, that is, to predict and control its subject matter (Hempel, 1969; Kolakowsky, 1968).

Not even radical behaviorism, however, founded as it is upon an extreme (Machian) positivism, is able to sustain this naturalistic position in the treatment of complex social experience in human affairs, notably in the economic psychology of purchase and consumption. It is further argued, however, that giving serious attention to, recognizing the unique viewpoint of, and incorporating the ontological concerns of such positivism is an inescapable component of methodological pluralism. The interpretation of consumer behavior to which radical behaviorism gives rise provides a unique source of meaning for purchase and consumption which can usefully enrich consumer research. First, however, it is necessary to elaborate upon the claim that methodologically pluralistic consumer research has become post-positivistic and to broaden the case for including perspectives based on positivism in its methodological canon.

FROM PLURALISM TO POST-POSITIVISM

The advocacy of pluralism which marked consumer research in the early to mid-1980s appears to have given way to a narrower focus in recent years. Although some authors have promoted a broad eclecticism in the range of epistemological standpoints of concern to other investigators, the thrust of such writing has tended toward the abandonment of natural scientific traditions in favor of a post-positivistic, hermeneutical orientation. Since hermeneutics constitutes a predominant method of post-positivistic inquiry in contemporary consumer research, the following argument concentrates on this interpretivist approach. Hermeneutics originated as a method of assigning meanings to written texts such as ancient theological documents that had been produced under radically different cultural conditions from those of the interpreter. Hermeneuticists generally maintain, despite their various nuances of approach, that human behavior is intentional, comprehensible by reference to aspects of the actor's internal life such as personal beliefs, understandings, intentions, wants, and internalized social rules (Betti, 1980; Dilthey, 1976; Gadamer, 1977; C. Taylor, 1977). Thus the central hermeneutical task is to reveal the actor's understandings of his or her behavior and situation, the meanings the individual identifies with that behavior, and the circumstances, especially social, within which it occurs. Such understandings may be gained by the investigator in two ways: through the sensitive interpretation of the actor's personal verbal reports and behavior, and/or in terms of the public meanings which provide the socially mediated rules that apparently guide that behavior (Geertz, 1973). Some versions of hermeneutics examine the ways in which social and cultural factors construct the *observer's* interpretation of the (unwritten) text provided by the actor's behavior and its context (Phillips, 1992).

It is sometimes argued that a *fundamental* and *essential* divergence between the subject matter of natural science and social inquiry makes a hermeneutical approach not simply desirable in social science but the sole legitimate method of investigation; social science has been portrayed over recent decades as more akin to the humanities rather than natural science (cf. Connolly and Keutner, 1988; Macdonald and Pettit, 1981; Rabinow and Sullivan, 1979; Schutz, 1962). The rationale underlying this distinction rests upon the argument that so-called "involuntary" *behavior* is caused while "voluntary" or intentional *action* stems from wants and beliefs and intentions (Harré and Secord, 1973). The import of such an argument is to exacerbate the estrangement of natural and social science, to make the methods of the former forever inapplicable in the latter (Phillips, 1987). In Geertz's semiotic conception, social inquiry is "not an experimental science in search of law but an interpretive one in search of meaning" (1973, p. 5). This all-or-nothing thinking has sometimes strongly influenced the advocacy of pluralism in consumer research with the result that it has become in practice the advocacy of post-positivism; the apparent argument is that the limitations of a frame of reference derived from positivistic science could be redressed only by turning exclusively to post-positivist, hermeneutical methods. The intellectual trend of the post-1980 philosophically enlightened consumer research has not, therefore, produced greater tolerance of alternative theoretical positions in general. But, in general, anyone who had expected an unrestricted "active interplay" of competing theories (Feyerabend, 1975), capable of generating novel critical standpoints and syntheses, would have been disappointed. To the extent that consumer researchers adopt any epistemology to the exclusion of any other, their discipline is marked not by genuine methodological pluralism but by a new retrenchment. By restricting inquiry through the omission of any available methodology, researchers limit the types of question they are able to ask. Pluralism is weakened, therefore, by the apparent exclusion by some authors of positivism from the authorized anthology of legitimate research paradigms. Misunderstood, "positivism" has become little more than a term of abuse (Hunt, 1990), and its potential contribution to a critical methodological pluralism based upon an active interplay of antithetical standpoints has been overlooked. This argument against the exclusion of positivism is not directed against critical relativism or the hermeneutical approach per se. By challenging the plausibility structures of all the paradigms brought into competitive interplay, methodological pluralism invites relativism (Berger and Kellner, 1981, p. 80). Nor is it, therefore, a claim that positivism is "true" in any singular sense. Rather, it is meant to draw attention to two reasons why an *exclusive* reliance on hermeneutics, its presentation as the sole legitimate method in social science to the exclusion of naturalism, is both unnecessary and untenable.

HERMENEUTICS AND SCIENTIFIC METHOD

Hermeneuticists are entirely justified in drawing attention to the special interpretive method that may be derived from social science's *conscious* subject matter. But to welcome hermeneutics is not to overlook the limited contribution to social inquiry of which this interpretive methodology is capable. Far from having disposed of the need for naturalism, the application of hermeneutical method leaves much for a traditional scientific approach to accomplish. Social science has tasks other than interpretation of this kind (Phillips, 1992). Much of the work of economists, for instance, relies on direct, intersubjective observation and objective recording of aggregate behavior patterns in the absence of any investigation of the subjective states of the individuals observed. An example in consumer research is the analysis of aggregate patterns of purchase frequency and multi-brand purchasing carried out by Ehrenberg (1972). Even this work is based to a degree on interpretation, of course: intersubjective observation leads to intersubjective understanding via interpretation. But it is far removed from hermeneutical interpretation which treats whatever is being observed as a text. By the adoption and execution of methodological naturalism, social enquiry reveals itself as natural science as well as a humanities subject amenable to the interpretive insights of hermeneutics (Phillips, 1992, pp. 18–19). In summary, while human self-consciousness means that interpretation is an inevitable component of social enquiry, its contribution is bounded by the use of methods that have more in common with traditional scientific method.

Moreover, the difference between interpretivist and naturalistic inquiry has been exaggerated by some critics of hermeneutical method as well as by some advocates thereof. The belief that hermeneutics is exclusively appropriate to the humanities and (therefore) the social sciences—a view whose origins can be traced to Dilthey (1976) and Habermas (1968)—would necessarily obviate the use of hypothetico-deductivism in these interpretation-based studies. In practice, however, hermeneutics, as applied in even the most entrenched humanities subjects, has been based on this method of inquiry which originated in natural science and which is assumed by many to characterize science itself (Popper, 1972). In theology, literary study, anthropology, sociology, and in consumer research, interpretivists resort openly to external empirical criteria of judgment and evaluation; moreover, the criteria used are those generally recognized as components of Popperian falsification (Kline, 1990; cf. Currie, 1993). It may seem superfluous to emphasize given that some advocates of hermeneutical method in consumer research do not dispute it. But, in view of the opinion of other consumer researchers who adopt the position that interpretation is antithetical to such "scientific" validation, elaboration of this point is necessary. In the course of examining this theme further, we shall also uncover some aspects of interpretation that have not been previously emphasized in consumer research.

The first emphasis is that hypothetico-deductive method is central to the humanities' research program as well as being appropriate to the evaluation of interpretive social science. Føllesdal goes as far as to argue that "the so-called hermeneutic method is actually the same as the hypothetico-deductive method applied to materials that are 'meaningful' (e.g., the systems of beliefs and values of human beings in action." Hence, "the hypothetico-deductive method is used wherever interpretation takes place" (1979, p. 319). Føllesdal illustrates this by considering the function of the stranger in Ibsen's *Peer Gynt*. The obvious and acceptable methodology is that of the natural sciences: five interpretations are evaluated by confronting them with the data (e.g., the text, the biography of the author, etc.). Social scientists and philosophers who have advanced this viewpoint, and its corollary that the natural sciences and the humanities are methodologically identical, come from a wide range of critical positions and include Berger and Kellner (1981), Harré and Secord (1973), Hirsch (1967), and Phillips (1987). Even in their approach to the humanities, hermeneuticists have generally sought a "warrant of assertibility" (Dewey, 1966; emphasized by Phillips, 1987), that is, they have recognized that their claims, in order "to be taken seriously . . . must be supportable with appropriate arguments or evidence" (Phillips, 1992, p. 108). Moreover, they have sought that warrant in the hypothetico-deductive method and other canons of appraisal founded upon scientific procedure and logic. A second point of emphasis is that even when interpretive accounts do not make explicit, or actually deny, their ultimate dependence on the marshalling of external evidence to test hypotheses, their reference to a world external to their pronouncements still makes them amenable to standard scientific testing. Students of psychoanalysis often claim that in this, as in other areas of hermeneutics, an interpretative account must be judged solely by internal criteria such as plausibility, coherence, consistency, comprehensiveness, and aesthetics (Stolorow, Brandchaft, and Atwood, 1987). This claim coheres with a more general belief that notions of scientific causality are misplaced in domains of inquiry where multiple interpretations are equally plausible (Schafer, 1980). However, Kline (1990) points out that while this may be true for "closed" systems, those unrelated to something beyond themselves, such as the interpretation of a Beethoven sonata (cf. Sharpe, 1988), it does not apply to systems that have an external referent, a sphere of activity beyond the interpretation which can be used to compare it with other explanations and by which it can be appraised. Such "open" systems include psychoanalytic interpretations, whose explicatory claims—for instance, those cast in terms of Oedipal conflict in childhood leading to current social difficulties—can be tested by observation, comparison, and evaluation, the essence of traditional scientific inquiry (Wolpert, 1992). Most, if not all, interpretations of consumer behavior fall unambiguously into this "open system" category: empirical correspondence remains an important criterion of the validity of such interpretations.

In light of these considerations, the distinction between positivistic science and interpretation is a convenience at best, denoting a series of methodological perspectives ranging from those most amenable to intersubjective agreement to those that rest to a greater extent on the viewpoint of the individual investigator. No stable discipline, it appears, can avoid either a body of consensually agreed "data," "facts," or "knowledge," or a conceptual and explanatory scheme that relies upon an interpretive extrapolation of that basic corpus. As we turn from this somewhat abstract consideration to a specific philosophy of behavioral science, radical behaviorism, it becomes apparent that this dichotomy is an essential element even in an extremely positivistic natural science. More important from the viewpoint of substantive consumer research is the possibility that a plausible interpretative amount of purchase and consumption, hitherto overlooked, can be derived from this initially highly positivistic system.

A PLACE FOR POSITIVISM

Three reasons emerge why positivism in general and radical behaviorism in particular should feature in methodologically pluralistic consumer research. First, if the aim is to generate as comprehensive a critical interplay as possible, it is counter-productive to omit any viable explanatory system. As noted, in general, such omission restricts the types of question that can be asked; in the specific context of the radical behaviorism which is so frequently omitted from inquiry in consumer research, it severely limits the types of question that can be asked about the environmental and historical determination of behavior. Contrary to the view that behaviorism has been superseded by successive paradigms such as cognitive science, it remains an active intellectual inquiry especially with respect to so-called mental phenomena such as thinking, reasoning, and rule-following (Hayes, 1989; Hayes and Chase, 1991). But, even if this were not the case, it would be necessary now to invent radical behaviorism in order to ask the full array of questions about consumer choice necessary to a comprehensive pluralistic inquiry. Psychology in general studies the individual as an ahistorical being; it de-emphasizes culture, history, and context. Cognitive psychology, still the dominant paradigm of consumer research, for instance, focuses exclusively upon the putative internal representations of the mind. Other structural schools of psychology give excessive weight to intraindividual factors such as genetic makeup, personality, and psychological constitution. But human behavior is not solely a matter of such organo-centric activities and processes as thinking and constitutional development: it is vitally shaped by what has happened to the individual, his or her *prior* behavior, and the consequences it has produced. The use of hermeneutical and other interpretive methods in consumer behavior has equally tended to abstract behavior from its historical and contextual antecedents. A full explanation of consumer behavior cannot be conceived or undertaken in the absence of this recognition and a concentrated attempt to overcome the lack of a contextual perspective. Second, social science cannot be entirely hermeneutical in the narrow sense of trying to account for or understand behavior in the absence of any reference to systems labeled "positivist." Even consumer researchers who have argued that positivism and interpretation lead to incommensurable outcomes (Ozanne and Hudson, 1989) may see a place for both. It is hopefully shown in this chapter that there is a more subtle relationship between positivism and interpretation than this allows. Third, so developed a paradigm as radical behaviorism has more to offer the growth of knowledge and understanding in consumer research than prescriptions for more effective retailing and minor components of grand theories. The epistemological basis offered by this philosophy of behavioral science, allied to the interpretive innovations proposed in this chapter, can provide consumer research with an alternative comprehensive model of purchase and consumption which promises both a new empirical and theoretical research program and a broader synthesis.

Several positivistically inclined disciplines which enjoy general application in social science, such as micro-economics, cognitivism, and psychometrics, have contributed extensively to consumer research. However, while behaviorism receives intermittent mention in marketing and consumer research, its contribution usually has been confined to the tactical management of promotional stimuli. The possibility that behaviorism provides an explanatory base for consumer behavior has often been explicitly ruled out of consideration. As a result, the unique explicatory stance of behaviorism, in which the causes of behavior are sought in a controlling environment rather than in intrapersonal states and processes, has been overlooked at a time when consumer research has increasingly encouraged methodological pluralism. *Radical* behaviorism has been especially denied epistemological consideration: indeed, the ontological and methodological implications of this paradigm (Skinner, 1938, 1950, 1963, 1974) have been explicitly rejected by authors who have expressed a preference for cognitive-behavioral theories such as those of Bandura (1977) and Staats (1975). This reluctance to bring radical behaviorism into the mainstream of consumer research is understandable on one level: the paradigm appears to have enjoyed its heyday in the 1940s and 1950s, only to be eclipsed by the cognitive science that emerged so strongly in the 1960s and which has dominated psychology ever since (Baars, 1986; Dennett, 1987; Leahey, 1987; Mandler, 1985). The uncompromisingly anti-cognitivist stance of radical behaviorism's founder may also have contributed: just a few days before his death, Skinner referred to cognitivism as "the creationism of psychology" (Vargas, 1990, p. 409). Few consumer researchers, or other social scientists, would presumably wish to controvert the prevailing self-image of our age, the post-Enlightenment view of men and women in charge of their destiny and liberty though the exercise of their rationality (Gay, 1966), by embracing so extreme an environmental determinism as that of radical behaviorism.

It may also be that a discipline whose members are increasingly aware of the implications of hermeneutical method find little to attract them in a philosophy of psychology that is so evidently positivistic in outlook, so intent on modeling its research methods on those found in the natural/physical sciences, and, apparently, passé. This chapter contends, nevertheless, that if consumer researchers genuinely are concerned to develop a pluralistic discipline which fully recognizes the value of alternative interpretational stances, radical behaviorism can no longer be denied its place in our epistemological canon. For, as is argued, far from being a paradigm that social science can disregard, radical behaviorism remains an intellectually challenging framework within which to comprehend human behavior, including those actions such as thinking, reasoning, and meaning which have conventionally fallen within the domain of cognitive science and hermeneutics. The results of the analysis may also surprise even those consumer researchers whose primary methodological and ontological preference tends toward naive realism and positivism. The following sections consider the ontological and methodological implications of radical behaviorism (Skinner, 1974) in the context of debate in consumer research about the roles of science and interpretation. As noted, radical behaviorism is chosen to illumine this debate because it rests upon a far more extremely positivistic basis than the *logical* empiricism which many interpretive consumer researchers have attacked (but which is actually more similar to their approved position than some of them imagined [Hunt, 1991]). Machian positivism, on which radical behaviorism is founded, deserves the attention of consumer researchers who would encourage pluralism because it is a major explanatory system hitherto overlooked. More important for the present purpose, however, is the interaction of scientific and interpretive functions that even this extreme positivistic position reveals and requires. While radical behaviorism provides a naturalistic account of behavior in laboratory and other relatively simple contexts, its role in the *interpretation* of complex human conduct raises many of the issues of method, validity, and reliability inherent in the hermeneutic task. It has been asserted previously that "open" explanatory systems, both positivistic and non-positivistic, derive a warrant for the conclusions they assert from observed reality. The chapter examines the implications of a system whose warrant is based on rigorous experimentation rather than, as is often claimed of hermeneutic accounts, solely on criteria such as internal consistency, aesthetics, elegance, or persuasiveness.

SCIENCE AND METASCIENCE IN RADICAL BEHAVIORISM

The problems of interpretation cluster around two issues: the nature of reality and the nature of measurement. Philosophers of science have latterly been busy explaining that science is about correlating phenomena or acquiring power to manipulate them. They stress the theory-laden character of our pictures of the world and the extent to which scientists are said to be influenced in their thinking by the social factor of the spirit of the age. Such accounts cast doubt on whether an understanding of reality is to be conceived of as the primary goal of science or the actual nature of its achievement. These comments from the touchline may well contain points of value about the scientific game. They should not, however, cause us to neglect the observations of those who are actually players. The overwhelming impression of the participants is that they are investigating the way things are. Discovery is the name of the game. The pay-off for the rigours and *longueurs* of scientific research is the consequent gain in understanding of the way the world is constructed. Contemplating the sweep of the development of some field of science can only reinforce that feeling.

—J. C. Polkinghorne (1984, pp. 1–2).

Ontology and Methodology

Radical behaviorism is inextricably bound up with the scientific career of B. F. Skinner (1904–1990), who founded and developed this philosophy of psychology (Skinner, 1938, 1950, 1953, 1963, 1974). Fundamental characteristics of his work include a positivism based upon biological economy and expediency, and an insistence upon inductive generalization, coupled with avoidance of any formalistic approach to scientific discovery. This includes even a refusal to formally design experiments: open curiosity rather than deliberate confinement of the possibilities for behavior patterns to emerge was the intended guiding principle (Skinner, 1956). None of this implies that radical behaviorism is value-free or theory-independent, or that Skinner's experimental space was a *tabula rasa* on which truth could spontaneously emerge. By the time he commenced work in psychology, at the graduate level at Harvard in 1928, the basis of radical behaviorist interpretation had been laid; it reflected Skinner's intellectual growth to that point which had encompassed elements of Baconian, Darwinian, Watsonian, and Russellian thought (Skinner, 1976), all of which inclined it toward environmental behaviorism. It was soon to add elements of the philosophies of science of P. Bridgman (1927) and E. Mach ([1896] 1959). A biographer (Bjork, 1993) even raises the possibility that Skinner's later emphasis on the efficacy of positive reinforcement over punishment derived from aspects of his upbringing.

The paradigm inaugurated by Skinner (1938, 1945, 1963), "the experimental analysis of behavior," consists of three separable elements (Blackman, 1980): *operant conditioning*, in which environmental factors determine the rate at which responses occur (Skinner, 1938)—see Box 3.1; *a single subject research strategy*, which proceeds inductively through the intensive analysis of individual behavior rather than the testing of deductive hypotheses by intergroup statistical comparisons (Skinner, 1950, 1961, 1969); and *radical behaviorism*, which explains behavior, including thought and other "cognitive" activity, by reference to contingent environmental stimuli rather than by intrapersonal states and events such as moods and attitudes (Skinner, 1974). (By "contingent" it is meant that the occurrence of the behavior now or in the future depends upon its having been followed in the past by consequential environmental events that have reinforced or rewarded it.) Radical behaviorism is the metatheory of the paradigm, that is, "a philosophy of science concerned with the subject matter and methods of psychology" (Skinner, 1963, p. 951, 1974, p. 3). Explanation in radical behaviorism consists in identifying the environmental elements that control the rate at which a response is emitted (Skinner, 1950) and, as the empirical analysis takes account of increasingly complex contingencies between discriminative stimuli, responses, and reinforcing/punishing stimuli, it is said to replace cognitive and other "mentalistic" explanations in terms of personality traits, attitudes, purposes, and intentions (Skinner, 1971, p. 18).

Behaviorism, in general, is an exploration of "what it means for psychology to be a natural science" (Zuriff, 1985, p. 8), a quest based on the twin criteria of *empiricalness* (scientific facts are derived through the

---

Box 3.1 The essence of operant behaviorism.

Treatments of operant conditioning are available in texts on learning (e.g., Catania, 1992a; Gordon, 1989; Lieberman, 1993; Schwartz, 1989). The paradigm is defined by the "three-term contingency": $S^D \rightarrow R \rightarrow S^R$, where S^R is the reinforcing consequence of a response, R, and S^D is a discriminative stimulus which does not elicit R (as it does an unconditioned stimulus in classical conditioning) but simply sets the occasions for reinforcement contingent upon the *emission* of the response, R. Despite the separability of the three components of this paradigm, radical behaviorist explanation rests in practice on the findings of operant conditioning experiments which show that the contingent consequences of behavior come in shape and maintain it. The "contingencies of reinforcement" which provide the basis of explanation comprise the behavior in question, the setting conditions in which it occurs (composed of discriminatory stimuli that signal an opportunity for reinforcement), those of its consequences that influence the rate at which it repeated, and the relationships among all of these. The discriminative stimulus, responses, and reinforcing/punishing consequence, each of which is a class rather than a single event, make up the fundamental explanatory device, the "three-term contingency."

Operant behaviorism is not, therefore, a stimulus-response (S-R) psychology (cf. classical conditioning). While radical behaviorism describes behavior as coming under stimulus control when responses are reinforced differentially in the presence of separate antecedent stimuli, the relationship between a discriminative stimulus and a response does not involve automatic elicitation of reflexive behavior. The discriminative stimulus alters the probability of a response by announcing the availability of reinforcement that is dependent on the emission of that response.

senses, wherever possible in the form of controlled experimental observation) and *objectivity* (independent of the individual preferences of the investigator, leading to publicly unambiguous findings rather than subjective interpretations) (p. 9). (*Radical* behaviorism, as is shown next, diverges somewhat from the latter criterion in principle, though much of its practice has endeavored to conform.) The result should be an intellectual exercise which is continuous with the rest of science, particularly, in the case of radical behaviorism, with biology (Smith, 1986).

The ontology and methodology of radical behaviorism are summarized in Boxes 3.2 and 3.3 which regroup the twelve essential characteristics of this explanatory system proposed by Delprato and Midgley (1992). *Ontologically*, radical behaviorism proposes that the explanandum of psychology is behavior and that its controlling variables are to be found in the extrapersonal environment. Current behavior is a function of the environmental consequences produced by similar actions in the past, though it may come under the control of immediately antecedent stimuli that signal similar consequences (the "three-term contingency"). Radical behaviorism is a materialistic philosophy: the universe is physical, and Cartesian notions of a mind-body duality are rejected. Changes to the organism and its behavior are biological, the result of an evolutionary past (the phylogenic history of the individual) and of a personal history of learning acquired during the lifetime of the individual (its ontogenic development). Operant behavior—to which most animal and human responses belong—that which *operates* on the environment, thereby producing consequences (rewards and punishments) that control its future rate of occurrence, includes language, thinking, consciousness, and science. The explanatory system applies, therefore, to all behavior which is not the direct result of evolutionary "contingencies of survival" or classical conditioning. Operant learning principles thus apply to "private" as well as "public" behaviors.

The *methodology* of radical behaviorism is intended to contribute to the prediction and control of behavior rather than its "understanding." Its explanation is descriptive rather than abstracted and theoretical, consisting in functional analysis which links behavior (always the dependent variable) to the independent (environmental) variables that control its rate of emission. Two such functional relationships are identifiable: *respondent* (Skinner's term for the response class occurring in classical conditioning) and *operant* (the response class relevant to operant or instrumental conditioning). This methodology requires searching for the laws that govern behavior-environment relationships, a deterministic stance. It is the environment, therefore, that *selects* behavior, not the individual who is simply a locus for the operation of "selection by consequences." Finally, psychology is reducible to biological terms in the sense that humans are zoological entities, but neither biology nor any other "lower level" discipline is adequate to account entirely for behavior. Behavior analysis is a discipline in its own right.

Box 3.2 Epistemological basis of radical behaviorism: Ontology.

Behavior as the Subject Matter

Behaviorism is uncompromising in its insistence that behavior is the proper focus of psychological inquiry. Watson, the founder of the movement, wrote, "Psychology as the behaviorist sees it is a purely objective experimental branch of natural science. Its theoretical goal is the prediction and control of behavior. Introspection forms no essential part of its methods, nor is the scientific value of data dependent upon the readiness with which they lend themselves to interpretation in terms of consciousness" (1913, p. 58). Behavior as Skinner defined it is the "action of the whole organism" (1975, p. 144) rather than that of any of its parts such as the actions of a muscle group. It is what the organism *does* (Skinner, 1938, p. 6) and is evident from the observation of the organism in relationship with its environment (Delprato and Midgley, 1992). Behaviorism is a subject matter in its own right and is neither an indication nor a confirmation of the existence of mental activity. "When you are studying behavior, don't claim to be studying something else: whether it's the operation of the cerebral cortex or cognition" (Smith, 1986, p. 272–275). Behavior may, however, take place within the organism in the form of perception, knowing, thinking, and so on.

The Locus of Behavioral Control

The "initiating causes of behavior are to be found solely within the environment" (Skinner, 1988c p. 73). The crucial variables are not found within the organism, though private, verbal events—which presumably take place within the skin—may act to signal the availability of reinforcement contingent upon the emission of a particular response, that is, as discriminative stimuli. These private events might conceivably be spoken of as proximate causes of behavior or catalysts for specific responses. But this still amounts to non-mental causation since what is within the individual is as physical as the external environment of behavior. The internal event is itself the product of environmental control, a response subject to reinforcing and punishing contingencies. Environmental causation includes genetic prefiguring.

Stimulus Control of Operant Behavior

Although operant behavior is shaped and maintained by its consequences (more accurately, the consequences that similar behavior has generated in the past), pre-behavioral stimuli play a part. Stimuli that are frequently paired with reinforcers/punishers and which occur immediately before the response in question come to signal the consequences of responding, to set the occasion for a response. They are known as discriminative stimuli because in their presences the organism discriminates (behaviorally) by

(continued)

Box 3.2 (continued)

emitting only that response which has previously been followed by either reinforcement or the avoidance/escape from aversive consequences. Discriminative stimuli have no power to elicit responses as antecedent stimuli elicit respondents. An antecedent stimulus may, however, come to control an operant response in the sense that it is followed by the response even though no reinforcement has been forthcoming on the previous several occasions; however, it retains such power of discriminative control only if it is paired more or less frequently with the reinforcer. Moreover, its power is determined by the previously acting contingencies of reinforcement and punishment which determine the learning history of the organism. The basic paradigm of operant conditioning and of radical behaviorist explanation is the "three-term contingency" consisting of a discriminative stimulus, a response, and its reinforcing or punishing consequences.

Materialism

Skinner denies that there are non-physical events or causes which are essentially mental. This is not to deny that, for instance, thoughts, perceptions, knowing, understanding, consciousness, and meaning exist, but it is to redefine them ontologically as behaviors. It is feasible to provide a comprehensive explanation of behavior without departing from the material realm.

Box 3.3   **Epistemological basis of radical behaviorism: Methodology.**

Purpose of Science

The purpose of science is prediction and control rather than the speculative theorizing and the testing of deductive hypotheses. Skinner's approach to theory rejected "any explanation of an observed fact which appeals to events taking place somewhere else, at some other level of observation, described in different terms, and measured, if at all, in different dimensions" (1950, p. 193). Such other events are often no more than "explanatory fictions" which bring inquiry to a premature end. But Skinner is in favor of theory of another kind, that is, empirically based and leading to sound interventions to solve practical problems. The hallmark of such theorization is pragmatism rather than intersubjective agreement among scholars.

Functional Analysis

The purpose of psychology, which is unequivocally an experimental science, is the isolation of reliable relations between environment (the independent variable) and behavior (the dependent). The aim is to

(continued)

Box 3.3 (continued)

establish functional relationships, those which "occur when a change in an independent variable results in a change in a dependent variable" (Delprato and Midgley, 1992). Functional analysis is thus concerned to establish three basic facts of observation, the circumstances under which behavior occurs and reliably varies being its controlling variables.

Classification of Behavior into Respondent and Operant

Skinner (1938) reaffirmed the phenomenon of classical (Pavlovian) conditioning, renaming its subject matter in the process as respondent conditioning. Respondents are responses elicited by prior stimuli; the pairing is the basis of stimuli; the pairing is the basis of stimulus-response (S-R) psychology. Respondent behavior is essentially reflexive and is sometimes referred to as involuntary. The relationship between stimulus and response implies a mechanical kind of causation (Delprato and Midgley, 1992). Operant behavior is behavior which operates upon the environment to produce consequences which determine the response's future rate of occurrence (Skinner, 1953, p. 65, 1971, p. 18). It is emitted by the organism and is sometimes somewhat misleadingly referred to as "voluntary." While it is not reflexive ("involuntary") behavior, it is still under the control of environmental variables, although these are sometimes difficult to detect, giving rise to the notion that the behavior is independent of the environmental stimuli that control it. Such functional relationships are described as response-stimulus (R-S). Identifying and describing the contingent relationships between a response and its reinforcing or punishing consequences are the essence of functional analysis.

Determinism

The scientific enterprise is deterministic, and its application to human behavior demands, no less than in any other sphere of scientific investigation, that behavior be shown to be lawful; prediction and control would be impossible if it were not so (Skinner, 1953, p. 6). Within this empirical epistemology, cause and effect relationships were reduced to correlations between observations and independent and dependent variables. Skinner's doctoral thesis, which was entirely theoretical, redefined stimuli and responses as correlation (rather than in terms of the "push" of the stimulus). Far from a system of mechanistic causation, therefore, radical behaviorism relies on functional relationships.

Organism as the Locus of Biological Change

The individual has been changed by his or her histories—evolutionary and environmental. Evolution has provoked physiological changes in the organism, including a propensity to be conditioned by the environment

(continued)

Box 3.3 (continued)

during the course of one's lifetime. In a complementary way, operant conditioning changes the individual biologically. Radical behaviorism is not, therefore, an "empty organism" philosophy. But the inner changes which correlate with behavioral changes are biological rather than cognitive. There is thus no reason to posit internalization, information processing, internal representations, storage, and so on, to account for behavior. Since none of these is amenable to biological analysis, cognitivism amounts to "premature physiology" (Skinner, 1986).

Generality of Behavioral Principles

The principles of respondent and operant conditioning are held by radical behaviorists to account for all animal and human behavior including that which is private—thinking, reasoning, knowing, understanding, and so on. Because reflex behavior constitutes such a small proportion of the repertoire of all animals, comparatively little attention is accorded respondent conditioning. By far the greater proportion is given to the psychology of the operant, commensurate with the greater proportion of behavior which is of this kind. Operant psychology thus provides an account of behavior that is unique to humans—the acquisition and use of language, that is, verbal behavior. Operant behavior in humans is of two broad kinds: contingency shaped, that is, determined by direct contact with the environment; and rule governed, that is, determined by verbal descriptions of contingencies. The analysis of verbal behavior and rule governance often relies on the inference of private events which are not directly amenable to objective scientific investigation.

Consequential Causality

Radical behaviorist explanation, the inevitable outcome of its ontology and methodology, is based on the selection of behavior by the environment on which it operates. The process is treated as homologous with that of natural selection: "Just as genetic characteristics which arise as mutations are selected or discarded through reinforcement," the assumption of "consequential causality" (Delprato and Midgley, 1992, p. 1517) is consistent with the rejection of mechanistic causation, including that of stimulus-response (S-R) psychology.

Reduction

The radical behaviorist position on reductionism is ambiguous. Delprato and Midgley (1992) point out that Skinner (1947, p. 31, 1975, p. 42, 1974, p. 215) embraced the possibility that physiologists would eventually produce a biological basis to which the phenomena of behavior analysis would be reducible. However, he also claimed that behavior analysis was a field in its own right, behavior an independent subject matter (1938, p. 433, 1961, p. 64, 1975, pp. 42–44). Perhaps Skinner's contention that operant psychologists were setting an agenda for physiological research (e.g., 1974, p. 215) was a means of reconciling these ideas, acknowledging that biology would one day substantiate behaviorism, which keeping behavior analysts free to pursue their own science at a higher level of analysis.

MACHIAN POSITIVISM

The radical behaviorist program was from its inception concerned to establish positive knowledge and avoid metaphysical speculation, to be demonstrably effective in the prediction and control of behavior rather than speculate about its supposed—but unverifiable by sense data—inner causes. The objection to inner causes, whether mental, neural, or hypothetical, is that they may prove no more than "explanatory fictions" which merely re-describe observations and, by offering a spurious explanation, bring inquiry to a premature end. The naive realism of the stance assumes no distinction between appearance to the scientific eye and reality (Zuriff, 1985, p. 250). The methodological program of radical behaviorism is derived directly from these premises: a science of behavior proceeds inductively, seeking functional relationships between environment and behavior, empirical regularities allowing both prediction and control, rather than theoretical sophistication based on hypothetico-deductive speculation (Skinner, 1969, pp. vii–xii).

The strongest influence on Skinner's philosophy of scientific psychology was the physicist E. Mach ([1893] 1974, [1896] 1959, [1905] 1976). Machian positivism understands cause in terms of the functional dependence of phenomena, "for that is all that can be observed" (Zuriff, 1985, p. 265; see also Smith, 1986, p. 185). Explanation is understood as description of what is directly available to experience and must not include reference to an unobservable realm of putative causes or to theoretical terms alleged to describe them. For Mach, "a valid explanation is nothing more than an economical abstract description of experience" (Zuriff, 1985, p. 265). In the same vein, Bridgman (1927), to whose thought Skinner was introduced in 1929, refused to entertain any role for unobservables in scientific investigation and explanation (Bjork, 1993, p. 99). Transferring this idea to the reflexive sphere of psychological investigation, Skinner found another justification for the parsimonious approach: theoretical entities, hypotheses, and unobservables deflected the scientist from the goals of prediction and control. The functional method avoided both hypothetico-deductivism and the temptation to interpose "explanatory fictions" between observer and observed; the scientist was thus more quickly rewarded for undertaking the painstaking tasks of investigation, his or her behavior more effectively reinforced by discovery (Zuriff, 1985, p. 260). Machian positivism, coupled with the Baconian insistence on empiricism led Skinner to a methodology of science that stressed "observation, classification, the gradual inductive establishment of laws, and the avoidance of over-generalization and metaphysical dogma" (Zuriff, 1985, p. 264). Mach had emphasized the continuity of science and the everyday working behavior of the craftsman: laws and concepts were therefore viewed as historically conditioned and contingent. The whole methodological approach is based on the belief that the investigator can separate the "genuine experiential import" of observations from any "superfluous metaphysical meanings" he or she might have been conditioned to "see." At one level, Mach's positivism was concerned with the parsimonious description of current facts (i.e., observations), but it was rooted in post-Darwinian evolutionary explanation. Science was believed to have evolved in order to make human adaptation and survival more probable; insofar as science made human control of the environment surer, it "promoted the survival of the species" (Bjork, 1993, p. 100). Hence Mach's criterion of scientific success was the extent to which knowledge facilitated the adaptation of the individual to its environment. Knowledge and truth thus were defined biologically rather than philosophically.

Nevertheless, there is clearly some confusion over the nature of the positivism that underlies radical behaviorism. Perhaps because both Skinner's system and the early *logical* positivism of the Vienna Circle stemmed from Mach—the group was initially known as the Verein Ernst Mach—and because of Skinner's passing interest in logical positivism during the thirties, radical behaviorism has often been portrayed as founded on logical positivism or the more sophisticated logical empiricism derived from it. Two full-length treatments by psychologists have assumed the connection (Koch, 1964; Mackenzie, 1977). However, as Smith comments, "Far from being a *logical* positivism, Skinner's positivism is grounded in biological expedience" (1986, p. 275). The logical positivists sought a philosophy of science compatible with the revolutions in physics brought about by the advent of quantum mechanics and relatively theory. These theories explicitly employed unobservables to explain physical phenomena at the atomic level; scientific facts were no longer based on direct observation of nature but depended on the frame of reference adopted by the scientist (Moore, 1985). Logical positivism initially accepted as axiomatic that (i) the sole route to knowledge was scientific method, (ii) metaphysical speculation deserved no place in scientific inquiry and explanation, and (iii) science required physicalist definitions based on intersubjective agreement on observations and measurements. The logical positivists' verifiability principle (Ayer, 1936) contended that statements were meaningful only if they were either *analytical*, for instance, definitional statements assumed by scientists, or *synthetic*, that is, they led to empirically testable deductions, "predictions that could be matched against sense data" (Moore, 1985, p. 55). This epistemological orientation is highly formalistic in its adoption of hypothetico-deductivism as *the* route to knowledge: scientific explanation was commensurate with scientific predictability. Logical positivism was also virtually synonymous with operationism: scientific concepts were expected to correspond descriptively to the experimental operations by which they were measured.

Radical behaviorism has several elements in common with this earlier logical positivism. As noted, Skinner readily accepted that scientific explanation consisted of generalizable descriptive statements and that concepts should be construed in observational terms (Moore, 1985, p. 56); hence he rejected explanations that appealed to a non-observational dimension, emphasized the quantitative description of actual phenomena, and accorded central importance to practical matters arising from the prediction, manipulation, and control of events. However, there are several key points of divergence between logical positivism and radical behaviorism. Radical behaviorism is anti-formalist, vehemently rejecting a hypothetico-deductive logic of inquiry (Skinner, 1969), which certainly characterized the logical empiricists between 1938 and 1971 (Churchland, 1986, pp. 254–255). Further, Skinner's operationism concentrated on the analysis of the research practice of the scientist (this is, consistent with the principles of biological economy, pragmatism, and adaptation found in Mach's philosophy), as compared with the logical physicalism inherent in the positivism of the Vienna Circle which required the intersubjective judgment of the scientific community to establish knowledge. Skinner subordinated logic to psychology: while logical positivists conceived science as "a linguistic phenomenon dealing with the logical syntax of language," radical behaviorism viewed science psychologically (in terms of the observed behavior of the scientist) and ultimately from a Darwinian functionalist perspective (Smith, 1986, p. 46). Most important of all is that, despite its initial concern with direct observation and operationism, logical empiricism came to incorporate non-physical events in order to increase its predictive accuracy. We have seen that Skinner always rejected an unobservable dimension, necessary to explanation of the observable. Moreover, whereas logical empiricism, when it was applied in psychology, came to distinguish a mental from a physical realm, Skinner spoke always of public and private events, both of which were physical in nature. That private events such as thoughts and feelings exist "within the skin" makes no difference to their ontological status (Skinner, 1974).

In this respect, radical behaviorism differs fundamentally from other forms of behaviorism and from cognitivism. Methodological behaviorism, for instance, insists on truth by (intersubjective) agreement and thus cannot deal with private events; it labels concern with the nature of thoughts and emotions as metaphysical speculation. Radical behaviorism accepts such private events as both real and part of its subject matter even though they are accessible to only one person, and it construes them as physical events, responses subject to similar environmental influences to those that control observable behaviors. They remain, therefore, within a scientific purview. Moore sums up the vital difference:

> The logical positivists and operationalists assumed license to construct any kind of entity and hence they kept in psychology all the old mentalistic explanatory fictions. Instead, Skinner argued, the doctrines of logical positivism and operationism should be employed to assess the extent to which terms were or weren't derived from actual contact with experimental operations. (1985, p. 58; cf. Phillips, 1992)

In summary, the positivism on which radical behaviorism is based is not logical empiricism with its inclusion of unobservables and consequent scientific realist ontology. Rather, it is a far more extreme positivism based on the original Machian view that science is description.

PRAGMATISM AS CRITERION OF TRUTH

The key to the entire philosophy of psychology espoused by radical behaviorism, which underlies both its scientific stance and its approach to interpretation, is its ultimate ontological position, pragmatism. It is by this that both the validity of its scientific endeavors in the laboratory and field experimentation and the interpretations of complex behaviors it bases on those endeavors must be appraised. Despite the extreme positivism radical behaviorism espouses, it is not concerned with the problem of scientific realism. In a tradition deriving from C. Peirce and W. James, it is *pragmatic* rather than realist, concerned not with discovering how an objectively available world is constituted and how it behaves but with what the world enables the investigator to accomplish. It is this underlying guideline to research that accounts for radical behaviorism's economy of conceptualization and communication, its view of the behavior of the scientist as the invention of rules under operant control, its stress on prediction and control as criteria of scientific truth, and its equating of explanation with description (Baum, 1994). Skinner's extreme pragmatism has no place for absolute truth; the criterion of *relative* truth (that is, relative to a particular historical and current context) is expediency or success (Morris, 1991); "good" and "right" are defined in terms of the capacity to reinforce (Zuriff, 1985, pp. 259–260). Since radical behaviorism thus avoids the question of whether there is a real world and how such a world must be approached, it is not concerned with issues of objectivity and subjectivity and the need to explain the world of observation by reference to a hidden world of explanation that lies beyond it. The requirement of science that description be economical leads to precise and rigorous methods of observation, though the entire enterprise is contingent upon what can be spoken of in the terms devised by the scientist, the most *useful* ways to talk about behavior, rather than on observation for its own sake. The emphasis is on devising concepts and terms that lead to control of behavior; constructs and principles which do not prove successful in this regard are discarded (Grant and Evans, 1994, pp. 8–9; see also Day, 1980; Skinner, 1957, 1969). This is the source of the theory-ladenness of radical behaviorism: its confinement of scientific discourse to the terms of the three-term contingency and its presupposition that behavior can be usefully spoken of in terms of its elements, period. Hence description can embrace private events such as thinking and reasoning as long as these are cast as behaviors in their own right and not accorded any causal status. Knowledge too must be understood and evaluated in relation to its function

(Zuriff, 1985, p. 257). However, the description, prediction, and control which behavior analysis seeks in order to demonstrate understanding and knowing is not necessarily that which leads to social engineering. Rather, the epistemological (as opposed to practical) prediction and control on which radical behaviorist pragmatism relies is first and foremost a question of demonstrating that behavior is a function of environmental factors (discriminative and reinforcing stimuli), and this can be accomplished experimentally: "That is, we understand behavior to the extent that we know how it works—knowledge gained through its analysis, a refined sense of 'successful' working" (Morris 1991, p. 131).

FROM SCIENCE TO INTERPRETATION

The research output of behavior analysts demonstrates comprehensively the environmental control of simple behaviors under experimental conditions. Any basic learning text details the achievements of the experimental analysis of animal behavior (e.g., Catania, 1992a; Lieberman, 1993), and research volumes (e.g., Blackman and Lejeune, 1990; Chase and Parrott, 1986; Hayes, 1989; Hayes and Chase, 1991) catalog progress in human operant experiments, especially those involving verbal behavior. The capacity of behavior analysts to bring operant behavior under stimulus control under laboratory conditions is not in doubt. But only a small proportion of behavior is amenable to rigorous experimental investigation: the bulk of (assumed) human operant behavior, that maintained by complex contingencies, eludes this technique (Kline, 1989). Yet none of this has impeded the claims of prescriptive and applied operant psychology in such realms of human activity as education, therapy, language acquisition, and even the design of cultures (Skinner, 1953, 1971). In behavioral domains such as these, which lie beyond the rigor of experimental control, radical behaviorism offers an account based on the extension of behavior principles gained in the analysis of simpler, more amenable contexts (the operant laboratory) to the wider realm. Perhaps the best-known example of radical behaviorist interpretation is found in Skinner's *Verbal Behavior*, in the introduction to which he points out that the interpretive method relies upon "an orderly arrangement of well-known facts, in accordance with a formulation of behavior derived from an experimental analysis of a more rigorous sort" (1957, p. 11). The warrant for such an account is constructed from the experimental analysis of behavior in simpler contexts; such an account is less than complete insofar as it alludes to contingencies that can only be analogously inferred, not directly observed and measured. Its plausibility derives from the principles gained in the experimental analysis of behavior and the assumption of continuity between the experimental conditions and those in which the interpreted behavior occurs. The resulting interpretive account falls short of the requirements of a radical behaviorist *explanation*;

"merely useful," its truth or falsity cannot be ascertained with the certainty available to the experimental scientist (Skinner, 1988b, p. 364).

Radical behaviorists claim that their science does not differ in this respect from others, that all sciences interpret when they cannot explain (Bethlehem, 1987). Skinner defines interpretation as "the use of scientific terms and principles in talking about facts about which too little is known to make prediction and control possible. The theory of evolution is an example . . ." (1988a, p. 207). The radical behaviorist interpretation of complex behavior thus also resembles those that deal with the geophysics of the earth's core, or the astrophysics of the sun. None is provable but each builds plausibly on the knowledge gained "under more favorable conditions" (Skinner, 1973, p. 261, 1974, pp. 226–232, 1988a, p. 208). Beyond the acknowledgement that radical behaviorism must interpret where it cannot explain, behavior analysts have rarely considered what form interpretation might take, how it should be evaluated and what implications it would have for prediction and control (see, however, Lee, 1988). The objective of hermeneutical analysis has been to uncover the meanings of remote texts and any appraisal of the nature and contribution of radical behaviorist interpretation can be reasonably expected to establish its credentials for conferring meaning. A central tenet of radical behaviorism is that meaning—the meaning of a response (Skinner, 1953, p. 36)—is to be found in its antecedents (the individual's learning history, plus current discriminative stimuli) and the consequences they have portended (the independent variables that control current responding).

These considerations are central to establishing what kind of account a model of consumer behavior based on a critique of radical behaviorism can offer. A severe indictment of the nature of a radical behaviorist account is made by Geertz (1973, pp. 6–7) in his elaboration of Ryle's (1968, 1971) distinction between "thin" and "thick" description. Geertz claims that radical behaviorism's explicative capacity is exhausted while it is still at the level of thin description, while anthropological interpretation requires and is capable of providing thick description. In Ryle's exposition of the difference between these descriptive levels, he speaks of a wink as (i) an involuntary muscle twitch, (ii) a conspiratorial signal, and (iii) a parody. In each case, from the viewpoint of what Geertz calls "an I-am-a-camera, 'phenomenalist' observation," a rapid contraction of an eyelid. But there are important distinctions to be made. While a twitch is not intended to communicate cultural meaning, a wink involves "communicating in a quite precise and special way: (1) deliberately, (2) to someone in particular, (3) to impart a particular message, (4) according to a socially established code, and (5) without cognizance to the rest of the company" (Geertz, 1973, p. 6). If a wink is executed as a parody of the involuntary action of the twitcher, however, a whole new set of cultural meanings is embedded in the blink of the eyelid.

The point is that between what Ryle calls the "thin description" of what the rehearser (parodist, winker, twitcher . . .) is doing ("rapidly contracting his right eyelid") and the "thick description" of what he is doing ("practicing a burlesque of a friend faking a wink to deceive an innocent into thinking a conspiracy is in motion") he's the object of ethnography. (p. 7)

Geertz's contention is that radical behaviorism is confined to thin description through some kind of conceptual impoverishment that prevents the behavioral scientist from appreciating the difference between what a camera would record and a rich and full account of the observed activity, which ascribes intentions, motives, meanings, and understandings to the actor whose behavior is under scrutiny. He continues,

> uncertain of his mimicking abilities, the would-be satirist may practice at home before the mirror, in which case he is not twitching, winking, or parodying, but rehearsing; though so far as what a camera, a radical behaviorist, or a believer in protocol sentences would record he is just rapidly contracting his right eyelid like all the others. (p. 7)

Geertz's understanding of radical behaviorism appears confined to its application to animal—and possibly human—responding in laboratory settings. Yet the type of description necessarily offered by radical behaviorism of behavior observed in the laboratory (the physical nature of which makes it unquestionably thinnish) need not be that which it provides, in its interpretive mode, of complex human behavior such as purchase and consumption. Insofar as the interpretive basis of radical behaviorism derives from the laboratory, however, the technique will always be subject to the criticism that it assumes too close a continuity between laboratory and "real life" environments. The next chapter therefore examines in detail issues that impede the continuity of laboratory settings and the complex contingencies that influence purchase and consumption. In each case, it argues that the discontinuities can be overcome, and a plausible explanation given of consumer behavior, through consideration of the meaning provided by a radical behaviorist account. It is subsequently argued that meaning is a property of the consumer situation and a behavior analytical model of this construct is presented and applied to the classification and interpretation of purchase and consumption.

4 The Meaning of Consumer Behavior

> Because semantic means are unconstrained, anything can be said of or written about any other semantic act, about any other construct or form of expressive signification. There is unbounded license of possible statement about each and every text, painting, statue, piece of music and, in natural consequence, on each and every secondary or tertiary comment or explication arising from them. Even as nothing in our physiological equipment for articulation or in the lexicon and rules of speech prevents us from uttering the irreparable and the untrue, so there is no conceivable arrest, no internal or external prohibition—except in the wholly contingent sense of censorship or taboo—on the enunciation of any aesthetic proposition.
>
> —George Steiner (1989, p. 60)

While, as Steiner points out, anything *may* be said, the aim of interpretation must be to produce statements that can be evaluated by reference to one or other reality system that is acceptable as having meaning and relevance to that which is deciphered and translated. The heart of radical behaviorism's interpretive stance is its unique location of the meaning of an act in the learning history of whoever performs it. Objective accounts of the environmental contingencies that apparently control behavior are frequently criticized on the grounds that they omit mention of the "subjective" appearance of settings and situations to the experimental participants themselves. But the investigation of this individual reaction is, to the behaviorist, a question of observing and accounting for a person's behavior within the situation, including that person's verbal accounts of what is going on. This can be achieved only by reference to the individual's environmental histories (Skinner, 1974, p. 77), for the meaning of an operant response is to be found in what has preceded it rather than in the current setting. It is not found in the discriminative stimuli of the present setting, nor is it found in the responses that take place there or in their outcomes. Rather, it can be located only in the history of exposure to similar contingencies in the past "in which similar settings have played a part" (p. 90). It consists in "aspects of the contingencies which have brought behavior under the control of the current situation" (p. 91). Meaning is defined, therefore, not in terms of the form or topography of a response, but in terms of its function, which is determined by the individual's learning history. The meaning of a response is found in the past contingencies that control the topography of current behavior and that empower current antecedent (discriminative) stimuli (p. 91). Topographies of behavior may resemble one another closely, but the meanings of the behaviors may differ because similar topographies can arise from different learning histories. Two customers may buy ties from the same assistant in the same store on the same day, but the meaning of doing so is quite different when the tie is bought as a present from when it is bought for personal use. The meanings do not depend on the reinforcer (say, an expensive formal tie bought as a present compared with a cheaper plain tie bought for everyday use). Rather, it lies in the past contingencies which make behavior in the current setting more probable if discriminative stimuli signal that this behavior will produce the reinforcement in question. In deciphering the meaning of verbal behavior, it is the "overall function of the behavior [that] is crucial" (p. 92). The essence of verbal interaction is that the listener is "disposed to respond" to a situation with which he or she is not directly in touch; he or she is in touch with it only via the mediation of the speaker, whose verbal response enables the listener to respond. Take a customer who is looking for a present for a relative's birthday, who cannot afford to pay more than £x. The sales assistant consults price lists and announces what the product in question will cost. Having heard the announcement, the listener is able to make the purchase. The elements of the "three-term contingency" are split between two people:

$$\text{Setting } (S^D) \rightarrow R_S \, [\rightarrow S^A]$$

$$S^D \rightarrow R_L \rightarrow S^R$$

where S^D is a discriminative stimulus, R_S the response of the speaker, R_L the response of the listener, S^A an aversive consequence, and S^R a reinforcer.

The responses are controlled—and given meaning—by a network of contingencies. The behavior of the listener is partly governed by a history of being reinforced as a result of believing or trusting the word of salespersons in similar settings (i.e., acting upon it). The speaker's behavior is partly controlled by aversive consequences: loss of a sale if the consumer's request for price information is not accurately and swiftly complied with. The salesperson may incur the anger of the customer if this information is not forthcoming or a reprimand from a supervisor if it is not accurately and persuasively given. Skinner points out that, for the speaker, meaning includes the stimulus that controls his or her verbal response (the announcement)—that is, the price figures printed in the list—and any "aversive aspects" removed by the response (anger, reprimand, dismissal). For the listener, meaning is similar to that of the price list if it were immediately available to him. It also includes the contingencies involving the gift (perhaps mutual obligations to observe birthdays) which ensure that a response to either the price list or the speaker's announcement is probable. It follows that meanings are not identical for both speaker and listener—*pace* communication theory.

Nothing passes from the speaker to the listener in the form of a shared meaning. "Meanings and referents are not to be found in words but in the circumstances under which words are used by speakers and understood by listeners" (Skinner, 1974, p. 93).

The Problem of Discontinuity

The warrant for radical behaviorism's interpretive stance must derive from the relationship between its accounts of complex behavior and experimental conditions under which its principles of behavior have been gained. Unlike the high degree of continuity among the situations in which biological principles have shaped evolution, and those found in the physical universe, there are two fundamental sources of discontinuity between the operant experimental space and the complexities of human social and economic life. They arise from issues of continuity between the animal subjects of operant experimentation and the human beings whose complex behavior is in question. They are not entirely overcome by the vast increase in the experimental analysis of human behavior (see the critique of radical behaviorist interpretation by Proctor and Weeks [1990]). The tendency of behavior analysts in progressively broadening the applicability of their conclusions, from the confines of controlled animal experiments to the complexities of human social, economic, and political activities, has attracted the criticism that they have extrapolated behavior principles based on an inappropriate analogue. As Mackenzie writes,

> The assumption of environmental generality, to put it excessively crudely, asserts that the Skinner box is representative of all environments. The assumption of speciational generality, equally crudely, asserts that the pigeon is representative of all species of organisms. The two assumptions together provide a warrant for extrapolating from the behavior of pigeons in Skinner boxes to the behavior of all animals in all environments, and specifically the behavior of humans in complex social situations. (1977, p. 160)

Each of these issues can be subdivided. Environmental continuity raises problems of the empirical availability of human genetic and learning histories, and the difficulty of providing a plausible behaviorist interpretation of behavior in settings where the elements of the three-term contingency can only be inferred rather than specified in operational terms. First, human learning histories, the source of the meanings of their actions, are elusive. While experimental psychologists can know the entire history of operant reinforcement and punishment of the animals with which they work, such information is simply not available in the case of adult humans; even in the case of pre-adults, it may be incomplete. Second, the elements of the three-term contingency which are specifiable in the operant chamber (in the case of animals) and the operant laboratory (in the case of humans) are no more than vaguely inferred in "real life" settings. Complex human behavior occurs in contexts that scarcely resemble the closed settings presented in operant experiments. Within the complex situations in which much human social behavior takes place, it is impossible to isolate the elements and their contingencies with the accuracy and certainty required of the experimental scientist.

The precise definitions of the elements of the three-term contingency as it is applied to animal experimentation must be replaced in the operant analysis of complex human interaction in social situations by an interpretative account based on an extension of operant theory. Although human operant experimentation is a growing field of activity, its results are still subject to the limitations of laboratory-imposed simplification. It is inevitable that, in the process of so extending operant explanation, terms which are carefully assigned in the laboratory acquire vaguer meanings—for example, when they are employed as surrogates in programmatic accounts of human verbal behavior (Schwartz and Lacey, 1982). Speciational continuity raises questions of the extent to which learning principles may be generalized. The key questions raised refer to the implications for operant interpretation of verbal behavior in humans, particularly the capacities to verbalize (i.e., think about and articulate aloud) the contingencies of reinforcement (whether accurately or otherwise), and for behavior to be rule governed rather than contingency shaped. From these considerations follows the possibility that reinforcement itself takes a rather different form in humans from that found in animals. As Richelle writes,

> Rule-governed behavior is more on the side of the intellect as opposed to emotion, of logical argument as opposed to intuition, of deliberation as opposed to impulse, of knowledge as opposed to know-how, of word as opposed to deed, of reason as opposed to faith, of truth as opposed to passion, of consciousness as opposed to unconsciousness, of culture as opposed to nature. (1993, p. 144)

Neither the problem of situational continuity nor that of speciational continuity raises insurmountable difficulties for an operant interpretation of consumer behavior. The experimental analysis of human behavior, noted already, has, during the last decade or so, produced a firmer basis for interpreting human activities from an operant perspective. However, it remains incumbent upon radical behaviorists to establish, first, an acceptable level of continuity between even these experimental situations and the non-experimental behaviors which are described on the basis of experimental findings. Second, they must demonstrate an acceptable degree of continuity between animal and human behavior. If either is lacking, the resulting account of complex human behavior will be limited.

ENVIRONMENTAL DISCONTINUITY

The Problem of Elusiveness

A recurring criticism of radical behaviorism as it applies to human conduct is that the genetic and learning histories of individuals are not empirically available to the researcher. This raises problems for a *scientific* explanation of consumer behavior or any other complex human activity: learning history in particular, the pattern of previous exposure to reinforcing and punishing contingencies and the consequences of responding to them, is central to any experimental understanding of the current rate of responding. The absence of personal histories also raises difficulties for interpretation which any model of consumer behavior based on radical behaviorism must address. The heart of the problem this poses for radical behaviorism's interpretive mode lies in the radical behaviorist conception of meaning. But the loss of learning history as a variable that can be used for prediction and control (both epistemological and practical) does not invalidate its use for interpretive purposes as long as it can be reliably inferred, for instance, from current behavior or verbal reports. Indeed, the necessity for constructing plausible learning histories is at the heart of all interpretive activities with respect to complex human behavior. (Because adult human participants in operant experiments also enter the setting with ready-made genetic and learning histories, their responses must also be interpreted somewhat by reference to an inferred past.) Exactly similar difficulties attend the efforts of anthropologists to interpret by providing a "thick account" of observations (Geertz, 1973; Ryle, 1968).

Current stimuli may also be elusive. Discriminative stimuli in the current behavior setting activate learning histories through their prior association with reinforcing and punishing consequences of acting in specific ways. These stimuli thus play a vital part in the creation of meaning, for they were also present in the past settings of purchase and consumption in which the consumer's learning history was established. An interpretative account must plausibly isolate the stimuli responsible for signaling meaningfully the contingent outcomes of possible current behaviors. This raises another crisis of identification, though it is not new: the loss of precision in generalizing from rigorous laboratory studies to human behavior in all its complexities is a problem which was eloquently and persuasively put over three decades ago. In a review of Skinner's *Verbal Behavior*, Chomsky argued that the account of complex behaviors in terms of operant conditioning amounts to no more than "analogic guesses . . . a metaphoric extension of the technical vocabulary of the laboratory" (1959, p. 29). Terms such as "discriminative stimulus" and "positive reinforcer," precisely defined and empirically available to all within the constrained context of the animal laboratory, reduce to nothing more than "vague surrogates" when applied to the analysis of the "real world" complications of human action and interaction. Furthermore, the conceptual extrapolation of elements of the three-term contingency from the operant laboratory, where they can be precisely defined in line with the requirements of objectiveness and empiricalness, to environments where their equally rigorous specification, control, and use in prediction are impossible suffers from the deficiency that the extrapolated principles are unfalsifiable (Lacey, 1974, pp. 39–40), which is to say no more than an interpretive account of behavior in complex, amorphous contexts inevitably incurs a loss of some of the rigor available in the carefully controlled laboratory.

The greater vagueness inherent in defining the discriminative stimuli that compose the current setting for consumer behavior (Wicker, 1979, p. 57) therefore has implications for an operant interpretation. Operant psychology originated in the animal laboratory: it was there that the operant response was first observed and differentiated from the respondent behavior central to Pavolvian conditioning (Skinner, 1938). The most significant ontological and methodological advance in operant psychology since that time has been the experimental demonstration of human operant behavior as verbally controlled (Catania, Shimoff, and Matthews, 1989; Lowe, 1979), based on Skinner's (1969) distinction between contingency-shaped and rule-governed behaviors (a dichotomy which will be further elaborated upon next). Both of these intellectual breakthroughs, like the research programs they initiated, occurred in laboratory settings.

A Solution: Behavior Setting Scope

It is an axiom of radical behaviorist metatheory that behavior is always controlled even when its environmental determinants are neither obvious nor externally imposed (Skinner, 1971). Nevertheless, it is reasonable to assume that a theory that originates in the laboratory will

> apply most easily to those real-world situations that most resemble the laboratory . . . [R]adical behaviorism, dealing as it does with prediction and control of behavior, applies in a more straightforward way to situations in the real world where the focus of control are most direct—prisons, factories, armies and the like. Radical behaviorism applies less obviously in situations such as family relationships where control is less obvious. But . . . it does apply meaningfully in those situations too. (Rachlin, 1987, p. 163)

It seems plausible to posit, therefore, a continuum of behavior settings from those in which behavior is most apparently under environmental control to those where the role of environmental stimuli must be inferred rather than (as in the laboratory) assigned. Lacey and Schwartz (1987, p. 170) describe the parameters of control in the *closed* settings that define the pole of the continuum typified by the animal laboratory. In such settings, only one reinforcer (e.g., a food pellet) is presented: an external controller (experimental scientist) determines the availability of reinforcers, designing and managing contingencies and states of deprivation without being personally subject to them: one specific behavior must be performed in order to access the reinforcers; and it is impossible for the subject to leave the setting (see also Schwartz and Lacey, 1982, 1988). A strong case can be made under such circumstances for an operant explanation since the elements of the three-term contingency—"a stimulus, a response, and the outcome the response produces in the presence of that stimulus" (Malott, 1986, p. 208)—can be pointed to unambiguously. Further, the manipulation of the stimulus and the outcome, and their relationship to the response, can be systematically and consistently associated with changes in rate of responding (Ferster and Skinner, 1957). Only settings devised for brainwashing, in which the regulator controls all the variables of life and death, resemble in real-world human contexts the closedness of the animal laboratory. When in the human operant laboratory, these elements are not so obvious, and the control exerted by setting stimuli can be debated. Moreover, much human behavior is influenced by rules, verbal statements of the contingencies, imposed by experimenters or deduced by participants, accurately or otherwise, from the apparent contingencies. "Real world" learning is also influenced by observation of the contingencies affecting the behavior of others, leading to imitation (Bandura, 1977). In the relatively open settings in which consumer behavior occurs, operant control is even more ambiguous. A dominant problem is that of equifinality. An operant class is an equifinal class: it may include responses that are topographically quite different but which belong together because they are functionally equivalent, that is, produce identical consequences (Lee, 1988, pp. 135–137). Ordering a book by mail has a form that is entirely distinct from asking for the same product in a bookshop, but both responses belong to the same equifinal class because they have the same outcome. A response that closely or exactly resembles another belongs to a different equifinal class if it produces functionally different results. Two consumers may enter the same store at the same time in exactly similar manners, but their responses belong to different operant classes if the first is reinforced by the purchase of a product while the second is reinforced by information about the availability and price of that product.

An operant interpretation must be capable of plausibly assigning discriminative and reinforcing stimuli to observed responses; equifinality makes this a difficult and complicated task because it reduces confidence that the interpretation is complete and unambiguous and it thus makes multiple interpretations possible (Lee, 1988). Nevertheless, it may be easier to resolve the problem of equifinality in considering the relative closedness of settings. (In order to avoid unnecessary repetition, relatively closed and relatively open behavior setting will hereafter be referred to simply as closed and open behavior setting, respectively; the comparative nature of the concept is always understood, however.)

Box 4.1 compares the idea of the consumer behavior setting as developed here with the concept of the behavior setting as construed in ecobehavioral science.

Box 4.1 **Comparison of the treatment of behavior settings in eco-behavioral science.**

We can clarify the nature of the consumer behavior setting, as an integral part of the BPM, by comparing it with the concept of the behavior setting as developed in eco-behavioral science (Barker, 1968, 1987; Wicker, 1987). The concept of the consumer behavior setting encompasses several features which Barker has identified. Moreover, like the notion of the behavior setting in ecological psychology, that of the consumer situation encompasses a synomorphic interaction; however, the two are not identical.

Behavior settings in ecological psychology are "small-scale social systems whose components include people and inanimate objects. Within the temporal and spatial boundaries of the system, the various components interact in an orderly, established fashion to carry out the setting's essential functions. To illustrate, in a gift shop, the temporal and spatial boundaries would be the hours the ship is open and the walls of the room it occupies. The shop's components include its employees and customers as well as inanimate objects such as goods for sale, display shelves, cash registers, money, and gift-wrapping materials. The orderly interaction of these components results in merchandise being displayed, bought, wrapped, and removed" (Wicker, 1987, p. 614).

The setting, then, consists of its participants, in interaction with their surroundings, a standard pattern of behavior, or program, and various levels of behavioral participation. The personal and inanimate objects of the setting tend to "fit together comfortably" (Wicker, 1979, p. 10), that is, to exhibit a synomorphic relationship. Behavior settings establish and maintain the means to effect the behavior program; the particular mechanisms by which this is accomplished are deviation countering (e.g., reprimands) and vetoing (e.g., exclusion of unruly members). Some settings permit deeper levels of penetration by the participants—a club, for instance, needs leaders and followers and a sustained pattern of multi-faceted interaction and participation; by contrast, a slot machine usually evokes only fleeting and infrequent participation

A major conclusion of work in eco-behavioral science is that behavior patterns are determined principally by the setting and its program rather than by the personal characteristics of its participants. An individual tends to behave similarly on two occasions separated by time but in the same location, but behaves quite differently in two other settings encountered sequentially. Moreover, the observed pattern of behavior in a given setting tends to persist irrespective of the individuals who participate.

The components of the behavior setting so defined can all be incorporated into the notion of the consumer situation as it has been developed in the BPM. The consumer behavior setting would be described as comprising discriminative stimuli arranged to facilitate specific behaviors, and the observation that the more interdependent the human and non-human components of the setting, the more probable is a specific

(continued)

Box 4.1 (continued)

pattern of response (e.g., Wicker, 1979, p. 11) is covered by reference to the closure of the consumer behavior setting's scope to proscribe alternative behaviors. The consumer behavior setting, as explained, does not include the individual, but the consumer situation involves a synomorphic interaction of the consumer and the setting.

What is missing from Barker's eco-behavioral science is any idea of what the individual brings to the setting. While his dismissal of individuality consisting in attitudes, personality traits, and so on, would be applauded by behavior analysts keen to avoid "explanatory fictions" (Skinner, 1950, 1963), some account of the inherited and learned histories of the individual, and their state variables, is necessary to make his or her sustained pattern of behavior in the setting intelligible. While observing the tendency toward conformity to a standard pattern of behavior in settings, Barker notes that some individuals do deviate from it (e.g., some consumers shoplift rather than obtaining purchases in a legitimate manner). But he treats this as an exception rather than analyzing why it occurs.

The main missing element, needed to account for the individual's precise approach, avoidance, and escape behaviors in a given setting, is his or her learning history. Whether or not this is empirically available, it is necessary to an explicatory rather than a purely descriptive account. Animal psychology denotes that its influence is real and that it accounts for the organism's current responses to immediate discriminative stimuli, even though it is rarely possible to record it, know it, and control it in the human sphere. As has been argued, the learning history explains what— along with state variables such as deprivation—transforms physical, social, temporal, and regulatory stimuli in a behavior setting into discriminative stimuli that promote specific behaviors. A theoretical statement as to how different setting types affect behavior in different ways needs the notion of a closed-open consumer setting continuum and that of the consumer's history of reinforcement and punishment which primes it.

SPECIATIONAL DISCONTINUITY

Behavior analysts assumed for decades that the principles they had first understood through animal experimentation would generalize across species (Miller, 1962; Morse, 1966; Skinner, 1938, 1969; Whaley and Malott, 1971). The behavior of humans was not expected to differ significantly from that of other animals, a view which stressed the physiological and evolutionary continuity of infrahuman and human species (Davey and Cullen, 1988; Perone, Galizio, and Baron, 1988). Attempts to apply operant learning principles to consumer and other economic behavior have also generally assumed interspecies generalizability (Alhadeff, 1982). However, the advent of widespread human operant experimentation demonstrated during the 1970s and 1980s how human behavior differs markedly from the patterns predicted from the influence of reinforcement schedules on animal responding (cf. Baron and Perone, 1982; Buskist and Miller, 1982; Buskist, Morgan, and Barry, 1985). As a result of this empirical differentiation of human operant performance from that of animals, difficulties arise in any attempt to interpret the behavior of one entirely in terms extrapolated from study of the other (Davey and Cullen, 1988; Lacey, 1979, pp. 364–366).

The Problem of Verbal Behavior

An early finding was that human behavior diverges from that of animals on fixed interval (FI) and fixed ratio (FR) schedules of reinforcement (see Box 4.2). Animal behavior on both of these schedules exhibits a pause

---

Box 4.2   Schedules and patterns of reinforcement.

A major determinant of the rate of emission of operant responses is the frequency with which those responses are followed by reinforcers, that is, the schedule of reinforcement. Study of the effects of different schedules has provided the most rigorous and voluminous evidence for operant conditioning available (Ferster and Skinner, 1957). When a response is reinforced every time it occurs, the procedure is known as continuous reinforcement (CRF). Such behavior is quickly learnt but extinguishes equally rapidly when reinforcement ceases. Physical responses such as turning a switch to produce light are best learned in this way. However, when less than every response is reinforced, in intermittent reinforcement, the behavior may take longer to learn but it also extinguishes slowly when reinforcement stops. Moreover, different patterns of intermittent reinforcement, varying according to the fixed or variable time intervals that separate reinforcers, or the fixed or variable ratio of responses to a single reinforcement, produce and maintain distinct patterns of responding.

FI schedules provide reinforcement when a given period of time has elapsed for a response made after that period; on variable interval (VI) schedules, the period of time that must elapse before a response is reinforced varies from reinforcement to reinforcement. FR schedules provide reinforcement when a specific number of responses has been performed, regardless of the time required, while variable ratio (VR) schedules are arranged such that a different number of responses is required to produce reinforcement on each occasion. Ratio schedules maintain a higher rate of responding than interval schedules. Fixed schedules maintain patterns of responding characterized by a pause after each reinforcement, after which responding resumes, often becoming rapid shortly before the next reinforcer is due.

The *interpretation* of complex behavior adopts the *pattern* rather than the *schedule* of reinforcement as its central analytical tool, however. That is, it takes the combination of high or low utilitarian reinforcement and high/ low informational reinforcement as its central means of explaining choice.

immediately after reinforcement is provided, followed by a gently increasing rate of responding. Human responding, however, is characterized by *either* a fast, continuous rate without a post-reinforcement pause, *or* a pattern marked by an extremely low rate in which one or two responses are preformed just prior to reinforcement. The difference is accompanied by distinct verbalizations of the contingencies: those showing the first pattern reporting that reinforcement was presented on a ratio basis, those following the second that it was available on an interval basis (Horne and Lowe, 1993). Another difference is that, while animal behavior is very sensitive to changes in schedule parameters, adjusting rapidly to novel contingencies, human behavior adheres much more rigidly to the original schedule parameters. Moreover, while animal behavior can thus be construed as "economical" in the sense that it maximizes the gains available for each response, human schedule behavior is not "rational" in the same way (Catania, Matthews, and Shimoff, 1982; Horne and Lowe, 1993; Matthews, Catania, and Shimoff, 1985). These differences have been explained by human verbalization in the form of both instructions provided by experimenters and the ability of participants to deduce rules of responding based on their observation of the contingencies in operation (Hayes, Brownstein, Haas, and Greenway, 1986; Lowe, 1979, 1983).

These demonstrations of the importance of verbal behavior in shaping non-verbal responding confirm a distinction put forward by Skinner (1969): that between behavior that is shaped through its direct contact with the contingencies of reinforcement and that which is governed by verbal descriptions of the contingencies (rules). Contingency-shaping is most likely to occur when the consequences of behavior are immediate and effective, that is, sizable, quick-acting, and probable (Malott, 1989; Malott and Garcia 1991); using a TV remote control leads to such instant and dependable reinforcement that channel "surfing" is easily learned. However, many of the consequences of human behavior are remote and not immediately effective, that is, small, delayed, and improbable; if these contingencies are to affect behavior at all, they must be verbally mediated and the behavior becomes verbally controlled or rule governed (Malott, 1989). Using gasoline that contains detergent results in changes that are undetectable from week to week, realized long term, and uncertain for the non-technical motorist. Without verbal rules acting as discriminative stimuli, outlining the likely outcomes of persisting in this behavior, and supplying motivation to act appropriately, few individuals would engage in behaviors such as buying "clean" gasoline, dieting, or quitting smoking. Rules indicate consequences of behavior that are not immediately obvious or which are effective only when they have cumulated over long periods. The recognition that so much consumer behavior is rule governed raises questions for its operant interpretation. Rules may not be "accurate" representations of the contingencies in as much as they misstate the relationship between an act and its outcomes, and omit important consequences of behavior while exaggerating the probability of others. Observation may not distinguish rule-governed from contingency-shaped behaviors and thus preclude a full interpretation. Some rules are private to the individual dedicating them and others may be unconscious. Categories of rules must be developed and the likely effect, operational identification, and functional (rather than topographical) significance of each type of rule made amenable to the interpreter. The potential difficulties in interpretation posed by equifinality are greatly increased by this facet of human behavior analysis. The complexities of contemporary marketing exchanges in affluent economies have no correspondent in animal societies let alone Skinner boxes and other experimental spaces. An interpretive analysis of the physical, social, and temporal contingencies of consumer choice imposed by advanced marketing systems is difficult; the implications of verbal behavior increase this difficulty.

A Solution: The Bifurcation of Reinforcement

We have seen that, while operant experimenters have generally assumed that the mechanism of reinforcement is identical across species, Wearden draws attention to what may be fundamental differences between conceptualizations of animal and human behaviors and the environmental conditions that maintain them. Whereas food and water, the ubiquitous reinforcers of operant behavior in animal experiment, have utilitarian benefit for the subjects, who are generally kept at 80% of their normal body weight, it is difficult to imagine that the tiny, even trivial, rewards presented to human participants in typical operant experiments, consisting as they do of points exchangeable for a few cents or small items of food, confer any such functional advantage. These reinforcers appear to possess neither utility nor exchange value for their recipients who, in some laboratories, have preferred to throw the snacks out of the window rather than even taste them. The performance of human participants in such studies is frequently erratic; their rate of scoring becomes orderly only when an element of competitiveness is introduced by the public recording of scores in the form of graphs (Wearden, 1988, pp. 199–200). The reinforcement in these cases appears not to stem from any hedonic or utilitarian benefits but from the feedback on the appropriateness and correctness of the performance that earned the food or money. This is consistent with the evidence that VI schedules of reinforcement frequently confuse human participants who cannot deduce what is required of them (Horne and Lowe, 1993). When informational feedback is made available to participants, they are more easily able to solve the problems set them even in the absence of nutritional or monetary rewards (Lowe, Harzem, and Bagshaw, 1978; Wearden and Shimp, 1985). Whereas FI schedules require participants to spend a few sessions in stabilizing their performances and, as noted, promote behavior that is insensitive to parameter changes, "informationally rich procedures" (Wearden, 1988, p. 203) result in smoother behavior patterns that respond "economically" to changes in schedule parameters.

This analysis reveals a level of complexity with respect to the contingencies that surround human behavior that has rarely been taken into consideration in descriptions of consumer choice based on extrapolations from animal behavior. Interpretation is confined to the information available to the behavior analyst, which may be scant (Lee, 1988, p. 137), leading to his or her drawing bold inferences about the learning history of the consumer, especially (in the light of Wearden's suggested bifurcation of the sources of environmental motivation with utilitarian and informational) the pattern of reinforcement that has sustained learned behavior. The sheer number and complexity of possible contingencies renders any interpretation incomplete (Lee, 1988, p. 138); only a small proportion of the pertinent contingencies may be obvious to the onlooker who must *inter alia* distinguish contingency-shaped from rule-governed behavior and propose the self-generated rules that may account for an individual's conduct as well as identify the public rules he or she is following. Such interpretations are always "fallible and always open to improvement . . . [no more] than hypotheses" (p. 138). This conclusion raises the possibility—indeed the necessity—of multiple interpretations even within a radical behaviorist stance, together with that of disagreement among radical behaviorist interpreters.

AN INTERPRETIVE MODEL OF THE CONSUMER SITUATION

These extensions of radical behaviorist interpretation from the rigor available to the laboratory scientist do not invalidate its quest for an account of the ways in which environmental forces rather than intrapersonal states and processes influence complex behavior. They are difficulties which accompany all attempts at sensitive interpretation of human behavior (e.g., Geertz, 1973) and, while they give an ironic twist to the Machian search for positive knowledge, they are not unique to radical behaviorism. Moreover, the quest for an interpretation of complex behavior is consistent with radical behaviorism's inductive approach. The task is not therefore to condemn its interpretive stance out of hand but to incorporate the findings and conclusions of the foregoing discussions into a framework that defines the dimensions along which interpretation should proceed. It is clearly not within the capacity of an interpretive model to present definitive portrayals or occasions of consumer behavior as operant activity. The aim of the following derivation of such a model is to sensitize researchers to the variety of behaviors and contingencies that must be taken into account. A model that uses the basic S^D-R-S^R paradigm would scarcely be adequate to capture the complexity and subtlety of these contingencies. Nevertheless, the model of the consumer situation is essentially an elaboration of this basic statement of radical behaviorist explanation in the light of the inadequacy of raw inductivism in the realm of interpretation.

The Scope of Consumer Behavior Settings

Interpretive radical behaviorism must first address the problem of environmental discontinuity. Given the criticisms of such diverse behavioral scientists as Rachlin (1987, 1989) and Schwartz and Lacey (1988), we can posit a continuum of behavior settings composed of the discriminative stimuli that precede current behavior (cf. Barker, 1968; Wicker, 1979). This continuum runs from the *closed* behavior setting of the animal laboratory to the *open* behavior setting in which a vacationing tourist plans a picnic. Both are characterized by discriminative stimuli that signal environmental control, but in the former there is no escape, and behavior for the hungry animal is determined by the structure of the Skinner box, while in the latter numerous possible courses of action are positively reinforced. Within this range lies a continuum of consumer behavior settings, from *relatively closed* to the *relatively open*. The former might be exemplified by the bank foyer in which customers are required (sometimes physically constrained by metal bars) to stand in line until they can be served. The physical surroundings—marble pillars, perhaps, or oak-lined walls—provide an air of seriousness and sobriety, signaling that frivolous behavior or, for that matter, any actions not related to the business of the day will not be reinforced and may even be punished. The social surroundings—serious-looking customers, industrious, dark-suited employees—also contribute to this atmosphere. Rules ensure that no customer steps forward until his or her turn arrives and is signaled and that only behavior specific to the transaction is conducted. Much of this behavior is under aversive control; it is governed by avoidance of the punishing consequences that threaten activity that is proscribed. If the consumer is to be satisfied he or she has little alternative but to be in the setting and behave accordingly. The relatively open consumer behavior setting is exemplified by the upmarket department store, Sears or Harrods, in which the consumer is seeking a luxurious gift for a close relative. Behavioral control is still apparent: the physical surroundings signal patterns of approved conformity, while the social context is likely to reward decorous behavior and preclude uninhibited conduct. But there are alternatives to being in the setting—other floors, other stores, other gifts. There are also rules that influence behavior within the store and the appropriateness of various products as gifts for the relative in question. But there is a greater opportunity for the consumer to devise his or her own rules and, since the object of purchase is a gift, to allow themselves some license in its selection. There is a multiplicity of reinforcers and different behaviors, combinations of exploration, rumination, imagination, and choice, which lead to them. Ultimately the store setting and the network of social moves are beyond the control of the individual consumer, but compared with the situation of the bank customer, he or she is relatively unconstrained in that his or her actions can take many forms and result in numerous outcomes.

The meaning of the behavior that transpires in either of these broad types of setting is also dependent upon what the consumer uniquely brings to it, his or her personal history. Part of this history is genetic, the result of an evolutionary past which has determined many of the individual's physical characteristics and propensities. Sex, body type, physical disadvantages, and so on, have far-reaching implications for consumption; they must be largely taken as fixed influences. The principal variable for the individual consumers is their learning histories, acquired during their lifetime, and capable of modification as they continue to purchase and consume. Meaning, in a radical behaviorist formulation, inheres in consumer behavior that is *situated*, located in terms of the antecedent and consequential stimuli that influence its rate of recurrence; meaning is found in the "consumer situation," a synomorphic concept that refers to the interactive effect of the behavior setting and the consumer's learning history. Both setting and consumer are integral to the definition of the consumer situation. It is the consumer's learning history that determines what elements of the physical, social, and regulatory setting will function as discriminative stimuli, for it is that learning history that determines what can act as a reinforcer or punisher for that individual and thus the probability of his or her behaving in such a way as to produce those consequences. A learning history of purchase and consumption, and their outcomes, accounts for the individuality or personality of the consumer, that is, how he or she is likely to react to a given behavior setting, what is a discriminative stimulus in the current behavior setting that activates that learning history: the individual's history of reinforcement and punishment can influence his or her current behavior only if the relevant elements of the setting are primed to signal the reinforcements contingent upon particular purchase and/or consumption responses. (Once again, note that we do not learn solely from direct experience of the contingencies; learning history also reflects observation and incidental learning without immediate reinforcement, the acceptance of rules handed down by others, and our tendency to devise our own rules based on observation and even imagination of contingencies as well as through the direct impinging of reinforcers and punishers.)

Utilitarian and Informational Reinforcement

We can draw further conclusions about the nature of the reinforcers that maintain approach/avoidance consumer behaviors. Basic behavior theory leads to the conclusion that these consequences will both reinforce and punish acts of purchase and consumption: reinforce it by providing positive satisfaction as the attributes of products and services are possessed and consumed; punish it as the opportunity to buy or use something else, or to save, is thereby foregone (Alhadeff, 1982). But, while reinforcing and aversive stimuli are inevitable consequences of consumer behavior, reinforcement of human behavior has two major varieties which arise from its speciational discontinuity with that of animals. As Wearden (1988) points out, reinforcement may be utilitarian *and/or* informational.

Utilitarian reinforcement, as the term is used by Wearden, refers to increases in utility, that is, use value, to the individual organism; although pleasure (which is generally associated with hedonism) is not the essence of reinforcement (a reinforcer is simply a consequence that increases rate of response), many utilitarian reinforcers will also be associated with pleasurable responses. Utilitarian reinforcement arises from the characteristics of the product or service obtained in purchase or used in consumption; this corresponds to the use of utility in economics to refer to "the direct satisfaction that goods and services yield to their possessors" (Gould and Kolb, 1964, p. 303, p. 740). Utility theory in economics derives essentially from the psychology of hedonism (Viner, 1925; Black, 1987; Griffin and Parfitt, 1987; Menger, 1956). Hence, while utilitarian reinforcement is akin to value-in-use, it derives not only from the functional performance of a product or service but also from the feelings associated with owning and consuming it. In addition to the functions performed by a product or service, utilitarian consequences of consumption include the positive affect generated in the process (Hirschman and Holbrook, 1982; Holbrook and Hirschman, 1982; Holbrook, O'Shaughnessy, and Bell, 1990). Utilitarian reinforcement refers, therefore, to all of the benefits derived directly from possession and application of a product or service, it is reinforcement *mediated* by the product or service; it inheres in the use-value of the commodity.

Informational reinforcement, by contrast, is symbolic, usually mediated by the responsive actions of others, and closely akin to exchange value. It consists not in information per se but in feedback on an individual's performance. Informational reinforcement attests to the level of correctness or appropriateness of a person's performance as a consumer; whereas utilitarian reinforcement stems from economic and functional payoffs of buying and using goods, informational reinforcement results from the level of social status, prestige, and acceptance achieved by a consumer by his or her efforts. It is usually publicly determined, judged by others according to the rules, and thus of primarily social significance. In as much as it is mediated by other people, it is *verbal* (Skinner, 1957), consisting in speech, gestures, and—where the individual provides his or her own informational reinforcement and thus becomes the "other" person—in private thoughts (Skinner, 1974). From the viewpoint of the consumer, informational reinforcement rests on a comparative judgment of how well he or she is using time and energy relative to other uses to which they would be put: "How well am I exchanging my time and effort for the acquisition of groceries?" If the consumer is being relatively inefficient, he or she may either speed up the shopping trip or postpone purchasing further items. If efficient, they can use the time and energy left over to accomplish something else. From the social viewpoint, the public consumption of a prestigious product or service is exchanged for the goodwill, praise, positive responses, and so on, of others, that is, for esteem and social status (Bagozzi, 1975).

The distinction between utilitarian and informational reinforcement has parallels in both consumer research and applied behavior analysis. Hirschman (1982) distinguishes "technological" innovations, stemming from changes in the tangible characteristics of a product class, from "symbolic" innovations, stemming from the new social meanings generated by a novel product. Research into environment-impacting consumer behavior has found that rewards of two distinct kinds influence the rate at which consumers will ride the bus or share transportation rather than use private cars, reduce domestic energy consumption, and avoid destructive waste disposal (Geller, Winett, and Everett, 1982). One class of rewards, "incentives," is primarily utilitarian—prizes, money, and gifts, for example—while another class, "feedback," is informational—records of the amount of electricity saved, miles foregone, personal recognition, and so on. While the first class consists in direct benefits of altered consumption patterns, the second is symbolic, conveyed verbally (including words and gestures) and has a wider, social significance. Moreover, a considerable volume of experimental findings indicates that these classes of reinforcer have separate and distinct effects on rate of responding (Cone and Hayes, 1980). Box 4.3 compares this usage of "utilitarian" reinforcement with recent developments in the idea of utilitarian consumption elsewhere in marketing studies.

Linking the Variables: Rule-governed Consumer Behavior

The consumer behavior setting also contains a special kind of discriminative stimulus in the form of *rules*. A rule signals the reinforcing and punishing consequences of behaving in a particular manner; it also derives its motivating power from the individual's learning history which determines the meaning of behavior in the circumstances. Learning history influences what can be a discriminative stimulus for the consumer in the current behavior setting. It does so in part by determining what will be a reinforcing or aversive stimulus (Foxall, 1992b).

A rule is akin to any other discriminative stimulus in that it sets the occasion for reinforcement contingent upon a particular response. Unlike other classes of discriminative stimuli, however, it is a *verbal* description of the relationship between behavior and its consequences (Poppen, 1989, p. 335). The verbal behavior of a speaker is mediated by another person, the listener; both speaker and listener will have been similarly socialized in the use of their common language (in the terminology of behavior analysis, both belong to the same "verbal community") (Baum, 1994). In considering consumers' rule-governed behavior, we are concerned with the verbal

Box 4.3 **Recent developments in the study of "hedonic consumption."**

It is useful to compare the use of these terms with recent developments in the study of hedonic consumption. Hirschman and Holbrook (1982) define some products (such as dramatic performances) as hedonic, while others are functional or utilitarian. The BPM, by contrast, attributes hedonic consequences to all usages of products and services and indicates that the utilitarian reinforcing consequences of such consumption may be high or low relative to that of other products and relative to the informational consequences of the consumption in question. Utilitarian qualities are not, in other words, intrinsic to a product or class of products; they are defined by reference to the identified consequence of gaining or using the product. What is socially designated as utilitarian or constitutes appropriate utilitarian consumption is culturally determined, and the operation of setting variables in signaling principally utilitarian or informational reinforcement depends, therefore, on the consumer's learning history.

The ascription of utilitarian reinforcement to the consequences of consumer behavior indicate the extent to which they are affective, emotive, or pleasant. However, defining utilitarian consumption in terms of personal, subjective pleasurable experience is necessary but insufficient by dint of its narrowness (cf. Holbrook and Hirschman, 1982). The definition must include the acquisition of goods that will give rise to further utilitarian experiences (such as money and other prizes, gifts, personal recognition, etc.). Informational reinforcement, in comparison, includes performance-related feedback and is more rational and objective, consisting of points, savings, recognition of attainment, and so on. Whereas Hirschman and Holbrook distinguish between utilitarian and aesthetic consumption, the BPM distinguishes utilitarian and informational consequences of consumption, categories that cut across theirs. Going to an opera, for instance, which they would designate aesthetic consumption, is indeed reinforced by utilitarian consequences if the consumer obtains hedonic satisfaction from it but may also be informationally reinforced if he or she wins status, say, by being seen at the opera.

The conceptual independence of utilitarian and informational reinforcement is further supported by the need for a plausible interpretation of such behaviors as saving, insuring, and giving which goes beyond the usual assumption that repeated acts must be followed by immediate utilitarian reinforcers. These actions are usually considered enigmatic in that none requires such palpable gratification to be presented soon after their performance: neither may receive immediate gratification and both incur costs before they produce positive reinforcement. It is rare for saving or gift-giving to receive no reinforcement at all, and even stuffing cash under the mattress and giving expensive presents are negatively reinforced in that they lead to peace of mind and discharge

(continued)

Box 4.3 (continued)

social responsibilities and obligations. The fact that some of these consumer behaviors occur in closed settings (taking out a mortgage related endowment or the reciprocal giving of birthday presents to close relatives) therefore explains some of this aspect. It is only when they occur in obviously open settings that they are less obviously operant. Moreover, most saving and insuring can be actually construed as the purchase of the products of banks and other financial institutions.

What is different about the purchasing of savings and insurance policies and gifts (when these arise in open settings) and the purchase of other, more tangible goods is that the former is often not followed by utilitarian reinforcement. However, it is reinforced informationally by stimuli that indicate level of progress and performance. Such informational reinforcement can be steady and cumulative in the case of savings and insurance as interest and bonuses accrue, and inasmuch as the giving of expensive presents confers social status fairly swiftly and conspicuously, or personal satisfaction feelings, in the case of gift-giving. Behavior setting variables also affect the topography and incidence of these behaviors—as discriminative stimuli promise later utilitarian reinforcement. Again, the implication is that both utilitarian and informational reinforcement must be posited in order to account for the observed behavior.

---

behavior of a listener, with his or her following of a rule enunciated by a speaker, usually another person, but, on occasion, the speaker may be the listener, as when one makes rules for his or her own conduct. As a rule, the consumer's rule-governed behavior may be mediated by another person or by the physical environment, or by both. Rule-following that is socially mediated is known as *pliance*: the listener behaves as instructed by another who is in a position to reward or punish subsequent behavior depending upon whether it conforms to the rule. A great deal of consumer behavior that is influenced interpersonally is pliance: a child who spends his or her pocket money as instructed by the parent who provided it complies with a rule that states the reinforcing consequences of so doing ("If you spend your money wisely, you can save more at the end of the week") and/or which signals the aversive consequences of non-conformity ("If you spend all your money on sweets again, you will have to go without pocket money next week"). Rules such as these are known as *plys*.

A consumer's rule-governed behavior that arises from rules speci-fied by another person who is not in a position to reinforce or punish his or her behavior is also common. This time the physical environment mediates the rule-following and the behavior is known as *tracking*: the rule is a *track*. When one consumer tells another how to get to the new supermarket ("Turn left at Duke Street, walk fifty yards, and turn right into Princess Road: the store will be on your left") the listener "tracks" the environment in order to get there. The speaker is in no position to supply reinforcement or punishment for the listener's success or failure in getting to the supermarket; only progress in getting there—finding Duke Street, noticing Princess Road and turning into it—can provide reinforcement. The same rule-governed behavior may contain elements of both tracking and pliance. For instance, finding the new supermarket may be no more than tracking if the speaker is never again encountered, but if meeting the speaker means he or she can enquire of the rule-follower's success in locating the store and give praise or ridicule, there is also an element of pliance. When the tracking and pliance inherent in a rule are complementary in that they require the same behavior to be enacted in response to both elements, the rule is known as a *congruent*; when pliance and tracking conflict, the rule is a *contrant* (Poppen, 1989). The identification of rules and their functions is especially important in radical behaviorist interpretation. Rules may act as surrogates for an individual's learning history by relating current discriminative stimuli to the utilitarian and informational reinforcement available in and signaled by the setting. Rules are, therefore, a link between the consumer behavior setting and the pattern of reinforcement (or punishment) most likely to reinforce (or inhibit) the consumer's current behavior. A rule represents verbally the relationship of a particular behavior to its environment; it is not only a discriminating stimulus in its own right but may also supply the meaning of the other discriminative stimuli in the setting. For instance, a rule may state "Drive on [response] only when the light is green [discriminative stimulus]" and thereby supply the significance of the light to the hearer. As a discriminative stimulus, a rule depends for its effectiveness in controlling behavior on the consequences of responding or not responding to it (Poppen, 1989); it cannot, therefore, be separated from the learning history of the consumer. The BPM (Figure 1.1, p. 9) assembles these interpretive dimensions into a model of the consumer situation. Consumer behavior is portrayed as the outcome of an interaction of the scope of the current behavior setting (a store, a home, an office) and the consumer's history of reinforcement and punishment (Foxall, 1992a). It has been argued that the meaning of a consumer response, viewed from the standpoint of operant psychology, is found in this interaction. That meaning inheres not only in the discriminative stimuli that constitute the behavior setting but also in what they portend by way of response-contingent outcomes, and that is determined for the individual by his or her learning history. Hence the consequences shown at the right of the figure—utilitarian, aversive, informational—are those signaled by the discriminative stimuli; their significance for current behavior derives from the role they have played in that learning history.

EMPIRICAL EVIDENCE AND OPERATIONAL MEASUREMENT

> Measurement should be viewed purely pragmatically, neither as desirable nor undesirable, but as useful or not useful in some application. Those who inveigh against measurement do not seem to eschew words like "few" and "many," which imply numbers. Yet it must be admitted that an obsession with measurement does result in a tendency to elevate method over substance. What good is a series of equations containing many unquantified or unquantifiable variables? It can in fact be misleading if it suggests measurement is possible.
>
> —John O'Shaughnessy (1992, p. 305)

It is natural to enquire at this point how far the explanatory variables incorporated in the model—behavior setting scope, learning history, and utilitarian/informational reinforcement—are empirically available, amenable to identification and measurement, and related to patterns of behavior predictable by the model. The validity of any interpretive account based on this model depends upon such considerations. In fact, there is extensive empirical evidence to support the view that the scope of consumer behavior settings exerts predictable influences upon behavior. First, studies of token economics, in therapeutic and other rehabilitative contexts, document the strong influence of environmental stimuli upon action within such closed settings. Second, applied behavior analysis, which has employed field experimentation to explore the influence of consequences upon consumer's environment-impacting behaviors, indicates a definite, though—in the more open settings involved—less exact, influence of environment upon action. These sets of empirical data also elucidate the distinction between utilitarian and informational sources of reinforcement.

The Token Economy

The essential components of a token economy are (i) tokens, (ii) back-up reinforcers, and (iii) rules. *Tokens* are a medium of exchange earned by pro-social behaviors that require the expenditure of time and effort. Because the material well-being of patients and other inmates who participate in token economics is not at risk—the basic necessities of life are provided regardless of how they behave—the acquisition of tokens is more analogous to consumer behavior under conditions of relative affluence than it is to earning an income. Participants may expend this time and energy as they wish: the point of the program is to encourage them to *spend* their time and effort productively (Lea, Tarpy, and Webley, 1987). *Back-up reinforcers* are additional material goods and services that may be obtained in exchange for tokens at rates determined usually by the staff of the institution concerned. *Rules* specify how consummatory behaviors shall be related to tokens and how tokens shall be exchangeable for back-up reinforcers. (Rules specifying how and when tokens are earned, lost and spent [Kazdin, 1981, p. 61] are often collected into a written manual for the sake of clarity and to avoid ambiguity. They may be posted up in the setting.)

In the terminology of behavior analysis, tokens are generalized conditioned reinforcers; obtaining them is contingent upon performing predetermined responses in accordance with a specified schedule (Kazdin, 1981; Winkler, 1980). Rules may state contingencies in several ways. Any individual's earned tokens may accrue simply to him or her. But there are other options. For example, the performance of the group as a whole may determine the allocation of tokens to each individual; alternatively, in "consequence sharing," the tokens earned by an individual are allocated not only to him or her but also to each of his or her peers. Back-up reinforcers purchased by one person may additionally go to each member of the group (Kazdin, 1981). Punishments or "response costs" may also be incurred—for instance, as fines for proscribed behavior. Tokens reinforce rule-governed behavior, notably pliance ("Make your own bed every day in order to receive x tokens"); they may also strengthen congruent tracking ("This is the way to make your bed properly"). Tokens, therefore, are or are related to informational reinforcement since they present evidence of the level of performance achieved by an individual. They are methods of performance feedback, status reports. As secondary, conditioned reinforcers, they obtain their control over behavior by association with back-up or primary reinforcers. For the most part the back-up reinforcers are utilitarian in nature: their control stems from the properties of the back-up items themselves, particularly the utilitarian functions they perform. Tokens, by contrast, control behavior principally through their symbolic nature and function: they are symbols of the amount of work done, of the spending power of those who own them and thus of their informal social status in the group.

All of this is suggestive of a closed setting. The contingencies are determined by agents who are not themselves subject to them. Moreover, the staff are subject to a quite different set of contingencies as a result of their training and career aspirations (Kazdin, 1981, p. 71). The conditions under which the token economy is operated may be relaxed by allowing tokens to be administered by peers or by self-administration of reinforcement (in which participants grant themselves points or tokens). But the scope of the setting remains essentially closed whatever the schedule and whoever decides it: the behavior of inmates is systematically monitored; certain behaviors are designated "pro-social" or "desirable," not by the inmates but by those who ultimately control the setting; reinforcers are similarly chosen by persons other than the inmates, as are the tokens; finally, the rules by which tokens might function as exchange media—the schedules and rules—are "externally" determined (Krasner and Krasner, 1973, pp. 354–355). The behavior modification inherent in the token economy involves "*planning the environment* so as to shape and maintain 'desirable' behavior . . . [it is] a *systematic* and *planned* approach" (p. 352). And Tarr speaks of such contexts as "closed economies" (1976, p. 1136). Battalio, Kagel, Winkler, Fisher, Basmann, and Krasner support the suggestion that token economies are closed behavior settings: "[T]he individual lives in the controlled environment . . . 24 hours a day . . . [subject to the] routine maintenance of controls." The token economy is "a therapeutic environment for an institutionalized population" (1974, p. 52). Given that inmates cannot usually physically leave the setting—wards may be locked, classrooms cannot be vacated except with special permission, prisons clearly confine—the reinforcers in question can be made entirely contingent upon prescribed behavior. The behaviors involved are relatively simple, as are the contingencies. Few, if any, alternatives are on offer; on the whole, there is no competitive source of supply of the utilitarian (back-up) reinforcers. It is predictable, therefore, that behavior in token economies will be orderly and that few, if any, inmates will deviate from the expected pattern. This has been borne out in those experiments, generally in therapeutic environments, which have found individual token economy behavior to conform to the patterns described by micro-economic theory and, overall, to be "exactly" like that found in a national economy (Tarr, 1976; Winkler, 1980, p. 271). In the case of micro-economic relationships, for instance, a study at the Central Islip State Hospital (Battalio, Kagel, Winkler, Fisher, Basmann, and Krasner, 1974) found that price/quantity demanded relationships were as predicted by neoclassical theory (Tarr, 1976, p. 1136): "[T]he data fulfill the fundamental theorem of the theory of consumer behavior . . . that compensated demand curves slope down . . . through systematically varying prices on a weekly basis over a seven week period, it was found that aggregate weekly expenditures raised in the manner predicted by consumer theory" (p. 1139). Of thirty-eight participants in the study, thirty-six "acted consistently with revealed preference theory"; the behavior of the remaining two, which appeared initially to contradict the theory, turned out on closer inspection to confirm it, though after a time lag (Battalio, Kagel, Winkler, Fisher, Basmann, and Krasner, 1974).

Evidence for the conformity of behavior in token economies to macro-economic expectations comes from a number of experiments in a state psychiatric hospital in Sydney, Australia (Winkler, 1980). The studies showed consumer behavior to vary with basic demand theory in three respects, confirming the predicted relationships between income and total expenditure, income and purchases of luxuries versus necessities, and the price elasticity of demand of luxuries versus necessities (p. 272). These studies took savings into consideration and found that when the stock of savings increased, the earning of tokens decreased; when excess saving stocks were available, moreover, any increase in the amount of reinforcement available became progressively less effective in the control of behaviors.

Are the behavioral changes effected in token economies maintained when the participant leaves the therapeutic community? While hundreds of studies indicate that token economies effect behavior change and do so more effectively than alternative methods (Kazdin, 1981, p. 69), it appears that behaviors often revert to pre-treatment levels when the principles are no longer used. The question of response maintenance and transfer is clearly of the utmost importance to the staff of the institutions involved and the social administrators who have devised and sought to benefit from the programs. It is also of great relevance to any attempt to generalize about the influence of the environment on operant behavior. Actually, the fact of behavior often returning to baseline levels when the individual is removed from the structures of the token economy are relaxed, though problematic for those directly involved in therapy and rehabilitation, confirms the importance attached by the BPM to the immediate setting as a determinant of current behavior. The means at the disposal of administration of token economy programs to effect long-term, post-treatment behavior change also support the BPM approach. The evidence is that response maintenance and transfer are feasible if the discriminative stimuli that control behavior in the token economy are established in the naturalistic setting. Strategies advocated for such response generalization, which provide evidence for this proposition, include the following (Kazdin, 1977, p. 196). First, similar contingencies must be implemented across the settings: this strategy increases response maintenance in the short term; moreover, when the contingencies are withdrawn completely, further response maintenance is more probable. Second, the contingencies should be gradually faded during training: the effect is to maintain a level of performance in the face of progressively decreasing reinforcer influence. Third, if reliance on discriminative stimuli is increased in the course of training, and if the relevant stimuli are repeated in the naturalistic environment, the probability of maintained pro-social behavior is increased. Fourth, response transfer is more probable if reinforcement has become progressively more intermittent during training, or if the time lag between the response and the reinforcer has been increased. Finally, encouraging the individual to take more personal control over his or her reinforcement makes response maintenance more likely. This includes the use of self-reinforcement (as when a person praises himself or herself for appropriate behavior), self-instruction training (in which rules are internalized and rehearsed), and the extension of discriminative stimuli so that aspects the individual prompt behavior (Hackenberg, 2009).

Applied Behavior Analysis of Ecologically Impacting Consumer Behavior

This evidence supports the BPM in two ways. It draws attention to the influence of consumer behavior settings on behavior in addition to the limited effect of reinforcers, substantiating behavior setting scope as a separate explanatory variable (though not an entirely independent factor, since the control exerted by discriminative stimuli depends ultimately on pairing with reinforcers and punishers). The strategies for response maintenance and transfer also raise an important issue for the study of consumer behavior: how far can the control of behavior be attributed to the environment when the setting is relatively open? The implication of treating behavior setting scope as a *variable* is that the more open the setting, the less specific will be the environmental control of behavior. The evidence produced by a large volume of research on the effect of consumer behavior on the natural environment and on attempts to change ecologically damaging behavior by means of contingency control also supports the treatment of behavior setting scope as an important variable in influencing choice. The studies typically have taken the form of field experiments with "real" consumers who have voluntarily agreed to take part, whose participation in the experiment must compete with their everyday activities, and who can leave the experiment or act contrary to its stated aims at any time.

Although the experimenters provide an additional source of refinement to those found in their lives in general, therefore, this is by no means the sole source of motivation and there are plenty of alternative behaviors available to the participant, each with its own set of contingencies. A feature of all of the settings involved is that positive reinforcement from *current* behavior (that which the experiments have sought to change or eliminate) is usually immediate and directly available to the individual who acts, while aversive consequences are usually delayed and relatively inconsequential for the individual because they are diffused among and felt by the community at large. In all these respects, the settings in which the field experiments have taken place can be regarded as open. Two things are striking by comparison with the findings on token economies. The changes in consumer behavior documented in the investigations cited can be traced to experimental manipulations of the consequences of behavior. But—our first observation—in contrast to the results of the token economy studies, the relationship between reinforcement and behavior change is less clear-cut, less orderly, and less likely to apply to all of the participants. A case can be made that the environmental consequences of behavior account for the rate at which it is performed.

The second observation is that here, too, two distinct functional relationships between behavior and reinforcement are apparent. Applied behavior analysis has used two sources of reward for pro-social behavior (Cone and Hayes, 1980; Geller, Winett, and Everett, 1982). *Incentives* include monetary rewards, prizes, and some tokens. Incentives share certain characteristics: they are tangible and usually physical. Moreover, they have direct utilitarian applications, represent or can be used to produce personal material gain, and their consumption leads to functional benefit, what we have called utilitarian reinforcement, and thus material well-being (Foxall, 1994c). They conform broadly to the pattern of utilitarian reinforcers described previously. *Feedback*, on the other hand, provides a different kind of reward. Consisting, for instance, of a record of consumers' performance such as feedback on the amount of electricity one had saved or the number of miles foregone by using public transportation rather than a private car, different forms of feedback show certain characteristics that are absent from incentives. They are largely symbolic and verbal, and provide a means by which one's behavior can be measured (the more the consumer walks to work, the greater proportionally is his or her saving of petrol). Feedback does not consist in utilitarian satisfaction, though when it measures material gains or savings (e.g., savings accumulated by not buying fuel for one's car or by reducing one's domestic energy consumption), they can be used to obtain and use utilitarian satisfactions. Praise and recognition probably fit into this category more easily than that of incentives (cf. Foxall, 1994c) because they confer social status and feedback on achievement. Feedback corresponds broadly to the informational reinforcement described previously. The applied behavior research shows that incentives and feedback have separate effects on the consumer behavior in question (though there is often a synergistic effect from combining them). The studies allow us to compare the effect of utilitarian reinforcement (incentives) with that of informational reinforcement (feedback), and both of these effects with that of prompts, which are verbal exhortations to act in a particular way. The first conclusion (Foxall, 1993b) is that utilitarian reinforcement is the single most effective source of motivation, followed by informational reinforcement, followed by prompts (which are generally of *no* effect on their own, since they are vague rules that do not encourage pliance: they propose behavior that is not mediated by anyone). The second is that various combinations of utilitarian and informational reinforcement are apparently applicable to the effective control of particular classes of consumer behavior (Foxall, 1995a). In the case of private transportation, high levels of both utilitarian and informational reinforcement appear necessary to reduce motoring. Prompts alone as potential motivators for riding the bus are ineffectual, but utilitarian reinforcements in the form of large cash incentives are particularly powerful. (There does not appear to have been a study in which feedback on driving miles foregone has been provided, though one might expect this to act in a synergistic fashion with the incentives.) The effective combination of high utilitarian with high informational reinforcement implies a connection with accomplishment. Where domestic energy consumption is concerned, prompts again are the most effective single consequence for reducing use and, although informational reinforcement—especially frequent feedback on energy utilization of monthly billing—has some independent effect, it is especially worthwhile in combination with utilitarian consequences. Both sources of reinforcement coupled with prompts prove even more effective. Utilitarian reinforcement alone, however, is demonstrably effective. The combination of high utilitarian with low informational reinforcement implies a connection with hedonism.

The same gratifying combination is not so easy to detect in the case of pro-social waste disposal. Fairly high levels of feedback are motivating—for instance, signs of the amount of waste appropriately disposed of—but utilitarian reinforcements are also effective. It is clear that applied behavior analysts have also relied heavily on the closure of behavior setting scope in this instance. Finally, what evidence there is of the environmental control of water consumption and conservation suggests—in line with the predictions of the BPM—that both utilitarian and informational reinforcement play minor roles and that the closure of the consumer behavior setting—for instance, through metering—is effective.

5 A Model of Interpretation

He who can interpret what has been seen is a greater prophet than he who has simply seen it.

—St. Augustine, *De Genesi ad Litteram*

We cannot do without people who have the courage to think something new before they can demonstrate it.

—Sigmund Freud to Wilhelm Fliess, December 8, 1895
(1985, p. 155)

The fact that it is possible to interpret token economy and applied behavior analyses as providing evidence for the model is highly supportive of the underlying variables and relationships it posits. But it is also necessary, before undertaking the interpretive reconstruction of actual consumer behaviors, to establish how the elements of the model can be identified and measured for purposes of new empirical research. This step is essential to the appraisal of the model itself and to understanding what sort of account of consumer behavior it is capable of producing. Moreover, in order to know the nature of the interpretation, it is necessary to determine whether and how empirical research following a more traditionally "scientific" approach might be undertaken within this framework. Knowledge so gained will also show the extent to which the model must be evaluated according to alternative criteria such as internal consistency, aesthetics, plausibility and integration of patterns of purchase, and consumption with a single explanatory framework. How far, then, can the elements of the model be made operationally measurable? The three key variables concerned are behavior setting scope, learning history, and behavior; since the discriminative stimuli in the current setting prefigure contingent consequences of various kinds (utilitarian reinforcement, informational reinforcement, aversive outcomes), some means of distinguishing and measuring may also be required. Note that all of these variables relate to the behavior of an individual consumer in a particular consumer behavior setting. This level of measurement and operational modeling corresponds, therefore, to the consumer situation.

COMPONENTS OF THE BPM

Behavior Setting Scope

The scope of a consumer behavior setting refers to the extent to which a physical, social, temporal, and regulatory environment induces a particular response such as purchase or continued use. Such scope can in principle be psychometrically assessed using scales based on the criteria outlined by Schwartz and Lacey (1988): *availability of and access to reinforcement* is a function of the number of reinforcers presented to the consumer, the means available to him or her to secure them, and the necessity of undertaking specific operations on which the reinforcers are contingent; the *degree of external control of the setting* is a function of how far marketers control access to the reinforcers, the nature of the contingencies imposed, and the feasibility (cost to the consumer) of escaping from or avoiding the setting.

Learning History

The need to obtain an operational measure of the consumer's learning history is more problematical. Clearly the quantitative radical behaviorist intent on scientifically explaining consumer choice must somehow reconstruct the learning history of the individual whose current probability of emitting a given purchase or consumption BPM response is to be accounted for (even predicted and controlled). It is clear nonetheless from the foregoing that consumers' learning histories are not empirically available to the researcher as are those of laboratory animals to the experimenter who has observed them from birth or, at least, from the point of their initiation into operant research. There may be no alternative here than to turn to verbal surrogates of a learning history, to ask respondents to report on the antecedents and consequences of this prior behavior (though this, of course, assumes a good deal of self-knowledge). Moreover, if the quantitative measurement of learning history is required, it should be noted that a sophisticated technology exists already for the measurement of consumers' evaluations of the likely outcomes of this future behavior: the theory of reasoned action (Fishbein and Ajzen, 1975), the theory of planned behavior (Ajzen, 1985), and the theory of trying (Bagozzi, 1992) are essentially methods by which respondents articulate their learning histories by reference to the consequences that specific "target" behaviors have previously wrought. The theory of reasoned action, for example, asks respondents to evaluate this belief that performing a particular response will have a specified consequence, to express their motivation to comply with the anticipated wishes of others with respect to the target action, and to forecast the probability that they will again perform this behavior under closely specified conditions (Foxall, 1983). The origins of this approach lie, moreover, in verbal operant conditioning (Dulany, 1968). In Dulany's theory of propositional control, the individual is assumed to form a rule or "verbal hypothesis" summarizing his or her learning history which describes the reinforcing and punishing consequences of performing a given act. The influence of such "contingency awareness" on current/future behavior depends also upon the individual's positive or negative evaluation of the consequences of similar behavior in the past, something which once again can be a function only of his or her learning history (Fishbein and Ajzen, 1975, pp. 298–301. Further, the attributes of the "product" under investigation could include both incentives and feedback in order to capture the effects, possibly differential, of utilitarian and informational reinforcement. There seems little doubt that psychometric scaling that elicits present verbal reports of learning history is feasible.

Behavior

Behavioral responses in consumer settings are also amenable to scaled measurement. At the operational level, consumer responses can be classified as *approach* (when positive reinforcement is accepted) or *avoidance* (when the individual avoids or escapes from an aversive stimulus). Approach-avoidance has been measured in a number of ways and, in the case of consumer behavior, can be operationalized as whether a consumer accepts a reinforcer (e.g., by buying a product) and by the length of time he or she spends in a purchase setting such as a store or a consumption setting such as a nightclub (Donovan and Rossiter, 1982; Mehrabian and Russell, 1974).

Utilitarian and Informational Reinforcement

Sufficient description has been made of utilitarian and informational reinforcers to suggest that they derive from separate sources and influence behavior in different ways. Utilitarian reinforcement derives from the intrinsic properties of the consequences of buyer behavior such as ownership of products; informational, from the extrinsic considerations of the level of social and economic performance achieved by the individual consumer through buying and using economic goods and services. This essentially qualitative distinction was supported by the differentiation of incentives and feedback in the applied behavior analysis studies and the token economy investigations reviewed previously. Some reinforcers contain elements of both sources of reward, however, and may be difficult to classify unambiguously. Money, for instance, has been treated as a utilitarian reinforcer in its own right by virtue of the access it provides to other utilitarian reinforcers such as products and services; but money "earned" by reduced consumption (of, say, domestic energy) might be thought of as also containing informational properties. Interpersonal praise similarly might have dual functions: it is desired as an end in itself for the intrinsic satisfaction it supplies, but it is also a sign of the progress made by an achieving consumer. The interpreter must make explicit his or her reasons for attributing some reinforcers predominantly to one or other category. The methods of interjudge evaluation and establishment of interjudge reliabilities is also available for the classification of relatively high or low utilitarian and informational reinforcement. A well-tried methodology exists for such an approach (e.g., Page and Iwata, 1986).

Testing Hypotheses

Combining the interactive effect of behavior setting scope and learning history, it would be possible to relate the consumer situation to consumer responses and to test simple hypotheses about consumer behavior in different settings—for instance, that a positively predisposing learning history of a consumer in an open setting would result in approach, and that an inhibiting learning history in a closed setting would lead to avoidance or escape. Indeed, there seems little doubt that a psychometrically testable model, incorporating the central BPM variables, could be both constructed and used, if successful, to predict consumer behavior (epistemologically certainly, though almost as surely practically too) and, if marketing prescriptions were written in its terms, perhaps to control it to a degree. The potential operationalizability of the model provides a clue to the empirical correspondence of its constraints, and empirical testing may enable us to check on its usefulness in prediction. But there are several reasons why such modeling and measurement are incomplete. First, quantitative investigation of this kind makes only narrow contact with the behavior under review and its context. It is useful inasmuch as it allows the basic relationships posited by the BPM to be tested in a general way but it results in a very "thin" description indeed of consumer behavior and its environment. Any methodology is limited in the range of answers it can suggest, just as the number of questions a theoretical stance can pose is prescribed; however, a purely quantitative technique is, in the present context at least, constrained. Second, the excessive reliance upon first-person reports inherent in this quantitative approach is antithetical to the spirit of behaviorist inquiry which stresses the direct observation of behavior in contact with its reinforcing/punishing consequences. Radical behaviorism has severely criticized attempts to explain behavior by reference to attitudes, intentions, subjective meanings, expectancies, purposes, and other "mentalistic" notions. The argument that there are cognitive precursors of overt behavior has been challenged on ontological grounds: we observe only the verbal behavior said to express them and that behavior is itself under the control of contingencies that are quite distinct from those which shaped the behavior during the learning history. All that can be recorded by scaling techniques is evidence of the individual's adaptation to the contingencies that control current verbal responding. Explanatory accounts of behavior in terms of purposes, intentions, and so on, simply shifts the environment into the head in order to present the causes of behavior as internalized rather than external to the individual (Skinner, 1977). Third, multi-attribute methods at best approximate a consumer's learning history as he or she recalls it. They cannot capture the variables to which the BPM has drawn attention in full: learning history, as has been argued, is the product of contingencies other than those which control such recall; behavior setting scope is a construct specifically designed to overcome the problem of "situational intervention" between the expression of an intention and the opportunity to act (Foxall, 2005). Since it is admitted even in the more sophisticated versions of such models that, because situational influences are constantly in flux, the only intention statement that is consistent with an act is that which immediately precedes it (Ajzen, 1985, p. 19), the idea of behavior setting scope is an advance on theories which omit situational variables and concentrate exclusively on the alleged cognitive determinants of behavior. Moreover, only the most detailed account of learning history, including knowledge of the probable effects on behavior of discriminative stimuli found in the setting, would suffice. Simply to use an interaction term as part of a quantitative exercise would hardly capture the richness of the "consumer situation."

There is no need, therefore, for the model outlined previously to be restricted to giving a programmatic account of purchase and consumption. Little psychometric ingenuity is required to enable the variables described to be operationally scaled and measured and to permit the relationship of a consumer's learning history and current behavior setting (including the significance of signaled utilitarian and informational reinforcers, and aversive consequences) to his or her current behavior. But, while the model appears capable of operational application and thus of empirical testing, the richness of the present analysis lies in the model's capacity to suggest an interpretation of broader aspects of consumer behavior.

OPERANT INTERPRETATION OF CONSUMER BEHAVIOR

Levels of Interpretation

Radical behaviorist interpretation is a reconstruction of the probable environmental causes of observed behavior; the environmental stimuli currently influencing observed behavior must be inferred from the factors that are known to control operant behavior in the laboratory and in field experimental settings. Such interpretation thus proceeds inductively. Three successive and interactive levels of interpretive analysis (summarized in Table 5.1) can be proposed.

The operant class. The first and most general level, that of the "operant class," categorizes consumer behavior as belonging to one or other of four operant equifinality classes, and, subsequently, to one of eight contingency classes. Equifinality indicates that all the members of a particular class of behaviors produce a similar pattern of consequences which maintain those behaviors. The maintaining consequences of an operant consumer behavior are the utilitarian and informational reinforcers with which it is consistently associated. (Aversive consequences do not maintain behavior; rather, they reduce its frequency, and will be considered later in the context of the second level of analysis.) On the assumptions necessary to this form

Table 5.1   Three Levels of Interpretive Analysis

Level of Analysis	Environmental Stimuli	Behavior Units
Operant Class	Pattern of reinforcement:	Operant Equifinality Class:
	Low/high hedonic reinforcement	
	Low/high informational reinforcement	
Contingency Category	Schedule of reinforcement (single, dominant)	Accomplishment, Pleasure, Accumulation, Maintenance
	Pattern of reinforcement, behavior-setting scope (generally inferred)	General pattern of behavior appropriate to relatively closed/ open behavior setting; subset of operant equifinality class
Consumer Situation	Pattern of reinforcement, relative strength of immediate reinforcement and punishment: reinforcer effectiveness, (multiple) reinforcement schedules, reinforcement delay, quantity of reinforcement, quality of reinforcement, aversive consequences	Approach, Escape, Avoidance responses including browsing, purchases, arranging credit, using, saving, buying alternative product, leaving the behavior setting.
	Personal learning history: related to and inferred from pattern of reinforcement, immediate reinforcing and aversive consequences signaled by discriminative stimuli	
	Behavior-setting scope: nature and effect of the following in increasing/decreasing consumer discretion and choice: physical discriminative stimuli, social discriminative stimuli, temporal discriminative stimuli rules	
	State variables: mood, ability to pay, availability of credit, deprivation/satiation, etc.	

of interpretation, that *all* consumer behavior can be functionally related to one or other pattern of relatively low/high utilitarian and relatively low/ high informational reinforcement, and that there are four such patterns of reinforcement which maintain purchase and consumption responses, and, therefore, four operant classes of consumer behavior (Figure 1.3, p. 11). (Again, in order to avoid repetition, these forms of reinforcement are hereafter spoken of as simply "low" or "high," though the comparative nature of their definitions is understood.)

Analyses of this higher-level, operant class level of analysis (Foxall, 1992a, 1992b, 1993) have led to the proposal that the four logically derived and functionally defined operant classes of consumer behavior might be labeled as in Figure 1.3. It was argued that the consummatory activities involved in survival as a human organism and in minimal effective functioning as a social being (including fulfillment of the responsibilities of citizenship) would be maintained by relatively low levels of both utilitarian and informational reinforcement. The behaviors involved in ensuring physiological well-being and basic social acceptance do not require high levels of either economic goods and services or recognition from one's fellow man: only the fundamental levels of nutrition, shelter, taxpaying, and meeting other social obligations need be met. Consumer behaviors influenced by relatively low levels of both utilitarian and informational reinforcement, and consistent with high levels of contentment and inertia, were termed *maintenance*. It was suggested that a second class of consumer behaviors is maintained by a relatively high level of informational reinforcement and a relatively low level of utilitarian reinforcement. Behavior which depends for its continuance on frequent feedback on performance or level of achievement comes into this category. Such behaviors would typically include discretionary saving for a particular item, collecting, and achieving cumulative rewards as in promotional deals. Utilitarian reinforcement is far from absent, and its attainment would usually be the ultimate goal of such behavior, but it is *relatively* less important in maintaining the day-to-day, week-to-week, or month-to-month responses that cumulate to achieve it. Informational reinforcement thus acts as a frequently given proxy for the ultimate utilitarian reward that is contingent upon perseverance. This class of behaviors, largely concerned with the satisfactions that accrue from meeting performance criteria, was termed *accumulation*. The third operant class of purchase and consumption contains behaviors that are maintained by relatively high levels of utilitarian but relatively low levels of informational reinforcement. All forms of entertainment, relief of pain, acquisition, and use of economic goods and services fall into this class. Informational reinforcement is not necessarily unimportant: it might be socially rewarding to be seen having or consuming such items (not failing to have them might also remove the possibility of social disapprobation), but the principal maintaining consequences are utilitarian. This class of consumer behavior, denoted by the receipt of utilitarian satisfactions, is known as *hedonism*. Finally, some consumer behaviors are maintained by relatively high levels of both utilitarian and informational reinforcement. This class of behavior includes anything which displays the consumer's overall level of economic and social attainment: working for badges such as advanced college degrees, being seen to buy and consume luxuries and other icons of wealth, and seeking further self-realization or improvement all figure here. Such items are not only intrinsically valuable to the individual; their conspicuous consumption shows forth his or her level of social status, honor, or esteem. This class of behaviors, leading to achievement that fulfills the consumer, is known as *accomplishment*. Accounts of this level of analysis have also tentatively attached a notion of the relationship between the dependent variables (observed behavior) and the independent variables (the inferred pattern of utilitarian and informational reinforcements maintaining them) in the form of a schedule of reinforcement. Many of the activities that fall into the maintenance class appear to be preserved by a fixed internal (FI) schedule; many, if not all, accumulation responses, on a fixed ratio (FR) schedule. Most hedonism responses are seemingly maintained by a variable interval (VI) schedule, and accomplishment is generally maintained by an apparent variable ratio (VR) interval (Foxall, 1990). Great care must be taken in suggesting schedules that maintain non-laboratory behaviors (Poppen, 1982), but an interpretation must make some rather bold conjectures.

These four broad types of consumer behavior are operant equifinality classes to which particular pre-purchase, purchase, and consumption activities are allocated on the basis of the *function* they perform, that is, the pattern of consequences they produce. This observation has two implications for the interpretation of consumer behaviors within this framework. First, consumer behaviors which are topographically quite different from one another may be allocated to the same equifinality class because they produce the same pattern of low/high utilitarian and informational reinforcement. Hence both attending a spiritual development program and searching for a luxurious present in a prestigious department store are classified as *accomplishment* because each is believed to be maintained by high levels of both utilitarian and informational reinforcement. Second, the obverse of the first, two topographically identical activities can be allocated to different operant classes of consumer behavior if they produce different patterns of reinforcement. Hence watching a performance of a Shakespearean play is *hedonism* if it is done solely for personal gratification but *accomplishment* if the play also forms the subject of an examination for which the viewer is consciously revising. It is also *accomplishment*, more subtly, if the viewer receives not only *hedonism* from the performance but also advances toward a personal goal of self-realization or personal (cultural) improvement (see also Foxall, 1990, 1994a).

The contingency category. A second level of analysis, that of the contingency category, allocates broad types of consumer behavior according to the scope of the behavior setting as interpreted by the observer as well as the general pattern of reinforcement. Within each operant class of consumer behavior, particular purchase and consumption activities differ depending on whether the behavior setting in which they occur is relatively closed or relatively open. There is a continuum of consumer behavior types, based on behavior setting score, within each operant class; however, the following exposition treats this factor as a binary variable, speaking only of closed and open consumer behavior settings. There are, therefore, on this simplified definition, two general contingency categories within each operant class (see Foxall, 1990, 1992b, 1993b). Figure 1.2 (p. 10) shows the eight contingency classes derived from considering utilitarian reinforcement, informational reinforcement, and behavior setting score as three separate binary variables. Responses within each of the four operant classes of consumer behavior derived previously differ topographically according to the scope of the behavior setting in which they occur. They remain equifinal, however, in that they produce the same general pattern of utilitarian and informational reinforcement. Simplifying the complex of contingencies by assuming binary variables, Figure 1.2 defines contingency categories by reference to three continua: from low to high utilitarian reinforcement, from low to high informational reinforcement, and from closed to open behavior setting scope.

These contingency classes define the eight combinations of contingency that can influence the rate of consumer behavior. They refine the elements of the environment contained in the three-term contingency: discriminative stimuli become the elements of the consumer behavior setting which determine its closed-open scope (physical surroundings, social surroundings, temporal orientation, and rules), while reinforcers become the inferred pattern of utilitarian and informational reinforcers acting on behavior. Figure 1.2 also proposes labels for the general patterns of behavior likely to be allocated (maintained by) each contingency category. Once again, these allocations are functionally determined. It is suggested tentatively, however, that maintenance in closed settings takes the form of *mandatory consumption*, for instance, payment of taxes for street lighting, the police and military services, and buying a television license; in open settings, it is *routine purchasing*, for instance, of groceries in a supermarket; accumulation in closed settings consists in *collecting*, for instance, collection of coupons, installment buying, saving up; in open settings, it is *token-buying*, for instance, accumulating "air miles" on frequent flyer programs; *hedonism* in closed settings often takes the form of *inescapable entertainment* such as watching an in-flight movie, while in open settings it takes the form of *popular entertainment* like viewing television or watching a rock video or opera; *accomplishment* in closed settings can be categorized as *fulfillment* including personal development and leisure activities, while in open settings it is characterized as *status consumption* including search for luxuries and radical innovations.

The consumer situation. This third, most detailed level of analysis relates specific consumer responses such as browsing, evaluating, purchasing, and using to the elements of the consumer situation in which they occur. Such behaviors are *approach* (when a positive reinforcer is accepted), *avoidance* (when the behavior is negatively reinforced by avoidance of an aversive event), and *escape* (when the consumer frees himself or herself from a currently aversive setting). This micro-level interpretation of consumer behavior involves identifying the discriminative stimuli that compose the behavior setting (and, wherever possible, the consequences to which they point); it also requires some assessment of the learning history of the individual. These two factors determine the *consumer situation*, the point at which consumer behavior is located (Foxall, 1992a). Here, the purpose of a radical behaviorist interpretation of consumer behavior is to reconstruct the meaning of an act for an individual consumer. We have seen that this meaning is ultimately related to the learning history of that consumer, something to which direct empirical access is denied the observer. An operant interpretation must concentrate, therefore, on those environmental factors which can be observed (or inferred) and documented, notably elements of the behavior setting, and both the pattern and the relative strengths of potential reinforcement and punishment signaled by the setting variables and available to the consumer who acts therein: the assumption here is that such reinforcing factors have operated on similar behavior in the past, in similar settings, and can, therefore, be used as a guide to the predisposing/inhibiting nature of the consumer's learning history.

Recognizing, therefore, that behavior is amenable to numerous interpretations, even within an operant framework of analysis, we can begin to answer the first question of operant interpretation, "What is this person doing?" (Lee, 1988, pp. 135–136). This requires that the meaning of the act be elucidated in terms of learning history (as far as this is available or can be inferred) and current setting; the analysis of the current setting must include an understanding of the role of likely consequences of behavior so that the problem of equifinality can be plausibly countered by reference to the outcomes of behavior in the setting. Only by isolating these consequences and relating them to the behavior can we respond to Lee's second question of operant interpretation, "What has been *done?*" The resulting description can be as scientistically "thin" as we wish, based on no more than a parsimonious account of the operational measures and their putative interrelations, or as interpretively "thick" as we wish, leading to an understanding of "how the action of interest makes a difference to the person's life. That is, what does the action produce or present that would not be produced or presented otherwise?" (Lee, 1988, p. 137). The more closed the setting, the greater the possibility of both a thin, scientistic interpretation and a thick interpretive account which can point to their referents with a degree of intersubjective agreement; the more open, the more speculative both accounts must be. Where should we look for such consequences? Any consumer behavior is both reinforced and punished; the strength of the behavior (its frequency and its magnitude on any one occasion) is the result of tendencies toward approach (leading to such positive reinforcement as possession and consumption of the utilities and information provided by a purchase) and those toward escape (leading to punishers such as loss of cash, an end to pre-purchase deliberation which may be satisfying in itself, forgoing other products). Whether approach (e.g., purchase) or escape (saving, buying something else) is the outcome depends upon which of these responses is the stronger (i.e., upon the learning history of the individual) (Alhadeff, 1982).

By the *pattern of reinforcement* is meant the effect of utilitarian and informational reinforcers used at preceding levels of analysis to ascertain the operant class of consumer behavior in question, that is, the relative levels of utilitarian and informational reinforcement. In this final level of analysis, however, the chief concern is to infer some aspect of the consumer's learning history from the (presumably) continued presence of this pattern of reinforcement. If the consumer's behavior is assumed to have been maintained by this pattern in the past, we must, within the confines of an operant reconstruction, assume that this pattern (or the discriminative stimuli that signal it) will continue to positively influence approach behavior in the current behavior setting. We must also, at this level, take the possible aversive stimuli of responding into consideration, both to indicate the strength of escape behavior acting against the strength of the approach behavior and to interpret the nature of any avoidance behavior in the setting. By the *relative strength of potential reinforcement and punishment* is meant the net outcomes or consequences signaled by the discriminative stimuli in the current behavior setting as contingent upon the purchase or consumption response. Alhadeff (1982) portrays purchase behavior as a vector of these two strengths or probabilities which are principally a function of the consumer's learning history. The strength of approach depends upon reinforcer effectiveness (which is, in turn, a function of the consumer's level of deprivation), the schedule of reinforcement (and here we must add to Alhadeff's [1982] analysis, the possibility that multiple schedules will be in operation in non-laboratory settings), reinforcer delay (the length of time by which reinforcement has followed the response in the past; the longer this interval, the weaker the response), the quantity of reinforcement, and the quality of reinforcement. The strength of escape depends upon how aversive the loss of money is to the consumer who must pay for the product (and this is itself a function of the reaction of others to previous purchases by the individual); the past results of losing the positive generalized reinforcer, money; and the result of having been prevented from acquiring other reinforcers as a consequence of having bought a particular product, the length of delay between the purchase and such punishing consequences, the quantity and quality of the money surrendered, and the reinforcement schedule (Alhadeff, 1982; Foxall, 1990, pp. 65–69).

What is missing from this interpretation, which extrapolates from operant research on animals directly to the consumer behavior of humans, is recognition of the situational and speciational discontinuities involved. We must, therefore, incorporate the elements of the consumer behavior setting into this account. These discriminative stimuli provide a link between the consumer's learning history and the reinforcers contingent upon current behavior. If those signaled reinforcers can be identified, along with the aversive consequences, and related to the physical, social, temporal, and regulatory stimuli that compose the setting, we can mitigate, though not entirely overcome, the absence of a full and reliable, empirically elicited learning history. At this level of analysis, behavior setting scope must be assessed by a thorough and detailed judgment of the extent to which the various sources of discriminative stimulus (physical, social, temporal, regulatory) promote or inhibit the behavioral choices open to the consumer. Finally, the analysis of the consumer situation requires an appraisal of the immediate state variables which may influence behavior in the setting: the consumer's state of deprivation/satiation with the reinforcers made available by the product, mood states, ability to pay, access to credit facilities, and so on. The third level of analysis is nested within the two earlier levels. Levels 1 and 2 locate the micro-accounts, of specific consumer situations, among the whole range of contingencies of learning presented by differing patterns of high and low utilitarian and informational reinforcement, closed and open consumer behavior settings.

INTERPRETATION IN ACTION

The purpose of the following analysis is to show the form that a radical behaviorist interpretation of consumer behavior might take. Only through such analysis can the nature of the BPM account be assessed. Although the four cases presented are original, they can be placed into operant classes and contingency categories (Foxall, 1993a). The four cases have been chosen because they are well-documented instances of consumer behavior, independently researched by psychologists or marketing specialists in three cases and based on accompanying literature in the other. All four cases also represent examples of marketing influence in the form of set enclosure and the manipulation of reinforcers and rules. The analysis of large groups awareness training is presented as an example of accomplishment. Attendance at the seminar suggests high levels of both utilitarian and informational reinforcement since the participant is seeking useful and applicable knowledge about how to make his or her life work more effectively, and because the seminar provides a check on progress toward personal goals and social attainment, social acceptance; it is an example of marked status consumption. The participant can be expected to be seeking (i.e., to have a learning history of being reinforced by) both incentives (the gains to be had directly from the service bought and consumed) and feedback (an assessment of performance as a person). The experience of eating at a Benihana restaurant is presented as an example of hedonism. The show-business aspect of the service suggests a high level of utilitarian reinforcement while informational reinforcement, not unimportant given the status implication of consumption here, is *relatively* low. Frequent-flyer programs are used to illustrate accumulation. Informational reinforcement, as one accumulates "air miles," is predominant (how well am I doing?), though ultimate reinforcement is likely to be utilitarian—owning and using the bonus which one has acquired. Finally airport waiting exemplifies maintenance. This activity is undertaken solely in order to consume another, primary reinforcer, though it entails a different kind of consumption, namely, of the airport facilities. Moving on to our second level of analysis, that of the contingency category, and believing that each of these four behaviors belongs to a relatively closed behavior setting, it is possible to describe the behaviors in greater detail. Large group awareness training is an example of fulfillment; dining at Benihana is inescapable entertainment, accumulating air miles is token buying, and airport waiting is mandatory consumption. Not all of the settings in which these behaviors typically occur are equally closed (Foxall, 1992a).

Accomplishment: Large Group Awareness Training

Large group awareness training (LGAT) stems from the "Human Potential Movement" which was influenced by Rogers, Maslow, and Mayo, by existentialism, and by various strands of Eastern philosophy (Finkelstein, Wenegrat, and Yalon, 1982). The movement emphasized that neuroses could be cured through "self-actualization" or the individual's development toward his or her full potential. Other sources of input to LGAT include Gestalt therapy, sensitivity training, encounter groups, and yoga. While LGAT may appear an unusual focus for the study of consumer behavior, the movement has a strong commercial footing, and, from the beginning, the key criterion of its success has been "consumer satisfaction" (Finkelstein, Wenegrat, and Yalon, 1982, pp. 516–517). Various programs now offer this approach to personal development training—"Lifespring," "Insight," "Relationships," and "Actualizations," for instance. The oldest, *est*, (standing for Erhard Seminar Training), now known as "The Forum," has been chosen for analysis here since it is "the only commercial large group training which has been studied in the professional literature" (p. 518).

The operant class to which consumer behavior of this kind belongs (our first level of analysis) is apparently accomplishment since high levels of both utilitarian and informational reinforcement maintain the responses involved. Utilitarian reinforcement is evident from the ability of the service provided to the consumer: self-management skills, emotional release during the program, and the resulting capacity to control one's life more effectively after the two compulsory weekends and the voluntary "postgraduate" meetings which the training offers. Informational reinforcement takes the form of feedback on the individual's performance in life (pointing out first the unworkability of his or her life to date), on the acquisition of the positive understanding and skills provided by the course, and—through the post-graduate meetings—continued performance feedback as the principles of *est* are put into practice in the real world. Both of these sources of reinforcement appear to influence behavior strongly relative to their effects in the other operant classes considered here (see also Foxall, 1990).

At the second level of analysis, that of the contingency category, it is apparent that LGAT takes place in a relatively closed setting, that of a hotel ballroom between the hours of 8:30 a.m. and about midnight on the Saturdays and Sundays of two consecutive weekends. Trainees also must attend a pre-training evening, when they are introduced to the rules that will govern their behavior in the ballroom sessions, and a three-hour mid-training session held on the Wednesday evening between the two training weekends. The rules to which they are introduced at the pre-training session, and which are generally followed throughout the training, require the consumer to forgo alcohol and non-prescription drugs during the sessions; to introduce no watch or other timepiece into the training room; to use toilets, eat, and smoke only during breaks; to remain in their seat, until they are called upon; to wear identification tags; and to avoid sitting close to anyone of their acquaintance (Finkelstein, Wenegrat, and Yalon, 1982; Fisher, Silver, Chinsky, Goff, and Klar, 1990; Rhinehart, 1976). The degree of pliance induced by the stating and restating of such rules and the means by which consumer behavior in the setting is personally mediated (see next) confirms that *est* takes place in a closed setting compared to other forms of Accumulation (e.g., the pre-purchase browsing for luxury items in a prestigious department store that is classified as *status consumption*). We may, therefore, justifiably refer to *est* and other LGATs as *fulfillment*. By contrast, Accomplishment in open settings—for instance, browsing for a luxury gift in a prestigious department store—provides the consumer with far more choice among alternative products, brands, and stores, and also confers more temporal control.

The essence of the case study of *est* is the identification of its methods of controlling consumer behavior *in the current setting* by means of rules and other discriminative stimuli which signal the positive and aversive consequences that are immediately contingent upon responses performed "here and now." This is the concern of the third level of analysis, that of the consumer situation. On the first morning of the training, 250 to 300 trainees assemble, wearing tags showing their first names, in a ballroom in which they are seated facing the dais which contains only blackboards, stools, and a lectern. The ground rules are reread by the assistant trainer who stresses their voluntary nature, though by now each trainee has agreed in writing to be bound by them. The trainer who now takes over is clean and smart and projects an air of authority; he or she is in total control. Trainees may address no one but the trainer and then only when called upon. The trainer terminates the interaction with the trainee by saying "thank you" (an informational reward since it may signal that the trainee has understood what is being said or has complied with some requirement). This "thank you" is also a signal for the audience to applaud (a utilitarian reward since it suggests approval and recognition). The rules emphasize the controlling features of the physical and social environment—social restraints (the power of the anonymous crowd) and physical constraints (the doors to the ballroom are actually locked)—and forbid familiar discriminative stimuli such as watches and clocks. At first, the sole behavior permitted of the trainees is speaking, when permission is granted, to the trainer, and later movements and actions are restricted to what the trainer prompts and allows. Some rudimentary conclusions can be drawn with respect to the learning histories of the trainee consumers. According to Fisher, Silver, Chinsky, Goff, and Klar (1990, pp. 36–38), *est* participants are typically female (60%), heterosexual (>90%), white (>90%), infrequent churchgoers (63% went "rarely"), middle income (>66% earned between $12,000 and $50,000), not living alone (>80%), and highly educated (fifteen years on average). Trainees are, however, more positively inclined toward self-improvement and change than a control group of peer-nominees; they also have a tendency to report a greater impact on their lives of negative happenings during the preceding year than do members of the control group even though both have roughly the same number of such negative events (p. 38).

More interesting is the reevaluation and redefinition of their learning histories during and as a result of the seminar training. Its transformation is closely related to the progressive assertion of instructional control by the trainer over trainees (Baer and Stolz, 1978, p. 49). Trainees are encouraged to give up their "act," their self-images and attempts at self-presentation of their beliefs about themselves, their titles, the rules by which they try to live, their wealth, knowledge of their reputation, techniques of self-defense, and so on. The trainer subtracts all of these defenses against the new knowledge he or she is trying to inculcate to wear down the trainee's ideas about the source of his or her personal status and worth. This procedure actually invalidates the trainee's learning history (as he or she is aware of/can verbalize it), especially that based on informational learning, that is, the result of performance feedback. Trainees are encouraged to give up their act in several ways (pp. 49–50). First, any self-assertion on the part of a trainee with respect to his or her personal status, position, or achievements is immediately punished; the trainee's assertions are ridiculed, he or she is called an "asshole"; and it is pointed out that the trainee's life does not work: why else are they here? Second, the trainer points out that trainees do not know even what they think they do; they do not know how true what they believe about themselves actually is. Third, trainees are led to disbelieve their own minds which are portrayed as "tricksters." Fourth, all attempts at escaping the contingencies are punished. Finally, the physical surroundings—a fifteen-hour day spent in a cool room, for instance—increases the probability that the trainer's instructional control will be effectively imposed; few trainees have a learning history which would enable them to cope with the closed behavior setting in which they now find themselves.

Several tactics allow the trainer to fine tune his instructional control strategy. He or she first tells them accurately how (bad) they are feeling, increasing the feeling that the instructor is always right. Then, he or she slowly increases their feelings of self worth. It is all part of the *est* philosophy that the trainee is already perfect, already doing an unexceptionable job of being him- or herself; the course aims at "enlightenment," but this is the realization that there is actually nothing to "get"—one is already complete and has no need to evaluate him- or herself or his or her progress, no need to set up standards for the self or others (Baer and Stolz, 1978, p. 57). It takes time for this full philosophy to be presented and for the trainees to "get it"—hence the length of the seminar training—but the road to self-realization or self-actualization begins now. Third, the trainer allows no counter-control: he or she is not open to suggestion, persuasion, or coercion from the floor. He or she ignores attacks on him- or herself while providing selective reinforcement for the trainee's self-disclosure, "sharing," and gradually transferring control from himself to the audience, allowing the informational reinforcement of his "thank you" (which implies some progress has been made) to be enhanced by the utilitarian control exerted by the group's rate of acceptance. As we have seen, the physical, social, temporal, and regulatory environment consists of discriminative stimuli that signal all the rewards and punishment within the control of the trainer and their relationship to specific behaviors—by trainees in the setting. The in-setting training also provides utilitarian reinforcers which have the effect of further reducing the power of the pre-training learning history and of strengthening the new patterns of behavior learned during the sessions. Not only are new skills learned; they are accompanied by the emotional release elicited during the nine "processes" of "experience algorithms" that trainees undertake with eyes closed. Each of these increases their self-awareness, that is, leads to a greater understanding of the contingencies that have influenced the trainees' behavior: "They immerse the person in feelings, attitudes, sensations, and judgments that might otherwise be avoided. Thus, they allow an appreciation of what the experiences in fact consist of" (p. 53). The trainee is encouraged to be in a position to articulate the contingencies that have shaped his or her prior behavior and emotional reactions, to practice self-management, and to gain control. In the process of reinventing the self, the trainee establishes or recognizes new reinforcers which strengthen the new self-image he or she has acquired.

Hedonism: The Managed Restaurant Experience

An example of hedonism is provided by the Benihana restaurant case (Sasser, Olsen, and Wyckoff, 1978, pp. 44–57) on which the following account is based. Each restaurant in the Benihana chain features Japanese decor and a Teppanyaki table at which a chef prepares and serves food directly to the customers, next to whose table the apparatus is located. At the first level of analysis, that of the operant behavior class, the experience of dining in this context is apparently reinforced by high levels of utilitarian reinforcement and a low but not insignificant level of informational reinforcement. Evidence of the former is provided, first, by the behavior of the chef (each of whom, like the waitresses who are the other personnel who deliver the service, is responsible for two tables): the chef prepares, cooks, and serves the food with flourish and panache—the restaurant is generally acknowledged to be in show business as well as the food-delivery industry, and the gas-fire Teppanyaki table, containing the grill and a ledge for the various implements used in cooking, lies at the heart of the showbiz. The native Japanese chefs are highly trained in a formal three-year apprentice-ship: Benihana cooking is mostly showmanship and requires such detailed training; chefs' behavior is controlled by competition among the chefs and through a travelling inspector. The product itself is highly visual.

The second, interrelated, aspect of utilitarian reinforcement is the food itself: highly palatable (to U.S. customers) "wholesome, familiar food, with unusual, unique and delicious preparation, served in a fun atmosphere." The Benihana marketing philosophy continues, "We want to intrigue the people celebrating an anniversary or taking Aunt Sally out to dinner. A Japanese restaurant would normally never cross their minds. We are saying we are a fun place to try, and there is no slithery fishy stuff" (Sasser, Olsen, and Wyckoff, 1987, p. 54). The menu comprises a limited range of typi-cally *American* foods—steak, shrimp, chicken—all of which are "middle American entrées." The limited accompaniments—bean sprouts, zucchini, fresh mushrooms, onion, and rice—are similarly standardized and invari-able. Exotically titled but familiar beverages are highly priced but served in cheap paper mugs. Informational reinforcement consists predominantly in the social status gained from taking guests to this unusual and novel restaurant, a useful additional reward for whoever is treating "Aunt Sally" or taking business colleagues for a short but unusual lunch or dinner prior to a business meeting perhaps.

At the second level of analysis, that of the contingency category, there appears to be strong justification for designating this consumer activity as inescapable entertainment, since the form of the showbiz is entirely beyond the control of the customer and there are numerous constraints on behav-ior which would lead to the view that the setting is closed. Consumers would not go to Benihana if the food were not intrinsically good to eat (and research shows that a high proportion of current consumers are returners). Therefore, the panache with which they are entertained while eating and drinking is an inescapable extra, albeit pleasant and rewarding in itself. For all that the customer is free to walk out or try to ignore such entertainment, the setting is very different from, say, watching television or listening to CDs or the radio in one's own home, where it is possible to switch channels or tracks at will and to escape entertainment altogether with ease. By com-parison, eating at home or at a fast-food restaurant provides more choice and control; other forms of entertainment are within the control of the consumer at each stage and at every moment: listening to music at home, watching television, walking the dog, for instance. The third level of analy-sis, that of the consumer situation, confirms this by identifying the specific physical, social, temporal, and regulatory discriminative stimuli by which the behavior of consumers is shaped and constrained. Even before they get to the dining area guests are assembled informally in the bar into groups of eight; each eight consists of groups and individuals who are strangers to one another. Each of these groups of eight is shepherded by a waitress to the table: the bench-style seats do not encourage lingering beyond about three-quarters of a hour; the limited menu makes for speedy ordering; the food is grilled, which also encourages speed of service; the chef "force feeds" customers by throwing them pieces of food during the cooking; meat is cut up to assist faster eating; the sole dessert, sherbet, is also quickly consumed and will begin to melt if it is left too long. The end of the "show" is signaled by the chef's bow: this puts the clientele under some pressure to leave, but if it does not have the desired effect, he can start to clean the grill in anticipation of the arrival of the next group of diners. In any case, the surrounding showbiz does not encourage extended discussions: "[N]ormally a customer can come in, be seated, and be on his way out in forty five minutes, if need be. The average turnover was an hour, up to an hour and a half in slower periods" (Sasser, Olsen, and Wyckoff, 1978. p. 48). The pace was set by the chef who controlled the proceedings, if only because his take-home pay depended on tips.

The rules, all plys, which maintain this behavior program include the following: you should take a seat in the bar as directed and order a drink or drinks; you should move to the table when directed; you should order and eat relatively speedily; you should watch the "show" rather than get involved in lengthy conversation; you should not converse at length with strangers; you should leave when the meal ends; you should not keep other customers waiting; once one person leaves, follow him or her out. These rule-governed behaviors are encouraged and reinforced by the discriminative stimuli at the disposal of the waitress and the chef, and reinforce positively and negatively by the smiles, greetings, gestures, and the appropriateness of the behavior of these personnel.

Accumulation: Frequent Flyer Programs

The frequent-flyer programs of major airlines provide an example of accumulation—a class of consumer behaviors in which informational reinforcement is particularly to the fore while utilitarian reinforcement is *relatively* unimportant. This case is based on information relating to the Qantas Frequent Flyer Program (Qantas, n.d.) which appears typical of many other schemes offered. Members of such schemes acquire a standard number of points for every kilometer or mile travelled with the airline (as associated carriers) for which they have paid a full fare. Business-class passengers accumulate points at a higher rate, and first-class flyers at a higher rate still. Members who purchase or consume other services—such as selected car hire, credit card use, and hotel accommodation—may add further "bonus" points to their total. Feedback is provided by statements frequently mailed to members of the scheme which detail distances flown, bonuses, and points accrued. This case provides insight into the relationship between utilitarian and informational reinforcement. The feedback provided by the accumulation of points is, as just noted, dependent upon the consumption of services that provide mainly utilitarian rewards—air travel, car rental, and so on—though some informational reinforcement may be forthcoming directly from the conspicuous consumption of some of these services that provide social prestige. Additional points may be earned by using the American Express Card issued in conjunction with the Qantas program under the American Express "Membership Miles" scheme. Moreover, the ultimate source of reinforcement is undoubtedly utilitarian—free air travel and other benefits. These "other benefits" combine utilitarian and informational reinforcement in an interesting way.

They include priority check-in at airports, an additional baggage allowance, priority baggage-handling facilities, and a booking service for concerts and plays in London, Australia, and the United States. These additional benefits are available to holders of a Silver Card, an item of performance feedback conferred when 70,000 points have been earned on international flights or 17,500 on domestic routes or a combination, within a twelve-month period. They are available only when the cardholder is paying full fare for a journey. When an even higher total of points is accumulated within a year (250,000 for international flights, 62,500 for domestic, or a combination) the member of the scheme may receive a Gold Card which confers further privileges—for instance, access to "Captain's Club" lounges at airports irrespective of the class of travel selected as long as the trip is international. Points must be redeemed within two years. Just joining attracts an informational reward—a White Membership Card that enables miles travelled to be tracked automatically as long as the card number is quoted when a reservation is made. Although this is the least documented case history described here, it is still possible to identify the three designated levels of analysis. The operant class to which the behavior under review belongs is accumulation. Informational reinforcement in the form of frequent/regular feedback on the number of miles travelled or points accumulated is the most important means of maintaining the behavior. That behavior is travelling with the designated airline on one's next trip. This does not imply that utilitarian reinforcement is either absent or unimportant: indeed, we have noted the interaction of the two sources of reinforcement and the way in which the informational is ultimately sustained by the utilitarian.

At the second level of analysis, the behavior of the scheme member takes place within a *relatively* closed consumer behavior setting. Having entered the scheme, it is more attractive to continue flying with the designated airline in order to realize both the informational reinforcement immediately available and the ultimate utilitarian reward contingent upon accumulation. To some degree the frequent flyer becomes locked into being loyal to that airline. The opportunity to purchase other services such as car rental further reduces the probability that the consumer will fly with another carrier since those services are contingent upon his or her having travelled with the airline that operates the scheme. By comparison, accumulation in the form of regular saving into a bank account or collecting part-works that build into a reference book or encyclopedia takes place in a relatively open setting. The consumer is not locked in to the same degree: it is possible to transfer a savings account to another bank whose interest rates have been increased; missing a magazine is not punished by irretrievable loss since it may be available by mail or when the part work is republished. (Recall that in the frequent-flyer scheme points must be used within a specific time frame.) The reinforcer obtained each week or month is an end in itself as well as being part of a growing whole. Thus continued accumulation is not compelled.

At the third level of analysis, the consumer situation is marked especially by rules which determine whether behavior will be followed by contingent reinforcement. Rules determine who is a member, how membership is defined, how points and bonuses will be added, how points (tokens) will be converted into back-up reinforcers, and so on. These rules are plys: compliance on the part of the traveler is at the heart of the entire enterprise. We can only assume that the traveler has a history of delayed utilitarian reinforcement supported by the apportionment of tokens that act as discriminative stimuli for further responding.

Maintenance: The Design of Airport Waiting

In maintenance, consumer behavior of a particular topography is all but *compelled* by the contingencies: the consumer has no escape from the performance of the behavior in question because so much depends upon it— usually a very significant utilitarian and/or informational reinforcer. In order to take an airplane to a necessary business trip or to an exotic holiday destination, it is necessary to reach the airport and to remain there for some considerable time prior to take-off. The direct positive consequences of this airport waiting are minimal, and the aversive consequences substantial. The following operant interpretation is based on the account by Sommer (1974, pp. 70–80). The classification of airport waiting as maintenance (level 1) follows from the preceding brief description: neither utilitarian nor informational reinforcement is other than fundamental—there is sufficient comfort to keep customers there without complaint and sufficient progress reports (e.g., in the form of announcements about the time remaining to wait until the flight is called) and other discriminative stimuli detailing the availability of the principle utilitarian and informational reinforcer—the flight—to maintain further waiting. The physical, social, temporal, and regulatory environment is sufficiently prescribed to enable this situation to be classified unambiguously as mandatory consumption (level 2). Sommer describes "hard" architecture as designed by those who know what is best for others (p. 2). It cannot be destroyed since it is "strong and resistant to human imprint"; to those who use it, it seems impervious, impersonal, and inorganic; and it is characterized by "a lack of permeability between inside and out." Of all the forms of architecture he considers, Sommer describes airport terminals as "among the hardest buildings in the land" (p. 70). By comparison, consumer behavior for food products, which also qualifies as maintenance, usually takes place in a relatively open setting: the consumer is not compelled to shop at any particular store or to select specific brands or products on all occasions (Ehrenberg, 1972; Foxall, 1992a).

Moving on to the third level of analysis, that of the consumer situation, it is clear that the scope of these consumer behavior settings is severely limited by the physical surroundings that comprise the terminal, by the implications of the physical context of social behavior, by time constraints, and by rules that influence where consumers can go and what they can do there. People have to spend considerable periods of time in airports, longer now that security checks often mean arriving two or three hours prior to departure. Sommer points out that "no agency or organization feels a responsibility for insuring that waiting time is pleasant or productive" (1970, p. 70). Such waiting time is especially long on trans- and intercontinental flights which are often delayed, overbooked, consolidated, or cancelled. The time is spent in a "cold, sterile and unfriendly building." The social and physical layout is fine for passengers who want to be alone, but there is nothing for those who would prefer "a reassuring and comfortable environment" (p. 71). Hence the passenger suffers first of all an arduous trip to the airport and treatment as a non-person by uninformed personnel, then is left to his own devices to find the right check-in desks, queues, seating areas, and pathways. The seating is such that all the chairs are identical and are bolted together—the consumer is again ignored. It seems that officials only become aware of the existence of the customer and his or her needs when he or she is in the plane and is highly cosseted, though even here the consumer is socially isolated. The seating in the waiting area, consonant with the entire building, is socio-fugal rather than socio-petal (Osmond, 1957); whereas the latter encourages social contact, the former isolates the individual, where there is crowding things are even worse since the psychological apartness is emphasized (Sommer, 1970, p. 73). As a result people occupy small spaces, reading books and magazines and thus avoiding interaction with others who are nearby. The layout of the airport is such that both children and adults are "restricted to a few role responses such as playing the insurance machine, walking up the down escalator, turning on the water fountain, riding the conveyor belt in the baggage section when the attendant is not present, inspecting the candy machine, checking out the waste baskets and pulling the levers on the cigarette machines" (p. 74). If children are to see the planes, they must often be lifted by an adult because of the high windows (this is not so true nowadays). Older people are also very isolated and their sense of separation is enforced by the institutional row of chairs. According to Sommer, airports seem deliberately designed to eliminate conversation among the passengers. The evidence for this is that the seats are fastened together with arm rests that demarcate each individual's permitted space; rows are back to back or arranged in classroom style facing the counter; chairs are identical since it is assumed that everyone is the same size and shape; there is nowhere to leave coats; and there is a need to put parcels, cabin luggage, coats, and so on, on a lap or on the floor nearby and to police them so they are not trodden on and that no one trips over them. The most important thing is that the chairs are unmovable; nobody is allowed to form them into a circle so that social interaction within a group is possible. Sommer sees in this socio-fugal waiting area

> a conspiracy to drive passengers out to the concessions where they will spend money. Any effort to humanize or provide amenities in the waiting area is a threat to the restaurant, cocktail lounge, news stand, and gift shop. No one, including the airlines, has a financial stake in the comfort of passengers in the waiting areas.

Therefore "passengers have no organizational representation to look after their interests . . . They are regarded by the airlines as merchandise to be shipped elsewhere and by the concessionaries as sheep to be sheared" (p. 79). Those with the greatest power and influence are bought off by being taken to their own luxurious lounges which are subsidized by economy passengers.

Overall the impersonal institutional atmosphere of the airport waiting area means that there is extremely limited social interaction even with the family group that one has arrived with. Bomb scares mean that passengers are routed through sanitized areas while family and friends are denied access to boarding areas. Moreover much of the architecture is identical from airport to airport (e.g., the restaurant). All of this is reinforced by a series of rules which make pliance the most obvious characteristic of consumer behavior in this setting.

6   Interpreting Consumer Choice

The basic fault of every form of positivism in the social sciences is the belief that the act of interpretation can be circumvented.

—Peter Berger and Hansfried Kellner (1981, p. 127)

There are numerous "styles" for doing science: the only constant is the need to measure one's ideas against the real world.

—Lewis Wolpert (1992, p. xiii)

CONTINGENCY CATEGORIES

A typology of consumer situations is defined by the independent variables of the BPM, the antecedent and consequential stimuli that control behavior. Depending on the relatively open or closed nature of the setting, the high or low levels of utilitarian and informational reinforcement available in and signaled by the setting, there emerge eight categories of contingencies which can be interpreted as influencing consumer behavior. Each is a distinctive combination of setting and reinforcer variables which elucidates particular topographies of purchase and consumption. The BPM Contingency Matrix (Figure 1.2, p. 10) summarizes the ways in which the independent variables combine to produce the eight contingency categories. Each of these contingency categories represents a class of purchase and consumption situations. An interpretive account of consumer activity should systematically relate known patterns of purchase and consumption to the contingencies on which they are maintained. The following analysis identifies fundamental classes of consumer behavior and the schedules of reinforcement that apparently control them. It then describes the topographies of well-known examples of purchase and consumption and infers the nature of the behavior setting and the pattern of reinforcement apparently controlling them.

MAJOR CLASSES OF CONSUMER BEHAVIOR

Purchase and consumption can, like any other behaviors, be classified according to the nature of their consequences, that is, according to the pattern of utilitarian and informational reinforcement on which they are maintained. The shaping and maintenance of complex behavior may depend on the effects of concurrent reinforcement schedules which reflect the influences of more than one combination of reinforcer strengths, but, for present analytical purposes, most if not all consumer behavior can be assigned to one or other of the major classes of consequence based on permutations of low/high utilitarian and low/high informational reinforcement. The four classes into which the consequences of consumer behavior are divided are accomplishment, pleasure, accumulation, and maintenance.

Accomplishment

Social and economic achievement maintain such behaviors as the acquisition and conspicuous consumption of status symbols, as well as the activities involved in seeking sensation and excitement or personal fulfillment, as long as these acts result in the accumulation of some measure of attainment: points, certificates, rites of passage, course completion, and so on, which mark progress. This general pattern of consequences, *accomplishment*, is likely to be produced by high levels of both utilitarian and informational reinforcement. Many of the behaviors designated accomplishment are apparently maintained on *variable ratio* (VR) schedules and, depending on the degree of openness of the behavior setting—the extent to which the situation and its reinforcers are controlled by either the consumer or the provider of the product or service—will be discussed subsequently in the context of Contingency Categories 1 and 2. In the case of the open behavior setting (Contingency Category 1) a typical example is the pre-purchase search for and comparative evaluation of information relating to luxuries or discontinuous innovations; in the case of the closed setting (Contingency Category 2), casino gambling provides a typical instance.

Hedonism

The outcomes of all forms of popular entertainment and of behaviors such as taking medication, which are controlled (negatively reinforced) by the alleviation of suffering or displeasure, are consequence which may be linked with a high level of utilitarian reinforcement but only a low level of informational reinforcement which, nevertheless, is neither absent nor unimportant. Such a pattern of consequences may be summed up as *hedonism*. These behaviors, which occur as if maintained by a *variable interval* (VI) schedule of reinforcement, are discussed subsequently in the contexts of Contingency Categories 3 and 4. In the open behavior setting (Contingency Category 3), an example is the TV game show, while in the closed setting (Contingency Category 4), a typical example would be in-flight consumption of meals or movies.

Accumulation

Consumer behaviors involving collecting, saving (notably saving up irregularly to buy something), installment buying, and responses to promotional deals requiring the accumulation of tokens or coupons have consequences that presumably embody a high level of informational reinforcement but a low level of utilitarian reinforcement, though the latter is neither absent nor, necessarily, unimportant. The pattern of consequences produced by these behaviors is readily described as *accumulation*. Such behaviors are apparently maintained on *fixed ratio* (FR) schedules and are discussed below in the context of Contingency Categories 5 and 6. An example of accumulation in an open setting (Contingency Category 5) is collecting packet tops to obtain a fairly trivial free gift, while accumulating air miles as one uses airline services exemplifies the relevant behavior in a closed setting (Contingency Category 6).

Maintenance

The obligatory activities involved in survival (e.g., regular food purchasing) and the fulfillment of social and cultural obligations of citizenship (e.g., the consumption of public goods for which taxes are paid at regular intervals) may be construed as involving relatively low levels of both utilitarian and informational reinforcement, though this does not mean that either is absent or unimportant. The consequences that control such behaviors may be described as *maintenance*. Note that maintenance does not refer simply to physical survival and well-being but includes the consumer's fulfillment of minimal social, cultural, and economic requirements of any member of the society, especially as he or she makes sense of their social existence through consumption. These behaviors are seemingly maintained on *fixed interval* (FI) schedules and are relevant to Contingency Categories 7 and 8. The routine weekly purchasing of food items and other fast-moving consumer goods in a supermarket is an example of the behavior in question in an open behavior setting, while mandatory consumption of public goods, for which compulsory taxes are levied, exemplifies such behavior in a closed setting. Figure 1.2 (p. 10) summarizes the relationship of these major classes of consumer behavior to the contingencies that maintain them.

ACCOMPLISHMENT IN OPEN SETTINGS

Topography and Reinforcement

Watching TV documentaries and dramas, reading literary novels, or playing a board game like *Trivial Pursuit* are all apparently reinforced by strong utilitarian and informational consequences. In each case, the arrangement of reinforcers maintains behavior on an extended VR schedule (i.e., the behaviors are emitted steadily at a high rate but reinforced relatively infrequently): it is necessary, for example, to watch the program or read the novel for a period of time or number of pages before a substantial reinforcement arrives in the form of a dramatic development or significant denouement. A familiar instance in the context of consumer behavior is the pre-purchase responses typical of consumer behavior for luxuries and discontinuous innovations such as TV satellite dishes, video recorders, exotic vacations, and home computers. The BPM accounts for these pre-purchase behaviors—which involve search for and comparative evaluation of data about products and services, and which are depicted in the cognitive model as extensive problem solving (Howard, 1989)—by reference to the high levels of both utilitarian and informational reinforcement provided by the products/services which are the subject of the activities. Most of these items are possessed and used for the pleasure or ease of living they confer, the well-being they make possible for the individual: they thereby provide extensive utilitarian rewards. But they are often status symbols and their conspicuous consumption also provides informational reinforcement: they attest directly, and often publicly and unambiguously, to the consumer's attainments, especially economic. Goods in this category are usually highly differentiated by novel function (in the case of innovations) or branding (in the case of luxuries). Some of the pre-purchase behaviors associated with these products—window shopping, browsing, search, comparison, evaluation, and verbal consideration—occur frequently and are apparently maintained by moderate to high VR schedules (which maintain regular and systematic responding). These pre-purchase behaviors are learned through small reinforcements and extinguish quite slowly. Even if the possibility of purchasing is remote, individuals receive utilitarian and informational reinforcement from potentially pre-purchase activities. These pre-purchase behaviors are voluntary and may take several forms, none of which is compelled. Consumption is usually undertaken in an open (e.g., domestic) setting, though deliberate conspicuous consumption relies on carrying out some specific contextual actions.

Behavior Setting

Purchase of luxuries or innovations typically occurs in open behavior settings such as a retail store; pre- and post-purchase behaviors also typically occur in open settings such as the home. The very considerable degree of openness of these settings is inferred from the relatively unrestricted access to a wide variety of competing reinforcers enjoyed by the (prospective) purchase. At the pre-purchase stage, leading up to the purchase itself, the marketer has comparatively little control over the consumer's actions. The particular contingencies that control the consumer's behavior are determined by his or her unique history of reinforcement.

The manufacturer of any given luxury/innovation has little direct control unless it has a monopoly and the capability of convincing the potential buyer—through advertising or demonstration—of the advantages of the product, or unless it can influence retailers to persuade the customer to buy. In the case of a genuine innovation, few customers are initial buyers (consumer innovators), and most such products fail at the stage of consumer acceptance.

Behavior Setting Summary

Availability of and access to reinforcers: (i) many reinforcers are available, none of which has special salience; (ii) there are many means by which the reinforcers may be obtained; and (iii) the consumer is not compelled to execute more than a minimal number of externally defined tasks in order to obtain the reinforcers. *Situational control*: (i) the marketer has comparatively little control over the behavior of the prospective purchase/consumer; (ii) the consumer has several, perhaps many, sets of contingencies to "choose" among; and (iii) the consumer has many alternatives to being in the situation.

ACCOMPLISHMENT IN CLOSED SETTINGS

Topography and Reinforcement

Extensive problem solving occurs in open settings which provide consumers with considerable scope for participation and exit: there is little if any compulsion to be in a specific purchase or consumption situation at all, and many sources of reinforcement compete for the individual's discretionary income and time; when they pall, the consumer can relatively easily extricate him or herself from the setting. When a similarly powerful combination of utilitarian and informational reinforcers is available in a closed setting, behavior also comes under the control of influential aversive stimuli, both antecedent and consequential, which make escape and avoidance less probable. The casino provides an appropriate illustration. Gambling in so closed a setting is an activity maintained by high levels of both utilitarian and informational reinforcement. It takes place in settings composed of discriminative stimuli which clearly signal both the positive consequences of approved approach behaviors and the potentially punishing implications of escape or avoidance responses which flout established rules and gaming conventions. As is the case with services in general, it is not possible to divide behavior neatly into pre-purchase, purchase, and post-purchase phases: purchase and consumption occur simultaneously.

Behavior Setting

Although several games may be available in the casino (cf. the bingo hall where there is but one) the principal reinforcer is winning (points or money). The main utilitarian reinforcement derives also from this source: pleasure and social approval stem mainly from winning, though a certain amount of enjoyment and prestige may be derived from being part of a somewhat exclusive social group, dressing appropriately, conforming to a specified code of behavior, and so on. Closely defined behavioral acts must be adhered to in order to participate, including obtaining membership, following codes of dress and deportment, entering the game at the right time and in an appropriate manner, and so on. Different games provide different discriminative stimuli for broadly similar operant responses, but some variety is possible; however, once the individual is in the setting, only conformity to the required behavior patterns can lead to the reinforcers. Access to the casino is strictly determined by its management who pronounce on membership rights and may deny entry on any particular occasion to anyone who does not conform to the required codes of conduct. The casino management has considerable control over access to the informational and utilitarian reinforcement represented by winning by virtue of its determining the schedule of reinforcement in operation (although the rules of a game such as roulette may be said to determine the schedule, the casino may have legal discretion over the favorability of the odds to the house, and over the amounts staked). Those alternative sources of reinforcement that are available are close substitutes, offering minimal variety. The casino managers arrange the physical and, to a degree, social environment, within the law, controlling lighting, the situation of tables, the clientele, all of which may be manipulated to ensure the continued presence of the punters where they are most likely to gamble—to the extent of serving drinks and even meals at the tables and providing opportunities to gamble in the restaurants. Although there are such obvious physical encouragements to gamble and, indeed, movement may be severely restricted on occasion, the most subtle control is social. Quitting, failing to take risks by staking inadequate sums, and so on, evoke social disapprobation which makes escape and avoidance less probable.

Behavior Setting Summary

Availability of and access to reinforcers: (i) only a few reinforcers are available and one has special salience; (ii) there are only a few, closely prescribed, means of obtaining the reinforcers; and (iii) clearly specified behaviors must be performed to obtain the reinforcers. *Situational control*: (i) access and deprivation are controlled largely by the casino management; (ii) the consumer has few sets of contingencies to choose among; and (iii) consumer behavior is controlled by contingencies imposed by agents not under the control of the same contingencies.

HEDONISM IN OPEN SETTINGS

Topography and Reinforcement

Some consumer behaviors are apparently maintained by principally utilitarian reinforcement: informational reinforcement is often also important but not to the extent suggested by consideration of VR schedules. Watching popular television game shows which provide near-constant entertainment, and the reading of mass fiction which contains a sensation on almost every page, seem to be maintained on VI schedules: even a short period of attending is reinforced and the consumer is meant to be little more than the passive recipient of transitory thrills. However, behavior is sometimes maintained on these schedules for long periods, even though variety, pace, and change seem to be required to ensure continued reinforcer effect and therefore sustained responding. Personal music players and the viewing of many television shows and movies have replaced for many people the more demanding cultural habits essential to the appreciation of literary and dramatic art forms. Instead, mass culture presents frequent and predictable, relatively strong and continuous utilitarian reinforcements which are not contingent on long periods of concentrated effort.

Informational reinforcement is more obvious on some occasions than others, as when game shows allow the audience to monitor their own performances against that of the competing participants, but it is not the main source of reward, and even in instances like this it has an entertainment function. Once again the schedule may at times resemble CRF but not every response is reinforced, though enough are to ensure a steady rate of responding. Constant reduction in attention spans—viewers are reported to switch TV channels on average every three minutes and some use split screens to watch two programs simultaneously—implies a search for reinforcement. Trying to overcome this, some television shows incorporate sustained reinforcement for very short periods of responding, for instance, the "happy news" bulletin format, pioneered in California, in which reports are made entertaining by featuring "action, pace, [and] an almost dizzy attempt to keep the audience from getting bored" (Tunstall and Walker, 1981, p. 123). Such broadcasts contain a series of sensational stories, each of which receives one or two minutes' concentrated coverage in a half-hour bulletin, interrupted by three two-minute commercial breaks and a five-minute weather forecast presented with similar non-stop pace.

Behavior Setting

Competing television channels and other electronic media provide many sources of highly utilitarian reinforcement with some informationally reinforcing content. The portable technologies involved extend the geographical scope of the open settings in which these behaviors occur. Many other activities compete for the consumer's attention, reducing the probability that consumption of these items will be sustained. The consumption behaviors in question are apparently maintained on low VI schedules, though sometimes reinforcement is almost continuous: mass visual communication present reinforcers in such a way that the audience's attention is maintained in face of strong competition. Although TV advertisements fulfill the primary function of presenting discriminative stimuli which signal rein-forcement contingent on specified purchase and consumption responses, they also reinforce viewers' sustained attention. However, time and place of consumption are generally within the control of the consumer, even to the extent that the consumer may apparently deliberately use the output of these media to negatively reinforce avoidance/escape from boredom or other aversive stimuli, as when, for example, he or she is faced by unremit-ting travel. Even among fans of a particular program or type of program, loyalty is relatively low.

Behavior Setting Summary

Availability of and access to reinforcers: (i) there are relatively many rein-forcers available, none having overriding salience for a sustained period; (ii) there are many means by which the reinforcers can be obtained; and (iii) although specific minor actions must be performed in order to access the reinforcers, reinforcement is thereafter relatively effortlessly gained. *Situational control*: (i) access and deprivation are for the most part controlled by the consumer; (ii) the consumer has numerous sets of contingencies from which to choose; and (iii) behavior is maintained by contingencies under the control of the broadcaster, but the existence of a wide range of competing reinforcers means that consumer behavior is flexible and relatively unpredictable.

HEDONISM IN CLOSED SETTINGS

Topography and Reinforcement

The consequences of the behaviors in question are potentially pleasurable but inescapable. As a result, consumption of these products and services may be passive rather than active. An example occurs in the situation in which long-distance airline passengers must purchase meals along with their travel, and which, like the in-flight movies which follow them, are consumed without alternative. A less extreme example is a visit to a museum or art gallery: the more "dutiful" such behavior is, the greater the closed-ness of the setting. Some products relevant to this class of situations are escape commodities, those which offer relief from acute discomfort—for instance, aspirin for the removal of toothache. Behavior in this category is maintained by the removal of an aversive stimulus, that is, negatively reinforced, apparently on a low VI schedule. Routinely consumed com-modities at the product level which are necessary to survival and growth (typically primary commodities like foodstuffs) also belong here: biologi-cal necessity dictates the aversive conditions that are ameliorated by pur-chase or, more usually, consumption of these items. Physical deprivation is a substantial determinant of reinforcer effectiveness, and reinforcement is likely to occur only when the relief promised by the product is swift (reinforcer delay is minimal).

Behavior Setting

Escape from the setting is difficult—physically impossible in cases such as that of the in-flight situation, and socially proscribed in other instances such as the museum visit. The consumer's current state of deprivation or the effects of previous deprivations may constitute part of the current setting by making the reinforcement contingent on food purchasing or taking medication more salient to the individual. The setting is closed not by other people who uphold rules but by physiological factors beyond the control of the individual.

Behavior Setting Summary

Availability of and access to reinforcers: (i) in the case of "inescapable entertainment" the consumer is forced to "enjoy" just one type of reinforcer; in the case of primary escape, there is only one really effective reinforcer—the relief of pain or provision of food, and so on; (ii) either the reinforcer cannot be avoided or comparatively few means are available to obtain the reinforcer; and (iii) the consumer usually cannot escape the reinforcers or must follow specific rules to obtain reinforcement. *Situational control*: (i) the marketer has considerable control over provision of the reinforcers, price, and so on; (ii) the providers have considerable control of the contingencies but are not, in their professional roles, subject to them themselves; and (iii) there is no real alternative to being in the situation.

ACCUMULATION IN OPEN SETTINGS

Topography and Reinforcement

Consumer behaviors requiring the systematic collection or accumulation of a specified number of tokens before a major reinforcement is provided are apparently maintained on a FI schedule. In the case of open behavior settings, these include purchases where payments are made prior to consumption, for instance, the payment of installments for a holiday which can only be taken once the full amount has been paid, or payments into a Christmas club. Saving with the intention of making a large purchase when a certain amount has accumulated would fall into this category. Promotional deals requiring the accumulation of coupons or other tokens before a product or service can be obtained also belong here. The important reinforcement is informational, though utilitarian reinforcement is not absent.

Behavior Setting

The behavior setting is influenced by agents other than the consumer who attempt to structure the stream of behavior by the arrangement of highly contingent reinforcers that shape and maintain sustained, sequential patterns of response. Marketers attempt to influence consumer behavior by increasing the quality and quantity of positive reinforcers that strengthen consumer approach and to reduce the quality and quantity of those that are likely to invite escape and avoidance. Both may be simultaneously accomplished through promotional deals that make an extraordinary reinforcement (such as a prize) contingent on repeat purchasing. The reinforcer in question is usually qualitatively different from the purchased items which makes it available, and is usually predominantly utilitarian rather than informational in character. The requirement that the promoted brand be successively purchased before the additional reinforcer is obtained reduces the probability of escape or avoidance such as purchasing an alternative brand. Indeed, products that arrive periodically in parts (such as the weekly and monthly magazines that build into encyclopedia) are promoted such that non-response (missing even one part) is punished: missed parts may become available again only after a period of time has elapsed and the series is rerun, or they may be obtained at additional cost and inconvenience. Competitions and deals demanding repeat buying to be effective also apparently change the schedule of reinforcement, albeit temporarily, for those customers not already loyal to the brand. However, consumers retain a considerable degree of discretion in these circumstances since the products in question compete heavily with alternative, more readily obtained reinforcers.

Behavior Setting Summary

Availability of and access to reinforcers: (i) there are several salient reinforcers; (ii) at least several types of response lead to the reinforcers; and (iii) highly specific tasks need not be undertaken. *Situational control*: (i) the marketer has limited control; (ii) the decision process is largely under consumer control; and (iii) there are alternatives to being in the situation; other sources of reinforcement, offering more immediate gratification, are readily available.

ACCUMULATION IN CLOSED SETTINGS

Topography and Reinforcement

These behaviors also involve collecting but through purchase-based token economies in which payment for one item provides token for another. The setting is said to be closed because the first item would probably be purchased anyway in some form or other and the consumer's income constraint makes it likely that the second or backup reinforcer would be obtained only in this way. The reinforcement for the accumulation of tokens is predominantly informational, secondarily instrumental, though the backup reinforcement may be either utilitarian or informational.

Behavior Setting

A recent trend in marketing involves the use of token-economy principles by making additional reinforcers contingent on prior purchasing: the practice is simply an extension of the familiar prize schemes open to collectors of cigarette cards or trading stamps. The "air miles" earned by frequent flyers on domestic and international airlines constitute informational reinforcers that are analogous to the tokens earned for pro-social behavior in therapeutic and connectional institutions (Ayllon and Azrin, 1968; Battalio, Kagel, Winkler, Fisher, Basman, and Krasner, 1974; Kazdin, 1983). Some hotels also offer gifts to customers who accumulate points by staying frequently. The collection of these tokens is reinforced by the gaining of additional free air travel or hospitality (an increase in reinforcer quantity) and/or by access to different types of reinforcer such as prizes (an increase in reinforcer quality). Purchase and consumption of the basic product, the air travel or accommodation originally demanded, are maintained by both the intrinsic utilitarian reinforcers they embody and the informational consequences of buying and using them. These extrinsic, informational reinforcers also act as discriminative stimuli, directing behavior toward the attainment and consumption of the additional (back-up) reinforcers offered. The use of tokens in this way may not only increased the loyalty of existing consumers but also increase overall demand, at least while the deal is operated (Chesanow, 1985). The degree of closedness in these settings is judged mainly from the high value of the eventual reinforcers and the even more convoluted matrix of contingent reinforcement arranged to determine a cumulative, sequential stream of behaviors. The closedness is also apparent from the fact that the consumer is likely to indulge in the primary behavior in any case and has incentives to remain brand loyal as a result of the token economy framework in which he or she is, initially involuntarily, engulfed.

Behavior Setting Summary

Availability of and access to reinforcers: (i) there are few if any means of escaping aversive stimuli other than conformity to the task determined by others; (ii) there is usually only one or a few closely specified behaviors to be performed; and (iii) very specific tasks are required and the whole behavior is rule governed. *Situational control*: (i) the authorities have extensive control: they can take away the individual's freedom, make him/her ineligible to receive products or credit, and so on; (ii) the authorities impose rigorous sanctions to which they are not themselves subject; and (iii) there is no alternative to being in the situation, if aversive stimuli are to be avoided and the negative reinforcement that removes them eventually provided.

MAINTENANCE IN OPEN SETTINGS

Topography and Reinforcement

A typical example of behavior in this category is the habitual purchasing of grocery items at a supermarket, the routine problem solving of the cognitive model (Howard, 1989). The BPM relates behaviors such as these to the discriminative stimuli found in the open settings in which they occur and the low intensity of both utilitarian and informational reinforcement contingent on purchase and consumption. The setting is nonetheless more closed than that in which limited problem solving occurs. The behaviors shaped and maintained in these circumstances are truly routine since the consumer has tried many brands in the relevant product class and typically chooses among a small repertoire of acceptable brands which are close functional substitutes, each presenting a variation on the same underlying formulation of physical ingredients and differentiated to a greater or lesser extent by marketing considerations (Foxall, 1990). The responses which produce specific reinforcers are well established, and, in spite of enormous marketing activity on the part of manufacturers and retailers, aggregate brand choice is remarkably stable over the medium term. Neither utilitarian nor informational reinforcement is unimportant since both pleasure and data are obtained in the course of such purchasing, but neither has the intensity characteristic of the situations in which innovative or luxurious products are evaluated and bought. Behavior (selection of a specific brand or store) is apparently maintained on low FI or VI schedules or by CRF, that is, reinforcers—usually small and identical on each occasion—follow most, perhaps all, requisite responses.

Behavior Setting

The relative openness of the behavior setting is determined at the brand level: there is so much choice that the consumer enjoys considerable discretion over different versions of the required product. However, purchase and consumption of many of these items, notably foods, are inescapable, and the setting is not as open as those typified by Contingency Categories 1, 3, and 5.

Behavior Setting Summary

Availability of and access to reinforcers: (i) there is a multitude of competing reinforcers: brands, makes, and so on; (ii) there are very many means to the reinforcers, purchase alternatives; the reinforcers are small anyway;

and (iii) trivial, if definite, tasks have to be performed to obtain the reinforcers. *Situational control*: (i) in spite of the manipulation of the physical and social environment within stores and shopping malls, supplier control is limited: there is so much variety even within a specific product class that the arrangement of the setting to promote specific brands has only temporary effects; as a result, manufacturers and retailers market multiple brands and practice vertical and quasi-vertical integration; (ii) the consumer largely determines the immediate contingencies or is not much constrained by them in the medium to long term; hence complete store and brand loyalty are, for most consumers, rare; and (ii) there are plenty of alternatives to being in the situation: alternative stores, brands, and products proliferate, and there are alternative situations, some of which do not entail purchase and consumption at all.

MAINTENANCE IN CLOSED SETTINGS

Topography and Reinforcement

Not all consumer behavior in closed settings is controlled by managers of private firms or public corporations: on occasion, consumption is mandatory. The consumer behavior relevant to this set of reinforcement contingencies is typically compulsory purchase and consumption of state-enforced escape commodities such as social worker intervention, taxation, and television licensing. Often in these circumstances, purchase and consumption are negatively reinforced: the consumer acts to avoid the punishments which non-compliance will bring. The informational reinforcements provide discriminative stimuli to further behaviors. Such behavior is often maintained on a schedule which approximates FI and includes the payment of taxes, TV licensing, and compulsory health or motor insurance. Some of the products relevant to this category entail a mixture of government and private goods. Motor insurance, for instance, is legally required, though most drivers are free to negotiate with a risk-bearer of their choice. Other consumer behaviors most obviously associated with these contingencies include the purchase of complementary secondary escape commodities such as pension-fund membership, or mortgage-related endowment assurance. Neither utilitarian nor informational reinforcement is entirely absent, but the product or service is purchased usually as a complement to another item which is the principal source of reinforcement. The secondary commodity is purchased only because its consumption is a prerequisite of more strongly reinforced purchase or consumption. It is often the eventual acquisition of the additional product or service and the reinforcement it confers that reinforces purchase of the secondary escape commodity. Hence payment of premiums for mortgage-related life insurance may be maintained ultimately by the promises of delayed gratification (the cash released on maturity of the policy) but more routinely by the removal of the threat of punishment (e.g., loss of the mortgage offer). Continued purchase of such escape commodities is often maintained on a FI schedule: minimal informational reinforcement, such as entries in an account passbook or on a monthly or annual statement, may follow each payment or a series of payments, and interest or bonuses may be added at known intervals. Yet, for the most part, such behaviors are maintained not by these positive reinforcers but negatively by the avoidance of the aversive consequences of noncompliance.

Behavior Setting

The closed nature of the behavior setting is a direct consequence of the network of contingencies of reinforcement and punishment established and maintained by authorities external to the individual consumer. Legal, social, moral, and marketing contingencies combine to present the individual little if any discretion over his or her behavior. The secondary responses must be performed if the reinforcers contingent on the primary responses are to be obtained. This pattern of reinforcement is not confined to products and services: patronage of particular stores is often a prerequisite of obtaining specific product or service related reinforcers. Often the discriminative and reinforcing stimuli available in stores are so arranged as to maximize consumers' patronage and to shape purchase responses. However, use of retail outlets occasionally offers little if any direct utilitarian or informational reinforcement, as when an individual must visit a remote airline terminal to obtain tickets, or an unattractive government office to obtain a passport.

Behavior Setting Summary

Availability of and access to reinforcers: (i) purchase or consumption may be compulsory or contingent on other purchase, consumer has little choice and may need seller's approval/advice on mortgages, insurance, status of consumer, and so on; (ii) there are few means to the reinforcers; these products are needed to obtain other reinforcers; and (iii) specific tasks are determinative, from filling in application forms to proving identity and status. *Situational control*: (i) the provider has considerable control; (ii) the contingencies are determined by agents not subject to them; and (iii) there is no alternative if the other reinforcers are to be obtained.

SAVING AND FINANCIAL ASSET MANAGEMENT

Several authors have identified categories of saving behavior and shown their significance in consumer psychology (Wärneryd, 1989a). Katona (1975), for instance, defines several kinds of saving: *contractual* (e.g., regular payments of life insurance premiums), *discretionary* (e.g., saving for a planned vacation), and *residual* (e.g., holding money in a current account against irregular expenditures). Lindqvist (1981) goes further by proposing a hierarchy based on four sequential motives for saving: *cash management*, the most frequent motive, arising from the need to synchronize unpredictable payments and cash availability; *buffer saving*, a reserve of funds to meet unforeseen emergencies and their financial consequences; *goal-directed saving*, for a better car or home, and so on; and *wealth management*, the creation and deployment of wealth in order to achieve more with the assets at one's disposal. A BPM analysis of saving avoids motives and goals as explanatory constructs and seeks to relate observed patterns of savings behavior to the contingencies likely to maintain them (Figure 6.1).

At early stages of the consumer life cycle, saving is related to maintenance. In open settings, such cash management consists of residual saving,

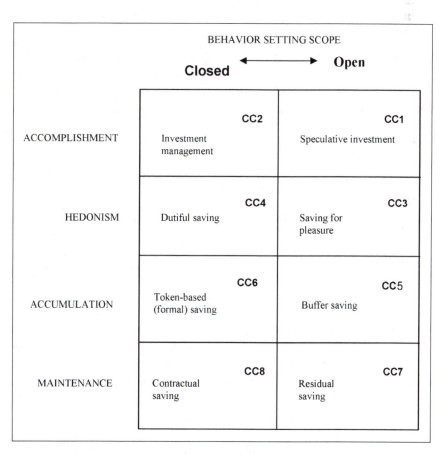

Figure 6.1 BPM interpretation of saving and financial asset management.

cash held in current accounts for the purpose of harmonizing receipts and expenditures, and saving by default. In closed settings, it takes the form of contractual saving, payments made for credit, insurance, pensions schemes, and so on (Katona, 1975). In both cases, it is likely to be predominantly contingency shaped rather than rule governed. The consumer comes directly into contact with the environmental factors that maintain these behaviors and, although some rules may affect specific choices (such as the plys that regulate the payment of premiums in contractual saving), the behavior is, for the most part, determined by its direct effects. Additional income is likely to be saved for purposes of accumulation, that is, with a view to gaining consumer durables, a better home, and so on. In open settings, it takes the form of a basic kind of discretionary saving, saving as a buffer against future misfortune (Katona, 1975; Lindqvist, 1981; Wärneryd, 1989a). This implies formal saving, the regular putting aside of funds into an account which attracts interest. In closed settings, the saving is of a token-economy kind which is described in Appendix 3. It consists of accumulating tokens (perhaps though the purchase of products which confer bonuses in the form of additional products—as in frequent customer programs that confer additional air tickets or free gifts—or by a commitment to saving regularly which, when adhered to, provides a higher rate of interest) which give access to other products or prizes which provide mainly utilitarian reinforcement. In both open and closed settings, initially at least, other rules of a specific nature are likely to influence consumer behavior; such rules specify, for instance, the rate of interest or the number of times a saving act needs to be repeated in order to earn benefits. Tracking is the consumer's likely verbal behavior as he or she follows instructions such as "Do this and that will follow"; to initiate and sustain early saving, however, some plying and augmentals may be necessary. The actual contingencies are likely to assume an important effect as regular saving is maintained by the addition of interest or other benefits.

Further gains in income and/or wealth are likely to lead to saving which will eventually facilitate higher levels of discretionary spending, perhaps on more luxurious items. In open settings, this could mean saving related to hedonism and fun: saving for vacations, luxuries, and entertainment equipment such a video recorders, camcorders, and the like. In closed settings, it would refer to dutiful saving, as for school fees for one's children, for instance. The benefits of such saving are long deferred, and rules are necessary to instigate and sustain this behavior; the contingencies are likely to assume greater control as saving plans mature, enabling spending, which motivates further long-term saving. Both of these are discretionary saving in Katona's (1975) terms, though of a more affluent nature than that which was described as accumulative saving. This is what Lindqvist (1981) refers to as goal-oriented saving (see Wahlund and

Wärneryd, 1987). The final stage is accomplishment, which manifests in asset management, the use of wealth to create more wealth (Lindqvist, 1981; Wärneryd, 1989b). In open settings, this wealth management takes the form of speculation for gain, and in closed setting as the management of investments. Rules play an important part in both cases: self-rules in speculative investment, and advice from others, such as brokers, in the context of investment management. Tracks and augmentals are likely to be particularly important.

The BPM approach does not simply re-describe the categories developed in other systems but relates patterns of consumer behavior with respect to saving and asset management to the changing patterns of contingencies likely to be operative at different stages in the consumer life cycle. However, it might be objected that, while the interpretation appears plausible, and at least indicates that a behavior analytical account of some specialized aspects of consumer behavior is feasible, it proceeds largely in terms of two components of the model. These are the scope of the behavior setting defined primarily in terms of the nature of the physical and social surroundings in which purchase and consumption occur, and the nature of the pattern of reinforcement apparently maintaining the chosen exemplar behaviors. An interpretative account of a broader sequence of consumer behavior is needed, if we are to adjudge the usefulness of the remaining variables in the model, particularly the role of consumers' verbal behavior. An appropriate sequence is that provided by the adoption and diffusion of innovations. Consideration of the sequence of consumer behaviors that occur over the product–market life cycle permits the extension of the applicability of the model in two ways. First, it allows assessment of the explanatory status of the setting and consequential variables that have not yet been covered, namely, effects of consumers' verbal behavior on their non-verbal responses, and the distinction between utilitarian and informational reinforcement. Secondly, it demonstrates the capacity of the model to account not simply for a sequence of consumer behavior within the context of an individual's economic experience but also for entire sequences of consumption responses involving diverse consumer groups and occurring within a broad social and economic context.

COMMUNICATION OF INNOVATION

Initial Versus Later Adopters

These four classes of consumer behavior can be viewed as a hierarchy. The successive lifestyles, which are a function of experience rather than age, of many consumers are likely to be characterized by maintenance, then accumulation, then hedonism, then accomplishment. Figure 6.2 proposes another sequence, by which the communication of innovations may be interpreted in a behavioral perspective. The rationale for this sequence is most apparent in considering the differences between the initial and later adopters (cf. Midgley, 1977; Rogers, 1983). The general argument is that initial adopters are drawn from those consumers whose behavior, for the product class/category in question, is described as accomplishment. This may be a general lifestyle characteristic of this group. They are experienced consumers who have a level of product knowledge and expertise in consumption plus a degree of wealth that allows then to make earlier adoption decisions and to act on them. They are not necessarily older than later adopters but, at least in the product class under consideration, are sufficiently economically socialized to act first. They should, therefore, differ from later adopters on all four explanatory variables posited by the BPM. Initiators, as opposed to later adopters, will exhibit differences in the pattern of utilitarian and informational reinforcement that maintains their behavior, a learning history that predisposes them toward earlier adoption, a susceptibility to the motivating effect of behavior-setting elements that encourage earlier adoption, and the presence of state variables that facilitate earlier rather than later adoption.

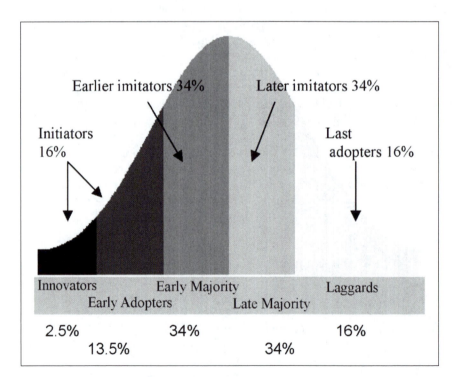

Figure 6.2   Adopter categories as defined by Rogers and the BPM.

Pattern of Reinforcement

By assuming that initiators' consumer behavior is characterized by accomplishment, the model understands that they are susceptible to relatively high levels of both utilitarian (pleasurable/utilitarian) and informational (social/symbolic) reinforcement. This is consistent with the evidence. Not only incentives, based on relative economic benefit and utility, but also social recognition and status motivate the first buyers of innovations (Bandura, 1986). The rewards of early adoption identified repeatedly in the diffusion literature may be classified as producing primarily economic benefit (utilitarian reinforcement) (Rogers, 1983; Gatignon and Robertson, 1991). Among the sources of economic advantage are some innovation characteristics usually treated separately but which are fundamentally related to the economic, technical, and functional benefits that are contingent upon adoption: relative advantage, compatibility, low complexity, and low economic risk.

These are elements in the consumer's learning process, which actually refers to a class of economic costs. All are concerned with the costs and benefits of integrating the innovation into an existing physical and social system, particularly with the joint effects (cost reduction and/or the release of synergy) of operating it alongside existing equipment or practices. Economic advantage consists in what has hitherto been described as incentives or utilitarian reinforcement (Gatignon and Robertson, 1991). Social benefit is the conferral of status, usually through the conspicuous use of the innovation, though sometimes through its highly visible purchase. The prestige which accrues from these consumer behaviors may derive from others' admiration of the economic relative advantages conferred by the innovation, but, unless the item is additionally amenable to social observation, it cannot deliver the additional social advantages which corresponds to feedback or informational reinforcement (Gatignon and Robertson, 1991). Not only are these sources of economic and social benefit known to be associated with the speedier diffusion of innovations; initiators perceive greater positive benefit (relative advantage, conspicuousness, compatibility) and lower negative consequences (risk, complexity) than do later adopters.

Learning History

Initiators generally have a shorter decision process than that of later adopters. They are venturesome, impulsive, able and willing to bear risks, and they make relatively rapid decisions to adopt. The new products they buy are discontinuous innovations, having maximal impact on current consumption patterns. Initiators need less interpersonal influence than later adopters, having less need for others to legitimize their adoption decisions. Midgley defines innovativeness as "the degree to which an individual makes innovation decisions independently of the communicated experience of others" (1977, p. 49). Moreover, initiators are more self-reliant and inner-directed than later adopters (Midgley and Dowling, 1978). But their behavior is far from spontaneous and innate. Initiators have greater expertise with the relevant product class, possibly deriving from their heavy use of the product and their opinion leadership (Gatignon and Robertson, 1991). Their capacity to recognize atypicality, to think in abstractions, combining product features, to deal with a large number of separate product dimensions, and to examine the environment for new products are also indicative of experience and expertise (Gatignon and Robertson, 1991). Their being less influenced than later adopters by interpersonal communications is the result of experience; like any other behavior, it is the outcome of a situationally determined learning history, the consolidated outcome of contingency-based learning and vicarious adoption with the product class, and exposure to the innovation in question mediated by mass communication.

These initial adopters model the new consumption behavior to the less active sections of the population and thereby initiate the market (Rogers, 1983). The behavior of the initiator group is associated with innovations that confer substantial relative advantage over currently used products and methods, both economic and social. In the terms of the BPM, such innovative adoption is maintained by high levels of both utilitarian and informational reinforcement. These consumers can afford to acquire the tangible benefits of innovative products; in the process of consuming them, they enhance their status and prestige (Bandura, 1986). Moreover, they can afford to undertake the early adoption of some innovations that fail: even this conveys to others that the adopter has the economic means and social standing to disregard the occasional loss. They have positive attitudes toward newness and progress, and are more likely than others to be offered credit and, if required, to accept it (Rogers, 1983).

State and Setting Variables

Initiators are affluent relative to members of the later adopter categories, risk takers who are eager to try the innovation for its own sake. There is no unequivocal evidence of their being older than other adopters. But they have higher social status, greater upward social mobility, and a more favorable attitude toward credit than later adopters. They also show more extensive social participation, are "cosmopolitan," have greater knowledge about innovations, and display more opinion leadership (Rogers, 1983), all of which are likely to be the result of more extensive consumer experience. Most crucially of all, and true of a wide range of product classes—including food, personal care items, domestic appliances, computers, and computer services (Gatignon and Robertson, 1985)—is that initiators are already established and heavier users of the product category in question. They are experienced users with a high level of product field expertise, which may account for the absence of communicated experience in their innovative decision making. Moreover, they are likely to have established relationships with retailers or other suppliers and to be able to arrange trial of the new product; the effect is to enlarge their learning history and enable quicker comparisons and decisions to be made.

Categories of Later Adopters

"People who strive to distinguish themselves from the common and the ordinary adopt new styles in clothing, grooming, recreational activities, and conduct, thereby achieving distinctive status" (Bandura, 1986, p. 150). But the capacity of an innovation to confer status is closely linked to its exclusivity: as it diffuses, it becomes commonplace. When the product is approaching the end of its life cycle, it has become a routine acquisition, appealing only to those who are tradition bound, economically limited, and so conservative as to try new (to them) products that have been severely tried and tested by preceding adopters. By the time these consumers (the last adopters) adopt it, the product has ceased to be an innovation in any radical sense: it may embody continuous improvements of a minor kind but its adoption is unlikely to have an extensive impact on consumption. These consumers, the laggards, are depicted in the diffusion literature as having no capacity for leadership, including opinion leadership: they are not, therefore, reinforced by high levels of informational reinforcement. What utilitarian reinforcement maintains their behavior is similarly of low intensity: only products that cannot fail are assumed.

Between the initiators and the last adopters are the earlier imitators (Rogers's "deliberate" early majority), and the later imitators (Rogers's "skeptical" later majority). The assignment of these adopter groups respectively to the contingencies maintaining consumer lifestyles marked by hedonism/utility and accumulation is not quite as clear-cut as that of the first and last adopter categories to accomplishment and maintenance. But the characterizations are supported by the diffusion literature. The earlier imitators are not leaders despite their fairly high level of social interaction: they are not reinforced primarily by informational consequences of their actions. Moreover, their interest is in "getting it right" when they try new products: they are cautious, taking time to deliberate before deciding. These actions suggest a high level of functional utility, utilitarian reinforcement. The behavior of the later imitators is negatively motivated. This group adopts an innovation only when it has become economically essential to do so—its members are not seeking utilitarian reinforcement, however. When they do adopt the item, it is principally for reasons of social pressure: they must finally adopt in order not to lose the honor or esteem of their fellows. Their adoptive behavior is thus negatively reinforced, but by considerations of informational reinforcement. Products adopted by these adopter categories are dynamically continuous; they embody improvements incorporated by manufacturers who by this time have experience of the market's requirements and may represent considerable extensions of the functional attributes of the innovation. They impact on consumption patterns and are purchased by groups seeking price and utility advantages.

Conclusion

This analysis indicates that it is feasible to present an alternative, though complementary, interpretation of consumer choice which attributes its changing topography to environmental rather than intrapersonal determinants. Whether these accounts must remain incommensurable remains to be seen, though the recent growth of cognitive ethology suggests that this is improbable. The chapter also demonstrates that it is possible to apply the metaprinciple of selection by consequences to expand the range of interpretations available to consumer researchers. By contributing to an interactionist (person x situation) approach to consumer behavior, the model and its interpretations appear in line with emerging thought on the most appropriate methodological approach to research. Current attention is focused on the empirical correspondence of the model and its testing, the implications of rule-governed, as opposed to contingency-shaped, consumer behavior, and the application of the model to the consumption of financial services and asset management (Foxall, 1993b).

A broader research theme is the relationship of operant classes to the competitive environment, to develop an ecological analysis of successive operants much as strategic theorists have related industrial structure to its competitive determinants. Since we are concerned with the population of consumer responses, competition is ultimately between the operant classes or "species" of consumer behavior, each maintained by its unique combination of environmental consequences (Table 6.1). What environmental conditions make each of these more likely than the others at a particular time? Why does selection among these variations occur when it does? It is also necessary to propose why not all eligible consumers join the requisite adoption category for a particular innovation—for instance, why not all who have reached the accomplishment stage even for the product class in question become initiators.

ENVIRONMENT-IMPACTING CONSUMER BEHAVIOR

Applied Behavioral Research

Applied behavior analysis has contributed substantially to knowledge of economic consumption as it adversely affects the physical and social environment (Cone and Hayes, 1980; Geller, Winett, and Everett, 1982). It rests critically and selectively on Skinner's (1953) behavior theory which stresses that the causes of behavior are found in its environmental consequences.

Table 6.1 Ecological Adaptation of Consumer Operants to Marketing Environments

Niche	Marketing mix	Consumer operant	Sources of hedonic reinforcement	Sources of informational reinforcement	Pattern of competition
Discontinuity	New brand in new product class	Accomplishment	High relative advantage	Conspicuousness Status enhancement	Between buying innovation, reusing current product, saving
	Heavy media communication		Compatibility		
	High price		Low perceived complexity		
	Exclusive distribution		Low perceived risk		
Dynamic continuity	Product improvement in original and new brands	Pleasure/utility	Very high relative advantage		
	Falling prices		High compatibility		
	Promotion limited, stressing functional improvements		Lower complexity	Status confirmation	Between buying original innovation (revised), new brand version(s), using old product saving
	Expanding range of outlets				
Continuity	More supplier entering	Accumulation	Avoidance of relative disadvantage of old product/method	Avoidance of low status	Between multiple version of brands in product class, old method (if available)
	More brand versions showing minor improvements		Very high compatibility	Social pressure to conform	
	Low prices		Very low complexity		

Table 6.1 (continued)

Niche	Marketing mix	Consumer operant	Sources of hedonic reinforcement	Sources of informational reinforcement	Pattern of competition
	Widespread distribution				
	Promotion stresses, social necessity, compatibility, low complexity				
	Vicarious learning and trial				
	Preponderance of buyer-dominated interpersonal communication				
Ubiquity	Proliferation of brands	Maintenance	Avoidance of disadvantage of failure to adopt Economic necessity	Avoidance of ridicule	Between multiplicity of similar brands (old method superseded)
	Tendency towards steady state market			Conformity to social norms	
	Line/brand extensions				
	Low prices				
	Commonplace distribution				
	Promotion minimal (new brand launches)				
	Interpersonal communication to the fore				

The applied field experimentation that characterizes this approach has explored how antecedent and consequential stimuli influence such consumer behaviors as excessive use of private transportation, over-consumption of domestic energy, littering and waste generation, and consumption of scarce resources such as water. The ultimate purpose has been to ameliorate these ecologically deleterious outcomes through the modification of consumer behavior (Winkler and Winett, 1982). Despite this theoretical underpinning and practical direction, the empirical findings produced by applied behavior analysts lack systematic organization and theory-based generalization. Despite comprehensive reviews and attempts to draw lessons from these findings (Cone and Hayes, 1980; Geller, 1989), behavior analysis lacks an integrative model of consumer behavior and the effects of intervention based on a critical evaluation of behavior theory.

Thus the field has tended to fall back on cognitive frameworks devised by consumer researchers (Schwartz, 1991) or the basic social marketing models derived from rudimentary marketing (Geller, 1989). Yet both of these approaches contain serious conceptual, methodological, and practical difficulties. Social marketing programs have been criticized on the grounds that they consist largely of informational and exhortative campaigns which do not generally use the full integrated marketing mix but rely to a disproportionate extent on social advertising. Further, the effectiveness of campaigns intended to change behavior by modifying attitudes have been questioned. Nor are these conclusions the result of theoretical preference or speculation uninformed by empirical evidence. There is abundant support from the research of cognitive psychologists themselves that, to the extent that they rely heavily on the use of persuasive communications to change pre-behavioral attitudes and values, social information campaigns have had little impact on consumers' conservation behavior. Despite vast general public knowledge about the potentially catastrophic consequences of failing to conserve energy, researchers report an inability to identify the required relationship between attitudes toward energy use and conservation; even those maximally informed are no more likely to save energy; nor does specifically informing people about the personal costs of current energy use and the benefits of reducing consumption affect behavior (Costanzo, Archer, Aronson, and Pettigrew, 1986).

However, applied behavior analysis indicates that simply informing people of the consequences of their actions is unlikely to modify their behavior unless they have been systematically exposed to those consequences in the past. The causes of behavior cannot be found in variables inferred from the behavior itself such as attitudes, and these inferences are not therefore legitimate targets for intervention. Social de-marketing based on applied behavior analysis can be systematically related to marketing mix management by a model founded on the behavior theory that underpins that analysis, elucidating the nature of both environmentally impacting consumer behavior and interventions designed to ameliorate its deleterious ecological effects.

First, the model and applied behavior analysis are described. Second, general propositions which must be fulfilled if the model accurately synthesizes the findings of the applied research of behavior analysts are derived. Third, the major target behaviors of this research—transportation, energy consumption, waste disposal, water use—are described in terms of the model; the model's capacity to encompass and explain the incentives and feedback that control each of these behaviors is a prime concern. Finally, the role of the marketing mix in influencing each class of environment-impacting consumer behavior is discussed.

Contribution of the BPM

Each of the classes of consumer behavior identified by the BPM is maintained by positive reinforcers, whether utilitarian or informational, but each has a downside which often does not impinge directly upon the consumer, at least not immediately. Social and public costs accrue to the community as a whole and not specifically to the individual consumer who is responsible for their being incurred. Consumer behaviors frequently take the form of behaviors that are damaging to the environment: for instance, seeking ever-greater accomplishments that provide utilitarian rewards and show forth one's status may result in the consumption of scarce and irreplaceable resources. Beyond a point, pleasure seeking may also have a deleterious effect on the environment through indulgent energy consumption. Accumulation brings with it the concomitant need to dispose of packaging and, in affluent societies marked by ever-shortening product life cycles, the products themselves. And, finally, the consumption of the basic commodities of life themselves, such as water, now threatens further consumption by depleting stocks.

Applied behavior analysis has been concerned for the most part to assess the extent to which contextual factors control the demand for products and services which have deleterious effects on the physical environment. Often, the unrestricted acquisition of short-term reinforcements by a limited number of individuals leads to long-term aversive consequences for all users. The utilitarian-reinforcing consequences of behavior are encountered quickly and directly after the action is performed, whereas the environmentally deleterious results of the behavior are encountered, if at all, indirectly and only after a period of time has elapsed. The immediate reinforcement of behavior with ultimately deleterious effects is so great, especially the utilitarian, and the aversive outcomes so remote, that the longer-term consequences can sometimes only be reduced or prevented through active self-management. The relatively open settings in which these behaviors typically take place and their maintenance by strongly utilitarian reinforcers mean that some closure of the setting has been advocated in lieu of self-management in order to compel a degree of pro-social behavior.

Applied behavior analytic programs incorporate a variety of behavior-related antecedent and consequent stimuli. Antecedent stimuli have consisted of prompts—that is, warnings, reasoned argument and facts, threats, pleas, and so on—relating to the deleterious effects of actions that exploit or pollute the environment. Two varieties of consequential stimuli have been employed: feedback, that is, information on the actual effects of individuals' actions, and incentives, that is, financial bonuses, praise, and encouragement. Antecedent prompts are intended to act as discriminative stimuli, signaling the aversive consequences of specific behaviors that impact the environment for ill. Feedback is essentially informational reinforcement, indicating the level of performance achieved by the consumer in, say, reducing his or her electricity consumption or private car mileage. Incentives are essentially utilitarian reinforcers, rewarding consumers with additional consumption goods or the capacity to acquire them for their pro-social behaviors.

General Propositions

If the BPM interpretation of consumer behavior is accurate, then it should be possible to present a plausible interpretation of the consumer behaviors that have been the concerns of applied behavior analysis in terms derived from the model. (i) It should be possible to identify the contextual factors that control them in terms of utilitarian and informational reinforcement and the setting variables that signal their availability. (ii) If specific classes of consumer behavior are maintained by defined patterns of high versus low utilitarian and informational reinforcement and on schedules that can be consistently inferred, we would expect intervention to succeed when it either maintains current levels of reinforcement or increases the level of one source of reinforcement without reducing that of the other. (iii) For consumer behavior, we should expect utilitarian reinforcement to play a broader role than informational and can predict that it would prove more effective in changing consumer behavior than either prompting or informational reinforcement alone. (iv) Successful intervention should also feature changes in the nature of the behavior setting, opening or closing it further in order to make pro-social behaviors more probable. (v) An integrated program of antecedent and consequential stimuli should work best when rules that link behavior and its consequences with a degree of specificity (rather than through vague prompting) are provided and supported. These general propositions can be tested by reference to the literature on environmental intervention based on applied behavior analysis. Full references to the following literature survey can be found in Cone and Hayes (1980) and Geller, Winett, and Everett (1982).

Private Transportation as "Accomplishment"

Of the environmentally impacting consumer behaviors with which applied behavior analysts have been concerned, the use of private automobiles, often carrying a single individual to or from work, falls into this category. Such behavior is apparently maintained by high levels of both utilitarian reinforcement—the fun of driving, control of one's journey—and informational reinforcement—speed, low and flexible journey times. In addition to these immediate sources of reinforcement, personal driving is powerfully maintained by intermittent reinforcements apparently available on a VR schedule: social approval, personal safety, simplification of journey-planning routines, all of which are contingent on the performance of a number of responses that varies among situations.

If this classification is correct, the research propositions developed previously would lead to the following expectations with respect to successful strategies of behavior change. (i) Since the current behaviors are maintained on high utilitarian, high informational reinforcements, de-marketing should attempt to replace the current behavior with alternatives similarly maintained, though utilitarian reinforcement is likely to be the more effective. (ii) The use of aversive stimuli, punishing motorists through taxes, tolls, and other uses of what essentially amounts to the price element of the marketing mix is likely to be counterproductive since the high levels of both utilitarian and informational reinforcement available from driving will compensate for attempts at punishment. (iii) The already open setting should be opened even further by the provision of effective competition to private driving: for instance, making buses more popular, comfortable, and socially acceptable. (iv) General prompts alone are unlikely to work, but discriminative stimuli, effectively linked to specific behaviors and their outcomes, may be effective: these should stress the rewards for bus ridership in terms of the personal gratification this provides rather than vague predictions of a remote better environment.

Evidence for the classification of private motoring as accomplishment and for the efficacy of the preceding strategy in social de-marketing is available from the findings of attempts to modify consumers' private transportation behavior which has been intended to reduce fuel consumption, urban congestion, and pollution by discouraging unilateral use of private cars and promoting public transportation. The most successful interventions have offered utilitarian reinforcement in the form of financial incentives: provision of small monetary rewards for riding the bus has, for example, increased the number of users of public travel services by 50–180% (Geller, Winett, and Everett, 1982). The need for principally utilitarian reinforcement, albeit coupled with informational reinforcement in the form of continuous and effective feedback, is indicated by the relatively unattractive pre-intervention pattern of consequences for bus ridership. Riding the bus and other strategies which avoid private transportation (such as walking, carpooling, and cycling) are at best minimally reinforced by utilitarian means by social contact and, eventually, feelings of fitness, and informationally by cost savings. But they are punished by aversive consequences: slowness, discomfort, danger, exposure, crowding, noise, inflexibility, unpredictability, and lack of control.

Discouragement of car travel has reduced mileage travelled by between 10 and 50% (Cone and Hayes, 1980). The provision of informational reinforcement plays a strong role in reducing driving but only in combination with utilitarian reinforcement; however, the two forms of reinforcement cannot in this case be effectively separated since each relies on the provision of the other. While feedback alone (on the number of miles travelled, operating costs, depreciation, social costs, etc.) had no effect on mileage travelled, performance feedback influences behavior by allowing the driver to monitor his or her behavior in order to achieve the incentives. Although utilitarian reinforcement once again emerges as the most effective single means of modifying behavior, its use in tandem with informational reinforcement has a mutually strengthening effect and provides a cost effective form of intervention.

In the marketing of alternatives to private car use, notably transportation by bus, which for many drivers is likely to prove highly disruptive of their journey routines, utilitarian reinforcement has been used almost exclusively and has taken the form of cash payments for riding the bus and, more cost-effectively, of tokens redeemable at stores and for additional bus trips. The use in this context of a variable person schedule of reinforcement (VP) in which every nth passenger is rewarded rather than every passenger not only reduces the costs of the transit program but indicates the relevance of a kind of VR schedule to the maintenance of behaviors in this category. The evidence is that this opening of the setting further by providing genuine competition to private motoring can be effective and that prompts alone are most ineffective.

Domestic Energy Consumption as "Hedonism"

Among environmentally impacting consumer behaviors, pleasure is exemplified by the over-consumption of domestic energy derived from fossil fuels, notably electricity for heating and lighting. The utilitarian reinforcements are high and closely related temporally to the responses that produce them—convenience and comfort. While informational reinforcement is less obvious, social approval may follow generous use of these resources in the company of others (meanness will certainly lead to social disapproval and loss of status). Punishments are real and may be severe (e.g., having to pay one's electricity and gas bills) but are remote in time and place from the usage situation and may be mitigated by staged payments direct from a bank account. The long-term consequences are remote: for instance, depletion of resources or social disapproval. Consumption behaviors are apparently controlled by a VI schedule: comfort and satisfaction depend upon employing the source of heat or light for a time that varies from occasion to occasion with the individual's task requirements and state variables (e.g., cold, hunger).

If this analysis and classification are correct, the following should be expected of a successful strategy of behavior change. (i) Since the current behaviors are maintained by high utilitarian and low informational reinforcement, any attempt to punish that behavior by introducing aversive stimuli (very high prices) or reducing utilitarian consequences, without a corresponding increase in utilitarian benefits, is likely to fail. (ii) Social de-marketing should concentrate on making the behavior (including avoidance) more involving, encouraging the avoidance of high bills and a feeling of self-gratification at saving energy and reducing pollution. (iii) If a sufficient level of utilitarian benefit can be guaranteed, the setting could be closed by increasing the costs of energy. Support for the classification of domestic energy use as pleasure and for the efficacy of this strategy comes from the attempted modification of consumers' domestic energy consumption which has used antecedent prompting, feedback, and incentives, separately and in combination. Alone, information relating to the environmental effects of pollution caused by high consumption of electricity at peak periods had little if any effect on peak usage. Greater effect was achieved by consumer self-monitoring of current energy usage: peak consumption reduced by up to 30% of mean baseline levels. Overall energy usage (i.e., peak and non-peak consumption) has also proved sensitive to informational feedback, even at times of steep increases in the price of energy. Combined feedback and monetary incentives have reduced peaking by about 65% of baseline, confirming the efficacy of combined consequences.

In line with the basic principle of operant conditioning that reinforcement must immediately follow the performance of a response in order for learning to occur, it has been demonstrated that daily feedback on overall energy usage, especially when combined with group feedback and mild social commendation for "pro-social" behavior can be effective. More practically, weekly or monthly feedback corresponding with normal billing periods is particularly efficacious. The combination of prompts and feedback with incentives (e.g., payments of up to $5 per week for reductions of gas/electricity consumption by 20% or more of baseline mean) is even more effective. Comparisons of the individual effects of the separate elements of persuasion (prompts, feedback, and incentives) indicate, however, that only incentives have an appreciable effect on behavior.

Waste Disposal as a Problem of "Accumulation"

Waste generation is a consequence of accumulation, but it is actually a problem manifested in the opposite of accumulation: disposal. Indiscriminate waste disposal has relatively few utilitarian benefits other than convenience, but its informational outcomes are extensive if subtle: it confers status through the assumption that someone else will clear up, and it may also imply conspicuous consumption. Such behaviors are maintained seemingly on FR schedules. Their long-term consequences are also remote: gradual spoliation of the physical environment, accruing social disapproval.

The general research propositions developed previously indicate that if this analysis and classification are accurate, the following will apply. (i) Given the assumed pattern of current behaviors being maintained by high informational and low utilitarian reinforcement, behavior change is likely to be accomplished by increasing such utilitarian consequences as aesthetic pleasure while not reducing informational feedback. (ii) The personal element in reinforcement should be especially effective. (iii) The encouragement of pro-social behavior can be achieved by paying people to return/recycle waste as long as the punishing consequence of doing so are moderate. (iv) Closing the behavior setting by providing bins should be effective. (v) Promotional appeals based on prompting in a general way would be ineffective, but modeling, showing the pro-social consequences of conformity, would also be effective.

The findings of applied behavior analysis in this area do indeed confirm the analysis and classification. Attempts at reducing littering have relied heavily on the use of prompts. The results have been generally disappointing unless the prompts were accompanied by positive reinforcement, usually utilitarian. Exhortations, lectures, and relevant general education have proved largely ineffective in this sphere. Even the attempt to reduce littering among children in a theater by manipulating the physical environment (providing bags for waste) had little effect. Combined with messages pointing out the disadvantages of litter, the provision of bags had a moderate effect. However, when a reward of one dime was given for each bag of rubbish, the decrease in littering was massive. Another form of utilitarian reward in the form of a ticket for a movie had a similarly substantial negative effect on littering. Similar results have been found in experimental studies of the reduction of littering in streets, and around and within buildings. Success is also apparent in the closure of the behavior setting, for instance, by providing more litter bins and devising trash cans that are fun to use, and by ensuring the initial cleanliness and attractiveness of the environment; all of these strategies have had some effect by bringing behavior under stimulus control, but only the presentation of positive reinforcers in the form of payments has any dramatic effect on behavior. Prompts, used alone, have little if any effect, perhaps because of their reliance on punishment for unapproved behavior: the individual who litters nevertheless and avoids immediate punishment is actually likely to be reinforced for his or her littering. The relative effectiveness of prompts and incentives indicated by litter studies has been confirmed by experiments aimed at increasing consumers' willingness to conserve irreplaceable materials through recycling. Attempts at increasing consumers' purchases of returnable bottles are a typical example. The use of prompts informing customers of the savings to which such behavior would lead and that they would be contributing to the fight against pollution have had mixed effects. Giving consumers small financial rewards for the reuse of such items as egg cartons, milk containers, and grocery bags, accompanied by in-store prompts and a pleasant and enthusiastic reaction by salespersons, has led to increases in custom.

Some attempts at increasing consumers' recycling behavior have had significant punishing consequences. The Bottle Laws enacted first in Oregon and subsequently adopted by several other states impose considerable transaction, inventory, and time costs on retailers who pass them on to their customers (Guerts, 1986). Both are penalized for their participation in the waste-reduction campaign, and, even though distributors are legally bound to comply, their consumers are in general unlikely to incur the costs involved in prepaying deposits and returning glass bottles unless they are adequately compensated for the punishing consequences of these pro-social endeavors. Experimental attempts to encourage the recovery of waste materials such as paper which can be recycled also indicate that prompts have minimal effects on behavior, while the provision of utilitarian and, to a smaller extent, informational reinforcers has a substantial reinforcing effect. Hence students offered prizes in contests and raffles are more likely to reduce wastage than those who are only exposed to educative prompting. The provision of convenient containers for the collection of recyclable waste is also significantly more effective than prompting on the promotion of appropriate pro-social behaviors perhaps because it achieves a degree of closure of the setting and the combination of prompts and suitable receptacles for the collection of waste has produced a combined effect on behavior greater than that expected from their individual contributions.

Domestic Water Consumption as "Maintenance"

Maintenance is exemplified as an environmentally impacting consumer behavior by the domestic over-consumption of water. Both utilitarian and informational reinforcements are low compared with those that control other the other classes of consumer behavior, though neither is absent: the luxury and status of having water continuously available on tap are easily taken for granted, but being able to drink, clean, bathe, and water the garden are indicative of comparative wealth and power; they are utilitarian and informational benefits directly related to the consumer's state of deprivation. The consumption behaviors in question are apparently maintained on FI ratios, most of the uses of water taking place at some time or other on most days or most weeks.

If accurate, this analysis and classification would suggest the following. (i) Punishment, especially involving price, would be especially efficacious in reducing consumption. (ii) Metering, to provide general association between behavior and its contingent consequences and to provide accurate and quick feedback on the outcomes of consumption, would be especially effective. (iii) Closing the setting by reducing the time and place during which water can be consumed would be effective. There is less experimental evidence for the behavioral economics of water consumption and conservation than for the other commodities and products considered, but the limited evidence suggests that this analysis and classification are correct.

A study of the conservation of metered water in Perth, Australia (Geller, Winett, and Everett, 1982), indicates that water consumption decreased by over 30% in both an experimental group provided with daily feedback on water use and a rebate proportionate to demand reduction, and a control group provided only with feedback, though change in climatic conditions may also have affected the results. The low elasticity of demand for water makes financial rebates less appropriate than for other classes of consumer behavior.

Social De-marketing

This survey indicates that the general propositions suggested previously are accurate. The BPM provides a coherent and plausible model of the role of antecedent and consequential stimuli in the shaping and maintenance of environmentally impacting consumer behavior. Utilitarian reinforcement is, as expected, the single most important influence on such behavior, but the three basic components of the model, used in optimal combination that varies depending on the class of behavior in question, exerts the greatest control. The most effective general strategy for behavior change indeed appears to be the maintenance of current levels of utilitarian and/or informational reinforcement plus the enhancement of relatively low levels of reinforcement, plus the manipulation of behavior settings to signal the consequences of modified consumption. Finally, different marketing-mix strategies can be extracted from the results of the applied behavior analyses for the four classes of environmentally impacting consumer behavior identified and described by the BPM. The fulfillment of the specific propositions put forward for each of these consumer behavior classes suggests the following generalizations, each well supported by empirical evidence and capable of serving as hypotheses for refinement and further testing.

Accomplishment. Modification of accomplishment behaviors, exemplified here by private motoring, requires the development of a radically more attractive product with strongly reinforcing utilitarian and informational attributes: this may even necessitate the creation of a different product. Price may be important too, but only when the new or thoroughly revamped product has been successfully launched and established: the price of the original might then be raised to punish its use. Until this point is reached, however, such a price rise would have little overall effect on demand for the original product given the abundant utilitarian and informational reinforcers it provides. Indeed, to the extent that private transportation is a prestige good, maintained by informational reinforcement that derives from conspicuous consumption, an increase in the costs associated with it might be counterproductive, encouraging rather than discouraging consumption. During the introductory phases of the new product, its price might be subsidized to ensure that consumers switched to its use: whether the price reduction has to be maintained indefinitely depends upon the effectiveness of the primary utilitarian and informational reinforcers provided by the novel product. As far as promotion is concerned, prompts are unlikely to have a strong effect on demand, though coupled with effective consequential stimuli they provide a necessary informative and persuasive role. However, advertisements containing modeling of the pro-social behaviors advocated would probably both increase awareness of the campaign and encourage imitative responses. Finally, as far as place is concerned, the behavior setting should be opened further by increasing competition and making the new product widely and flexibly available.

Hedonism. Consumer behavior modification in the case of hedonism is more subtly changed through the provision of increased, relatively rapid, and regular information on consumption. This information can be seen as part of the product provided by the utilities companies. The maintenance of utilitarian reinforcement is important and, since the overall goal of the campaign is a reduction in energy use, this must be accomplished by the encouragement of personal and domestic arrangements which promote thermal savings (e.g., better insulation, the wearing of more heat-efficient clothing, and the elimination of useless energy consumption such as the illumination of unoccupied rooms). These factors, which might be considered part of the place element of the marketing mix since they determine the location of consumption, contribute to the closure of the behavior setting. Price might also be used to deter over use of resources, but, given the highly utilitarian consequences of energy consumption, it is unlikely to have a strong independent effect on usage.

Accumulation. The single most cost-effective means of reducing littering is probably the closure of the behavior setting. Since litter is itself a discriminative stimulus for further littering, the provision of bins, bags, and other containers that encourage disposal is likely to have a cumulative effect on behavior. Prompting alone also has some effect on litter disposal if it is directly related to the means of acting pro-socially, for instance, by pointing out what to put, where to put it, and when. The behavior setting for recycling can be closed by the provision of containers for bottles, plastics, papers, and so on, in convenient positions for consumers to use. Utilitarian reinforcement remains a strong influence on behavior, though it will often be an expensive alternative: competitions and variable person schedules appear to be the most effective means of changing behavior, especially if coupled with promotional campaigns emphasizing modeled pro-social behavior. The costs involved in some pro-social behaviors presently punish the consumer—for instance, in the case of returning bottles and other packaging; either these costs must be reduced through the collection of waste materials or the financial recompense for their return must be expanded until behavior is economically controlled.

Maintenance. Finally, in the case of maintenance, exemplified by water consumption and conservation, it is important to control the behavior setting by installing water-conserving methods (e.g., smaller cisterns), by encouraging the use of rainwater for garden watering, and by the opportunity to use water less expensive than fully purified drinking water for some domestic purposes such as flushing toilets. The alternative place strategies (rationing, standpipes, etc.) are politically unacceptable and usually unnecessary except during emergencies, though metering is probably an essential prerequisite of most systems of behavior modification based on consequential stimuli, whether informational or utilitarian. Price might be used to overcome overuse, though again this would be politically acceptable only within close bounds.

7 The Nature of the Interpretation

> *. . . the same act that may be perceived as free may also and at the
> same time be perceived as causally bound.* Two different percep-
> tions are involved then, the first being attentive to man's subjective
> self-understanding as free, the second being attentive to the various
> systems of determination. The two perceptions are not logically con-
> tradictory, but they are sharply discrete. Both on the level of ordinary
> everyday consciousness, and on the level of theoretical reflection, two
> discrete relevance structures are involved, both applicable to the *same*
> phenomena. Clearly, the relevance structure of any empirical science
> is limited to perceptions of causal determination. Therefore: *Free-
> dom cannot be disclosed by the methods of any empirical science;
> sociology most emphatically included.* For this reason, it would be
> an impossible undertaking to devise a type of sociology that would
> include within itself the category of freedom even in its minimal phil-
> osophical sense. What is possible is to insist . . . that the perspective of
> sociology as of any other empirical science is always *partial* and that
> other perspectives are possible—including the perspective of human
> beings as acting freely.
>
> —Peter Berger and Hansfried Kellner
> (1981, pp. 96–97; emphasis in original)

The persistence of theories of behavior that stress *either* the intrapersonal
or the environmental determinants of action appears as inevitable in psychology as the coexistence of both wave and particle theories of light in
physics. Neither provides a comprehensive account, but each is necessary
to a full understanding. However, the cognitive theories of behavior which
have predominated in consumer research have led investigators to emphasize the intrapsychic determinants of choice at the expense of the environmental. One result is that the field lacks a theoretical perspective on
the consumer as an individual situated within a system of external contingencies which determine his or her purchase and use of products and
services. It is improbable that models derived within a cognitive perspective
can supply the needed purview. Cognitivism's metatheoretically prescribed
search for explanation in hypothesized intrapersonal structures and processes, together with its lack of detailed consideration of personal learning histories, renders it an unpromising source of contextual frameworks
within which to comprehend consumer behavior *in situ*. The BPM explores
the implications for consumer research of an interpretive stance derived
from behavior analytic *methodology*—that the rate at which responses

are performed is a function of the consequences of similar behavior in the past—and *ontology*—that behavior is a function of the environment rather than of intrapersonal perceptual events, traits of character, or cognitive information processing. Other publications have presented the critique of orthodox behavior analysis from which the model is derived (Foxall, 1990) and shown its relevance to an understanding of marketing practice (Foxall, 1991a). Several accounts of the nature of behavior analysis as applied to consumer research have appeared (e.g., Foxall, 1987), and these basics will not be repeated here. Instead, this chapter refines and extends the BPM and evaluates its conceptualization of consumer choice. In doing so, it differs from most current formulations of cognitive consumer theory by (i) emphasizing *behavior* as the dependent variable in consumer research, rather than pre-behavioral organocentric processes or events that may or may not be reliably associated with action; (ii) presenting a thorough theoretical perspective on the environmental influences on consumer behavior, showing how the contingent consequences of behavior can be related to the explanation and interpretation of the rate at which that behavior is performed; and (iii) showing how a behavioristic theory, to which increasing allusion has been made in the consumer research literature during the last decade, can provide a synthetic interpretive framework for the contextual understanding of purchase and consumption.

Preceding chapters have proposed an approach to the interpretation of consumer choice and marketing management based upon radical behaviorism. However, in contrast to earlier attempts to cast consumer behavior in operant terms, it has taken into account the differences between animal and human behavior which prevent a simplistic extrapolation from the animal laboratory to complex social and economic behavior. This has meant, of course, taking note of human operant experiments, but it has also meant recognizing that results obtained in any experimental setting have some inadequacies as a basis for interpreting such complexity. The astrophysicist who explains what is happening at the center of sun on the basis of laboratory experiments, and the evolutionist who accounts for remote biological change by reference to the simpler adaptations he or she has observed (to use Skinner's examples), can expect far less discontinuity between the experimental situation and that which they seek to understand than can the psychologist moving between the operant chamber or human behavior laboratory and complex consumer choice in the real world. These chapters have demonstrated, nonetheless, that a *functional* analysis of the complex human behavior involved in consumer and marketer behaviors is feasible, that it is possible to portray consumer choice as systematically related to environmental contingencies that shape and maintain it. The three levels of analysis summarized in Table 5.1 provide a means of conceptualizing contingency relationships and a method for their identification and interpretation. The proposed interpretation differs markedly from the experimental analysis of behavior, as it does from interpretive accounts such as those hermeneutical exercises which proceed in terms of the actor's intentions, understandings, and subjective meanings. But it also has something in common with each of these approaches to knowledge and understanding. Its functional analysis is clearly guided by the ontology, if not the methodology, of the experimental analysis of behavior, and its interpretive stance requires a particular self-awareness on the part of the analyst.

As has been argued, two sources of discontinuity between the experimental source of operant interpretation and the complex subject matter which provides its material must be addressed by the psychologist engaged in operant reconstruction of consumer behavior. First are the situational differences, which make the precise identification of stimuli and responses much harder in the complex setting, and the specification of the individual's learning history almost impossible. Second are the speciational differences, notably the use of language by humans (and the far more subtle and complicated use of verbal behavior by consumers than is the case in human operant experiments). The approach taken in the construction and use of the BPM has involved two variables which seek, not to overcome in a fundamental base or to do away with these discontinuities, which are real enough, but to show how *any* interpretive system based on radical behaviorism might accommodate itself to them. Situational discontinuity has given rise to the idea of a continuum of closed-open consumer behavior settings, and to the use of surrogate measures (qualitative and quantitative) of the consumer's learning history. Speciational discontinuity has given rise to the notion of informational as well as utilitarian reinforcement in humans. Together, they have suggested the concept of the "consumer situation" as an interpretive device. These variables also suggest how the science and interpretation of consumer behavior may differ. The argument was made earlier that while the (narrowly defined) scientific/positivistic approach is usually amenable to the falsifications inherent in hypothetico-deductive logic, interpretation may or may not be: it may be possible only to compile evidence *for* some interpretations rather than to examine them in a way that will lead to their crucial evaluation. The continuum of consumer behavior settings is a starting point for this distinction:

CLOSED			OPEN
consumer behavior settings	S^D, R and $S^{R/A}$ are specifiable and open to operational measurement for empirical research. Prediction and control are possible because dependent and independent variables are knowable.	S^D, R and $S^{R/A}$ may have to be inferred; variables not known with sufficient precision to predict and control at micro-level of brand/store, or possibly even at macro- level.	consumer behavior settings

Although interpretation may have a scientific basis and promote knowledge through "scientific" (falsificationist) procedures, in the particular instance of a radical behaviorist account of consumer behavior, there are certainly going to be interpretations that are not open to hypothetico-deductive logic. The following *continuum of consumer situations* makes this distinction even clearer:

SPECIFIABLE CONSUMER SITUATIONS	Closed setting	Open setting	UNSPECIFIABLE CONSUMER SITUATIONS
	Learning history (somewhat) known	Learning history far from fully known	

The discriminative stimuli that compose the closed consumer behavior setting can be relatively accurately specified and related to behavior, hence a clearer (if incomplete) picture of the consumer's learning history, the meaning of a given response in that setting for him or her, can be reasonably well inferred. In the open setting, by contrast, it is much more difficult to specify the controlling variables: learning history can be only vaguely inferred. The consumer situations occurring in the former context can be studied "scientifically," using the measures developed earlier; to the extent that they invite or require interpretation, it can presumably be given with some interpersonal concurrence. But in the latter case, that of the "unspecifiable consumer situation," evidence *for* the proposition of environmental control, which is not so obviously amenable to "scientific" testing, is the best one can do. But we can make a virtue of such necessity, for this is the very stuff of guided thick description (Ryle, 1971).

"THIN" VERSUS "THICK" DESCRIPTION

How thick, then, is the description of consumer behavior provided by the BPM? It will be recalled that Geertz (1973) argues that a twitch of the eye, a wink, a parody, and the rehearsal of a parody each conveys different levels of physiological impulse (the first) and cultural meaning (the rest), of which only the first is apparent to the radical behaviorist. To argue, as the behaviorist might, that twitching, winking, parodying, and rehearsing are topographically diverse—a parody involves a slower and deeper contraction of the eyelid than a wink or a twitch, rehearsal requires the repetition of stylized winks which invite ridicule, and the context of each of these behaviors differs in ways that make its meaning apparent—would be fair comment but might somewhat miss the point. Let us assume, apparently with Geertz, that the acts are topographically identical but that they convey alternative meanings. What is being argued is that the radical behaviorist is, of all people, singularly unable to make the cultural distinctions on which a comprehensive interpretation relies. This is absurd as well as ill-informed. Radical behaviorism has never claimed that topography is the key to understanding or that understanding is limited to topography. As has been argued previously, the meaning of a response is apparent from its effects, its consequences for further behavior, its function, and, most importantly, the learning history of the individual who performs it. A twitch is an example of respondent conditioning, something which is apparent to the observer from consideration of the occasions on which it occurs, its frequency and persistency, the reactions of other observers, and perhaps its physiological antecedents. A wink is an operant response which can again be systematically related to the limited range of setting occasions on which it occurs and to its social antecedents and consequences. A parody is similarly distinguished by *its* accompanying contingencies of reinforcement and the learning history of the parodist. Accounting for the variety of meanings of such a response is central to operant psychology, especially in its interpretive mode. To claim that radical behaviorism would be confined in each of these instances of observation to a bald topographical account of the movement of an eyelid is so far removed from what behaviorists have claimed and demonstrated for many decades that it suggests a serious misunderstanding of the research program of radical behaviorism.

There is, moreover, reason to believe that radical behaviorism provides an interpretation of cultural complexity which is a unique contribution to a comprehensive account of human social and economic behavior. Ryle points out that "[t]he thinnest description of what the rehearsing parodist is doing is, roughly, the same as for the involuntary eyelid twitch, but its thick description is a many-layered sandwich, of which only the bottom slice is catered for by that thinnest description" (1971, p. 482). Geertz's mistake lies in his assumption that radical behaviorism can provide only descriptions of the lowest levels, nothing about what the actor is thinking, nor about his or her past and future behavior (cf. Dennett, 1983, 1987). True, a thick description requires reference to success and failure, to deliberation as to the likely consequences of behaving in a particular way. Descriptions at a higher level of sophistication than the thinnest ought also to consider the individual's learning history: "Learning a lesson at one level presupposes having learned lessons of all the levels below it" (p. 483). Radical behaviorism, the study of the contingencies of behavioral reinforcement, is uniquely qualified to contribute to such thick interpretation. It would be impossible to provide a comprehensive account of complex human behavior without it. Each of the levels of interpretive analysis pursued previously—of the operant class, contingency category, and consumer situation—provides a successively thicker description, a more elaborate interpretation of what is going on (what the consumer is doing) by relating observed behavior to an increasingly sophisticated framework of contingencies. The analysis of consumers' rule-governed behavior, something of which Geertz appears unaware, permits the extension of radical behaviorist interpretation to successively higher levels of sophistication in accounting for the complexity of consumer choice. We can, moreover, posit a fourth level of interpretive analysis—that of the personal consumer—which attempts to render intelligible the choices made by a single consumer in terms of the context in which it occurs. Such interpretation would take account of the self-rules generated by the consumer and his or her working out what he or she is doing in operant terms. This qualitative approach, the subject of current investigation, is closely related to hermeneutical method (Chandler, 1993; Dougher, 1993) and promises to extend the continuum of scientific-interpretivist analysis even further away from the positivist pole.

The BPM interpretation of consumer behavior is, in one important respect, akin to the psychoanalytical interpretation of literature. It is based on an underlying model developed in a remote context (the operant laboratory and operant field studies; cf. the clinical setting) whose application to the immediate domain is plausibly based on an assumption of continuity. As a *scientifically based interpretation*, it depends upon the evidence that exists for the underlying model and the grounds for asserting the remote context as a reasonable analogue of the immediate, that is, for accepting the continuous nature of the two realms. If either fails, the interpretation ceases to be scientifically based. As a *heuristic device*, however, it might have a life independent of the scientific work as long as it renders the immediate situation more intelligible, that is, if its accounts can be accepted as plausible in their own right on a common sense understanding of what motivates consumer choice that does not demand a scientific foundation. This distinction may well apply to all interpretive systems. It appears to be the possibility of divorcing the interpretation from a scientifically demonstrable basis that alarms some critics of hermeneutics in consumer research. But this chapter has argued for the inevitability of an account of consumer behavior that is *more or less* based upon a scientific model but which offers interpretation rather than explanation, understanding rather than demonstration. Even when the initial model of behavioral ontology and methodology is positivistic in the Machian sense, as is the case for a radical behaviorist perspective, some degree of metascientific extension is inescapable once the behavior under review is complex (e.g., "real world" consumer behavior) rather than simple (confined to the laboratory or field setting). The only way in which consumer researchers can maintain the narrowly scientific status of their work is to limit it to the laboratory or statistical sample survey, neither of which replicates consumer experience. The alternative we have proposed is to be aware of the problem of moving from one realm to the other and of the steps that must be taken in accommodating the discontinuities that separate them.

A PRAGMATIC EVALUATION

The problems inherent in trying to evaluate alternative paradigms and competing theories have been a recurrent theme of earlier work on the BPM (Foxall, 1990). Given the difficulty, perhaps impossibility, of conducting crucial experiments and of definitely rejecting a hypothesis, we might profitably employ the pragmatic criterion and ask what a particular account of behavior uniquely enables us to do: what can we accomplish with this theory that would be impossible without it, or if we relied on one of its alternatives? This raises two subcriteria. (i) What technology can be used to test this theory? That is, what does this approach enable us to do, usefully, with the world? And (ii) what can we accomplish intellectually by applying this approach? That is, what do we now better understand as a result of its application? In both cases, the Jamesian pragmatic equation of the truth of a theory with its usefulness is being adopted (Baum, 1994, p. 124), a relativistic standard which will differ according to the context in which it is applied. Since science explains by describing phenomena in familiar terms which correspond with our experience (Mach, [1893] 1974), and since truth is understood instrumentally (James, 1907, p. 49), one explanation is truer than another if it explains more of the phenomenal universe. As Baum puts it,

> The idea that the sun and stars move around the earth explained only why they move across the sky; thus it is less true than the idea that the earth orbits the sun while rotating on its axis, which also explains why we have seasons. According to pragmatism, however, we will never know whether the earth *really* revolves around the sun; another, truer, theory could conceivably come along. (1994, p. 21)

The BPM provides an understanding of how marketing management works, what it does, which, at least, supplements existing accounts which do not consider the context in which consumer behavior occurs and, at most, supplies an alternative general theory of marketing. On this view, marketing operates the two fundamental ways: it influences the scope of consumer behavior settings and it manipulates reinforcers, both of which tend to shape and maintain specific responses. The means by which marketing management seeks to perform these functions naturally incorporate the marketing mix, the four Ps of product, price, promotion, and place-time. But the model increases understanding of the effects of using the marketing mix by drawing attention to its two fundamental functions. Hence the use of product variables enters into the management of behavior setting scope by creating and arranging physical discriminative stimuli (product features, brand attributes) in store displays and use contexts. Product also includes issues of the quality and quantity of reinforcers. Price is concerned principally with aversive consequences of buying and, perhaps, using a product; however, it is also a discriminative stimulus for the quality and quantity of reinforcement contingent upon the actions. Numerous controlling elements contained in the model enter into place-time or distribution: the physical, social, and temporal aspects of retail contexts, for instance, as well as reinforcer delay and the scheduling of reinforcements. Finally, promotions entail the manipulation of regulatory stimuli, the creation and presentation of the rules that link discriminative stimuli with reinforcing (and, on occasion) aversive outcomes. The art of marketing management inheres in the coordinated and consonant arrangement of the discriminative and reinforcing stimuli that compose the mix.

The aim of the BPM framework is to re-describe consumer behavior as a realm of activity *shaped by its context*, a prominent part of which is the marketing environment. In re-describing marketer behavior, it is, therefore, providing an additional account of a familiar territory. Marketing management has been described already as cognitive activity in a host of textbooks and chapters; the BPM research program is recasting it as operant behavior. The principal motive in doing so is to provide an understanding of environmental influence on consumer choice and the role of marketing as a predominant shaping force therein. The purpose is not to provide further prescriptions for marketing management. A re-description of what marketing managers are doing is unlikely to throw up such prescriptions of itself, though managers and consultants may well find the constructs that compose the model and its exegesis useful in their work. The extent to which marketing as a social and economic technology confirms the model in use is an empirical question yet to be settled. At this stage, it is necessary to confine a pragmatic assessment to an intellectual review. However, understanding how marketing works, what it does, is a prerequisite of making it work more effectively and of formulating necessary macro-marketing policy to regulate it. The contribution of the BPM lies in its showing how marketers attempt to influence consumer behavior by manipulating environmental variables, a theme which current marketing theory generally neglects. The widespread emphasis in consumer research on intrapersonal causation of behavior—on the causal status of attitudes, intentions, and other cognitions—means that we have no more than the rudiments of a theory of how situational factors impinge on purchase and consumption. *Yet extrapolations of findings from either experimental settings or from social surveys ignore the unique personal learning histories of the participants and those of the populations to whom the extrapolation is applied.* The BPM presents a framework within which consumer behavior may be located or situated at the intervention of the consumer's learning history and the discriminative stimuli that compose the current behavior setting. Thereby the model provides a functional account of consumer behavior which makes the use of the radical behaviorist philosophy of psychology and evolutionary explanation, thus far strenuously avoided in consumer research. In doing so, it introduces several analytical concepts to consumer

research: the scope of consumer behavior settings, the bifurcation of reinforcement into its utilitarian and informational *functions* (better than saying there are two distinct *kinds* of reinforcement), the central element of the
consumer situation, a functional classification of consumer operants, and
an original approach to the interpretation of consumer behavior.

SUMMING UP

To exclude explanatory systems that have their origin in positivism from
active consideration in consumer research is to lose a vital contribution to
the epistemological richness of our discipline. So long as consumer researchers remain in ignorance of the meanings of positivism, using the word as
an epithet whose historical significance must be pointed out to them, so
long will the relationship of science and interpretation be obscured. For,
contrary to the anti-positivist stance assumed by many advocates of relativism in consumer research, progress in our discipline requires serious
consideration of the essential oneness of science and interpretation in the
advancement of understanding. Both experience, leading to empirical evidence, and interpretation, conferring order and meaning on sense data,
are essential elements of any system of knowledge derived from the world
of phenomena. Moreover, attempts to separate them, to promote one at
the cost of disparaging the other, show misunderstanding of their interactive contribution. Observations that produce data are inescapably theory-
laden, while the appraisal of explanatory systems—whether "scientific" or
"hermeneutic"—requires contact with an empirically available realm. The
balance and interplay of experience and interpretation, and the questions
each poses for the other, lie at the heart of the problem raised by pragmatic
inquiry for the philosophy of science. Consumer research has generally
tended toward imbalance: initially dominated by positivist methodologies
and ontologies that placed it firmly within a realist framework of knowledge production, it now shows signs not of the relative equilibrium and
mutual understanding that would come of tempered redress of this over-
emphasis, but of sharp dichotomization, opportunities for rapprochement
notwithstanding. On one hand lies a retrenchment into a positivism that
refuses to listen to the claims of relativity (let alone relativism—see Peter,
1992) or, on occasion, even pluralism; on the other, an ofttimes uncritical
lurch into hermeneutic analysis that threatens to sever consumer research's
links with its scientific past.

It may be characteristic of contemporary consumer research that the
mutual indispensability of science and interpretation is tentatively suggested in the absence of any deeper investigation of their reciprocal
interdependence. There is an important reason why the renaissance of
philosophical considerations in consumer research has failed to produce
greater balance and tolerance: metatheory has been pursued for the most

part in the abstract, separated from detailed examination of actual theories or research programs. As a result, differences between conceptual and epistemological stances have become exaggerated. An adversarial model of research practice is an inevitable consequence of seeing "ontological disjunction" between concepts derived within alternative frames of reference as an unsuitable sign of incommensurability (Anderson, 1986). A primary contention of this chapter is that there may be far less incommensurability than consumer researchers have of late been encouraged to see, though what there is of fundamental significance. This chapter has argued, first, that to the extent that hermeneutical method has relied on hypothetico-deductive logic, it has been consistent with a broad scientific approach to the growth of knowledge. Second, and more important, it has sought to show in depth the dependence of even the most extreme positivistic scientific methodology on interpretation. In the case of radical behaviorism, the pervasive role of interpretation is apparent at three levels. First, this philosophy of psychology cannot be exempted from the theory-dependence of observation, the inescapable construction of facts in light of pre-existent theoretical standpoints which determine how observation is organized and structured and its outcomes interpreted (Popper, 1972). This is true even of operant experimentation in the closed setting of the animal laboratory where responses may be attributed to classical as well as operant conditioning (Garcia, McGowan, and Green, 1972), or to cognitive processing (Griffin, 1974); it is equally true of rigorous animal training where responses that run counter to the operant conditioning hypothesis have been portrayed as resulting from phylogenic intrusions (Skinner, 1983). Second, as shown in detail, an operant behaviorist account of complex human activity such as purchase and consumption is overwhelmingly interpretivist. Situational and speciational discontinuities between even the human operant experiment and the behavior in question make the interpretive stance inevitable. Several of the ontological components of radical behaviorist philosophy of science—such as materialism and determinism—are purely arbitrary assumptions whose veracity cannot be ultimately demonstrated. Even natural science does not universally accept such assumptions (Stevenson, 1974). Both of the discrete perspectives of determinism and free will are available to researchers, but social *science* can do no more than commit itself arbitrarily to a deterministic stance (Berger and Kellner, 1981, pp. 96–98). Behaviorism, like other approaches to science, may adopt a relevance structure which assumes causation but its practitioners should be sufficiently self-aware as to understand that other interpretations are not only possible but inevitable and desirable. As Berger and Kellner put it, the adoption of a deterministic stance "cannot be used to deny ontological validity to the category of freedom" (p. 98). Nor is the assumption that the environment is the sole source of causation for human behavior sufficient to rule out intrapersonal initiation: neither can be demonstrated with scientific finality, and much of the recent work in radical behaviorism which has dealt with verbal behavior and rule-governance has simply *interpreted* covert verbal discriminative stimuli as "non-initiating causes" which are subject to environmental control, as are the overt responses which they temporarily govern. Similarly, the monistic assumption inherent in materialism may be a simplifying assumption for a scientific approach, but it is ultimately an act of faith if it is used to apply ontological limits to explanation. Third, it is also clear that the ontological position of radical behaviorism rests fundamentally upon an interpretation of the nature of private events. The construal of thought, imagination, will, and so on, as *behaviors* (Skinner, 1945, 1957, 1974) presupposes an ontological status which cannot be substantiated or denied by scientific inquiry. It is a metaphysical assumption rather than a demonstrable proposition (Ayer, 1936). The same can be said of the deterministic assumption on which radical behaviorism proceeds: like free will, determinism belongs to the realm of superstition rather than that of science (Ayer, 1990).

These are not arguments for the overthrow of radical behaviorism; they imply only that the nature of the knowledge produced within its interpretive perspective must be understood and accurately construed by both radical behaviorists themselves and those who seek to employ this perspective in applied areas such as consumer research. Radical behaviorists have often assumed an aggressive posture vis-à-vis cognitivism and other systems that allegedly rely on explanatory fictions, equating behaviorism alone with a genuinely scientific approach. But the recognition that, beyond the confines of the operant laboratory, radical behaviorism offers "not science but interpretation" indicates that its account of complex human social behavior is of a different order from that of relatively simple animal or human responding in controlled experimental settings. Moreover, while radical behaviorism finds both its objective and its scientific justification in its capacity to predict and control, no such technological seal of approval is forthcoming for its interpretative discursions. The resulting interpretation of consumer behavior from a radical behaviorist perspective is "plausible" (to use Skinner's criterion) in two respects. First, it provides a coherent and comprehensive classification of observed (indeed, well-documented) patterns of consumer behavior in terms of the operant paradigm, albeit modified and extended in the context of the complex social behavior with which consumer psychology is concerned. Behavior setting scope, learning history, and utilitarian/informational/aversive consequences supply an alternative framework in which to comprehend a broad range of purchase and consumption activities, one which redresses the imbalance of current theories of consumer choice in which purchase and consumption are essentially placeless activities. Second, the model and the interpretations that stem from it appear to be consistent with the empirical evidence gained from hundreds of experimental studies of animal and human behavior. There is an external, empirical warrant of assertibility for the interpretations proposed. But the account provided is far removed from the Machian positivism on which radical behaviorism, as a philosophy of psychology, was founded. Skinner perhaps anticipated such a conclusion in stating that interpretation is distinct from science, providing not an explanation but an account that is "merely useful." But in view of the criticism leveled at cognitivists and other who have "left the dimensional system of science," it is part of that usefulness to point out how far radical behaviorist interpretation differs from the intentions of radical behaviorist science.

Radical behaviorist interpretation cannot be considered objective (in the sense of intersubjective) or quantitative; it need not be nomothetic, outsider, or etic. It is not clear whether it can avoid teleology in its analysis of verbal behavior. Certainly, from the point of view of *logical* positivism, much interpretation would fail the test of verifiability (Ayer, 1936). The enterprise is far removed from prediction and control and has much in common with the framework of hermeneutical method: presented with a text, observed consumer behavior, the radical behaviorist interprets it on the basis of experimentally confirmed operant conditioning. In doing so, he or she adds to the hermeneutical process a source of meaning, itself derived from a radical behaviorist *interpretation*, based on the likely functional consequences of behavior and its probability of occurrence as determined by the actor's learning history and the current behavior setting. The meaning of a radical behaviorist interpretation stems from this. Finally, our exploration of the possible form of a radical behaviorist interpretation of consumer behavior is consistent with a view of the growth of knowledge outlined elsewhere (Foxall, 1990). It can now be restated, again briefly, in terms akin to Skinner's view of the psychology of science which relies on an empirical approach to the behavior of scientists. Paradigms, philosophies of science, will always attract staunch adherents who do not deviate from the basic principles of ontology and method set forth by the paradigm makers. Perhaps it is the existence of the resultant "pure" research communities that has led to the notion that paradigms are incommensurable by virtue of their being disjunctive at the conceptual level (Anderson, 1986). But, as researchers interact, through literary communications as well as on a personal basis, paradigms clash, interplay, and erode one another. For, while core research communities may be impregnable, paradigms are human artifacts stemming from the behavior of scientists, and thus open to modification, change, and above all synthesis. Syntheses attract adherents of their own who do not find the core propositions of the paradigms that are merging at the edges incommensurable. (The social component of scientific progress, that is, growth of knowledge, has depended on such syntheses even when it has entailed gross distortion of one or other viewpoint: Catania [1992b] suggests that Darwinism enjoyed a period of rapid growth and acceptance because some of its mutations appeared entirely reconcilable with religious views.) The adherents of the synthesis can, therefore, test hypotheses derived from the merger or construct interpretation suggested by it. While crucial experiments cannot determine the veracity of one or other of two theories that are incommensurable, they can confirm elements of one or other theory to the synthesists or confirm the synthesis itself—if only to its adherents. Surprising as it may seem, this chapter has not argued for radical behaviorism but for toleration—of paradigms, of ontologies, of methodologies. Above all, it is a plea for consumer researchers to avoid tearing their discipline apart through an unnecessary and unworkable distinction between science and interpretation. To take sides in this debate is to risk losing the purpose of consumer research, which is to learn about consumer behavior. Something beyond both science and interpretation is required in order to accomplish that, an element of creativity which is easily forced out by too close an adherence to current vogues in the philosophy of science, a preoccupation with the manner rather than the matter of consumer research.

Afterword

> Science is rooted in creative interpretation. Numbers suggest, constrain and refute; they do not, by themselves, specify the content of scientific theories.
>
> —Stephen J. Gould (1981, p. 74)

This book has been concerned with only one phase of the BPM research program, albeit one that is central, integral, and ongoing. In order to preserve the contribution of its content to the ambience of the theoretical/interpretive phase of the program, it has been based on a monograph (Foxall, 1995b) which described an early denouement of that phase. It is supplemented from other writings of the 1990s era of the program. In order to put it into context, however, it may be useful to mention here some of the developments that have followed the early interpretive period with which this volume is primarily concerned. The questions raised by interpretation have underlain all of the work that has been undertaken subsequently, and this concern has extended particularly into the current philosophical and theoretical phase. A thorough examination of the role of interpretation in a science of behavior, *Context and Cognition: Interpreting Complex Behavior* (Foxall, 2004) is concerned with the need to go beyond the radical behaviorist philosophy of psychology in order to present a comprehensive account of behavior, while retaining the concept of operant consumer behavior as the basis of explanation. This theme has been extended in two works that have applied this thinking to consumer choice: *Understanding Consumer Choice* (Foxall, 2005) and *Explaining Consumer Choice* (Foxall, 2007).

I feel confident in concluding from this monograph that radical behaviorism can contribute substantially to our understanding of consumer behavior simply through its descriptive approach to it subject matter and the role of the BPM as an interpretive device. In other words, the BPM research program has been vindicated, not by the particular conclusion I have just come to, but insofar as it has been possible to come to a conclusion with respect to the status of radical behaviorism in consumer research. Subsequent research indicates that, beyond this, the BPM, still conceived and deployed as a model derived from radical behaviorism, can predict consumer behavior and explain them as *operant*, that is, controlled by their environmental consequences. This applies to consumers' verbal and emotional responses (Foxall, 1997; Foxall and Greenley, 1999; Foxall and Yani-de-Soriano, 2005), as well as to their product and brand choices which have been explored by means of matching theory and research and behavioral economics (Foxall, James, Oliveira-Castro, and Schrezenmaier, 2007). Both radical behaviorism and the BPM, as explanatory methods that do not rely on intentional concepts, have been shown highly relevant to the prediction and explanation of aspects of consumer behavior that are not amenable to such treatment by alternative methodologies. Similarly relevant results are also strongly suggested by the experimental program of research that has recently begun (Sigurdsson, Saevarsson, and Foxall, 2009). At the same time, the use of the BPM as an interpretive device has continued to bear fruit (e.g., Fagerstrøm, Foxall, and Arntzen, 2009). And a number of suggestions made in the course of this treatment of the BPM as essentially an interpretive device have been taken further: for example, the role of multi-attribute models such as the theory of reasoned action and the theory of planned behavior has been elaborated, especially with respect to the empirical assessment of learning history (Foxall, 2004, 2005). Further, the whole question of how a radical behaviorist interpretation of complex behavior is to proceed, begun in *Consumer Psychology in Behavioral Perspective* (Foxall, 1990), has been pursued in detail (Foxall, 2004). As a result, even more portentous developments have been forthcoming in the theoretical and philosophical components of the research program. The development of a framework of conceptualization and analysis that includes neuroeconomics, intentional explanation, and cognitive insights has extended the BPM paradigm immensely, without losing the fundamental insights and uses of its extensional basis (Foxall, 2005, 2007a, 2007b, 2007c, 2008).

Current work involves all five phases of the research program: conceptual development includes the incorporation of neuroeconomics into the explanatory basis of higher-order forms of the model; theoretical development is concerned with the construction of higher-order models that incorporate intentionality and cognition; empirical research concerned with affective responses to consumer environments is suggesting new ways of conceptualizing the relationship between contingencies of reinforcement (notably the patterns of reinforcement revealed by the model) and emotion; the behavioral economics work has been extended to the combination of considerations of price elasticity of demand and matching theory; and the philosophical basis of the program is being extended along the lines just outlined with respect to models of intentional behaviorism and super-personal cognitive psychology. But at the heart of the entire program is a fundamental understanding of how consumer behavior can be interpreted as an environmentally sensitive element of complex human functioning.

Bibliography

Ajzen, I. (1985). From intentions to actions: A theory of planned behavior. In J. Kul and J. Beckmann (Eds.), *Action Control: From Cognition to Behavior*, (pp. 11–39). New York: Springer-Verlag.

Alba, J. W., and Hutchinson, J. W. (1987). Dimensions of consumer expertise. *Journal of Consumer Research, 13*, 21–26.

Alhadeff, D. A. (1982). *Microeconomics and Human Behavior: Toward a New Synthesis of Economics and Psychology*. Berkeley: University of California Press.

Allison, J. (1983). *Behavioral Economics*. New York: Praeger.

Anderson, P. F. (1986). On method in consumer research: A critical relativist perspective. *Journal of Consumer Research, 13*, 155–173.

Anderson, P. F. (1988). Relative to what—that is the question: A reply to Siegel. *Journal of Consumer Research, 15*, 133–137.

Ayer, A. J. (1936). *Language, Truth and Logic*. London: Gollancz.

Ayer, A. J. (1990). *The Meaning of Life and Other Essays*. London: Weidenfeld and Nicolson.

Ayllon, T., and Azrin, N. H. (1968). *The Token Economy: A Motivational System for Therapy and Rehabilitation*. New York: Appleton.

Baars, B. J. (1986). *The Cognitive Revolution in Psychology*. New York: Guilford.

Baer, D. M., and Stolz, S. B. (1978). A description of the Erhard Seminars Training (*est*) in the terms of behavior analysis. *Behaviorism, 6*, 45–70.

Bagozzi, R. P. (1975). Marketing as exchange. *Journal of Marketing, 39*, 32–39.

Bagozzi, R. P. (1991). The role of psychophysiology in consumer research. In T. S. Robertson and H. H. Kassarjian (Eds.), *Handbook of Consumer Behavior* (pp. 124–161). Englewood Cliffs, NJ: Prentice-Hall.

Bagozzi, R. P. (1992). The self-regulation of attitudes, intentions, and behavior. *Social Psychology Quarterly, 55*, 178–204.

Bandura, A. A. (1977). *Social Learning Theory*. Englewood Cliffs, NJ: Prentice-Hall.

Bandura, A. (1986). *Social Foundations of Thought and Action*. Englewood Cliffs, NJ: Prentice-Hall.

Barker, R. G. (1968). *Ecological Psychology: Concepts and Methods for Studying the Environment of Human Behavior*. Stanford, CA: Stanford University Press.

Barker, R. G. (1987). Prospecting in environmental psychology: Oskaloosa revisited. In D. Stokols and I. Altman (Eds.), *Handbook of Environmental Psychology* (pp. 1413–1432). New York: John Wiley and Sons.

Barker, R. G. (and Associates). (1978). *Habitats, Environments, and Human Behavior*. San Francisco: Jossey-Bass.

Baron, A., and Galizio, M. (1983). Instructional control of human operant behavior. *Psychological Record, 33*, 495–520.

Baron, A., and Perone, M. (1982). The place of the human subject in the operant laboratory. *The Behavior Analyst, 5*, 143–158.

Battalio, R. C., Kagel, J. H., Winkler, R. C., Fisher, E. B., Basmann, R. L., and Krasner, L. (1974). An experimental investigation of consumer behavior in a controlled environment. *Journal of Consumer Research, 1*, 52–60.

Baum, W. A. (1994). *Understanding Behaviorism: Science, Behavior, and Culture.* New York: HarperCollins.

Belk, R. W. (1975). Situational variables and consumer behavior. *Journal of Consumer Research, 2*, 157–167.

Belk, R. W. (Ed.) (1991). *Highways and Buyways: Naturalistic Research from the Consumer Behavior Odyssey.* Provo, UT: Association for Consumer Research.

Belk, R. W., Sherry, J. F., and Wallendorf, M. (1988). A naturalistic inquiry in buyer and seller behavior at a swap meet. *Journal of Consumer Research, 14*, 449–470.

Berger, P. L., and Kellner, H. (1981). *Sociology Reinterpreted: An Essay on Method and Vocation.* New York: Anchor Press/Doubleday.

Berry, L. L., and Kunkel, J. H. (1970). In pursuit of consumer theory. *Decision Sciences, 1*, 25–39.

Bethlehem, D. (1987). Scolding the carpenter. In S. Modgil and C. Modgil (Eds.), *B. F. Skinner: Consensus and Controversy* (pp. 89–97). New York: Falmer.

Betti, E. (1980). Hermeneutics as the general methodology of *Geisteswissenschaften.* In J. Bleicher (Ed.), *Contemporary Hermeneutics Versus Science?* London: Routledge.

Betzig, L. (1989). Rethinking human ethology: A response to some recent critiques. *Ethology and Sociobiology, 10*, 315–324.

Bjork, D. W. (1993). *B. F. Skinner: A Life.* New York: Basic Books.

Black, R. D. (1987). Collison, Utility. In J. Eatwell, M. Milgate, and P. Newman (Eds.), *The New Palgrave: A Dictionary of Economics* (pp. 776–779). London: Macmillan.

Blackman, D. E. (1980). Images of man in contemporary behaviorism. In A. J. Chapman and D. M. Jones (Eds.), *Models of Man* (pp. 99–112). Leicester: British Psychological Society.

Blackman, D. E., and Lejeune, H. (Eds.) (1990). *Behavior Analysis in Theory and Practice: Contributions and Controversies.* London: Erlbaum.

Boden, M. (1972). *Purposive Explanation in Psychology.* Hassocks, UK: Harvester.

Branthwaite, A. (1984). Situations and social actions: Applications for marketing of recent theories in social psychology. *Journal of the Market Research Society, 25*, 19–38.

Bridgman, P. (1927). *The Logic of Modern Physics.* New York: Macmillan.

Brown, S. (1994). Marketing as multiplex: Screening postmodernism. *European Journal of Marketing, 28*(8/9), 27–51.

Burgess, R. L., R. N. Clark, and Hendee, J. C. (1971). An experimental analysis of anti-littering procedures. *Journal of Applied Behavior Analysis, 4*, 71–75.

Buskist, W. F., and Miller, H. L. (1982). The analysis of human operant behavior: A brief census of the literature. *The Behavior Analyst, 5*, 137–142.

Buskist, W. F., Morgan, D., and Barry, A. (1985). Interspecies generality and human behavior: An addendum to Baron and Perone. *Journal of the Experimental Analysis of Behavior, 6*, 107–108.

Calder, B. J., and Tybout, A. M. (1987). What consumer research is . . . *Journal of Consumer Research, 14*, 136–140.

Calder, B. J., and Tybout, A. M. (1989). Interpretive, qualitative, and traditional scientific empirical consumer behavior research. In E. C. Hirschman (Ed.),

Interpretive Consumer Research (pp. 199–208). Provo, UT: Association for Consumer Research.

Catania, A. C. (1992a). *Learning*. Englewood Cliffs, NJ: Prentice-Hall.

Catania, A. C. (1992b). B. F. Skinner, organism. *American Psychologist, 47,* 1521–1530.

Catania, A. C., and Harnad, S. (Eds.). (1988). *Selection of Behavior: The Operant Behaviorism of B. F. Skinner*. New York: Cambridge University Press.

Catania, A. C., Matthews, B. A., and Shimoff, E. (1982). Instructed versus shaped human verbal behavior: Interactions with nonverbal responding. *Journal of the Experimental Analysis of Behavior, 38,* 233–248.

Catania, A, C., Shimoff, E., and Matthews, A. B. (1989). An experimental analysis of rule-governed behavior. In S. C. Hayes (Ed.), *Rule-governed Behavior: Cognition, Contingencies, and Instructional Control* (pp. 119–150). New York: Plenum.

Chalmers, A. F. (1982). *What Is This Thing Called Science?* 2nd ed. Milton Keynes: Open University.

Chandler, M. J. (1993). Contextualism and the post-modern condition: Learning from Las Vegas. In S. C. Hayes, L. J. Hayes, H. W. Reese, and T. R. Sarbin (Eds.), *Varieties of Scientific Contextualism* (pp. 227–247). Reno, NV: Context Press.

Chase, P. N., and Danforth, J. S. (1991). The role of rules in concept formation. In L. J. Hayes and P. N. Chase (Eds.), *Dialogues on Verbal Behavior* (pp. 205–235). Reno, NV: Context Press.

Chase, P. N., and Parrott, L. J. (Eds.) (1986). *Psychological Aspects of Language: The West Virginia Lectures*. Springfield, IL: Charles C. Thomas.

Chesanow, N. (1985, June). Prize flights: All about frequent flier programs. *Savvy,* 67–69.

Chomsky, N. (1959). Review of Skinner's *Verbal Behavior. Language, 35,* 26–58.

Churchland, P. S. (1986). *Neurophilosophy: Toward a Unified Science of the Mind/Brain*. Cambridge, MA: MIT Press.

Cone, J. D., and Hayes, S. C. (1980). *Environmental Problems/Behavioral Solutions*. Pacific Grove, CA: Brooks/Cole.

Connolly, J., and Keutner, T. (Eds.) (1988). *Hermeneutics Versus Science?* South Bend, IN: University of Notre Dame Press.

Cooper, L. G. (1987). Do we need critical relativism? *Journal of Consumer Research, 14,* 126–128.

Costanzo, M., Archer, D., Aronson, E., and Pettigrew, T. (1986). Energy conservation behavior: The difficult path from information to action. *American Psychologist, 41,* 521–528.

Couch, J. V., Garber, T., and Karpus, L. (1979). Response maintenance and paper recycling. *Journal of Environmental Systems, 8,* 127–137.

Creel, R. E. (1987). Skinner on science. In S. Modgil and C. Modgil (Eds.), *B. F. Skinner: Consensus and Controversy* (pp. 103–111). Philadelphia: Falmer.

Crick, F. (1988). *What Mad Pursuit: A Personal View of Scientific Discovery*. London: Weidenfeld and Nicolson.

Currie, G. (1993). Interpretation and objectivity. *Mind, 102,* 413–428.

Danko, W. D., and MacLachlan, J. M. (1983). Research to accelerate the diffusion of a new invention. *Journal of Advertising Research, 23,* 39–43.

Darwin, C. R. (1859). *The Origin of Species*. London: John Murray.

Davey, G. C. L. (1981). Conditioning principles, behaviorism and behavior therapy. In G. C. L. Davey (Ed.), *Applications of Conditioning Theory* (pp. 189–214). New York: Methuen.

Davey, G. C. L., and Cullen, C. (Eds.) (1988). *Human Operant Conditioning and Behavior Modification*. Chichester: Wiley.

Dawkins, R. (1976). *The Selfish Gene.* New York: Oxford University Press.

Dawkins, R. (1982). *The Extended Phenotype: The Long Reach of the Gene.* Oxford: Oxford University Press.

Dawkins, R. (1986). *The Blind Watchmaker.* London: Longman.

Dawkins, R. (1988). Replicators, consequences, and displacement activities. In A. C. Catania and S. Harnad (Eds.), *Selection of Behavior: The Operant Behaviorism of B. F. Skinner* (pp. 33–35). New York: Cambridge University Press.

Day, W. (1980). The historical antecedents of contemporary behaviorism. In R. W. Rieber and K. Salzinger (Eds.), *Psychology: Theoretical-Historical Perspectives* (pp. 203–262). New York: Academic Press.

Delprato, D. J., and Midgley, B. D. (1992). Some fundamentals of B. F. Skinner's behaviorism. *American Psychologist, 47,* 1507–1520.

Dennett, D. C. (1978). *Brainstorms: Philosophical Essays on Mind and Psychology.* Montgomery, VT: Bradford Books.

Dennett, D. C. (1983). Intentional systems in cognitive ethology: The "Panglossian Paradigm" defended. *The Behavioral and Brain Sciences, 6,* 343–390.

Dennett, D. C. (1987). *The intentional Stance.* Cambridge, MA: MIT Press.

Deslauriers, B. C., and Everett, P. B. (1977). Effects of intermittent and continuous token reinforcement on bus ridership. *Journal of Applied Psychology, 62,* 369–375.

Dewey, J. (1966). *Democracy and Education.* New York: Free Press.

Dickerson, M. D., and Gentry, J. W. (1983). Characteristics of adopters and non-adopters of home computers. *Journal of Consumer Research, 10,* 225–235.

Dilthey, W. (1976). *Dilthey: Selected Writings.* Cambridge: Cambridge University Press.

Donovan, R. J., and Rossiter, J. R. (1982). Store atmosphere: An experimental psychology approach. *Journal of Retailing, 58,* 34–57.

Dosi, G. & Orsenigo, L. (1988). Coordination and transformation: an overview of structures, behaviours and change in evolutionary environments In Dosi, G, Freeman, C., Nelson, R. Silverberg, G. & Soete, L. (Eds) *Technical Change and Economic Theory* (pp. 13–37). London: Pinter.

Dougher, M. (1993). Interpretive and hermeneutic research methods in the contextualistic analysis of verbal behavior. In S. C. Hayes, L. J. Hayes, H. W. Reese, and T. R. Sarbin (Eds.), *Varieties of Scientific Contextualism* (pp. 211–221). Reno, NV: Context Press.

Drucker, P. F. (1955). *The Practice of Management.* London: Heinemann.

Dulany, D. E. (1968). Awareness, rules and propositional control. In D. Horton and T. Dixon (Eds.), *Verbal Behavior and S-R Behavior Theory* (pp. 340–387). Englewood Cliffs, NJ: Prentice-Hall, Englewood Cliffs.

Ehrenberg, A. S. C. (1972). *Repeat Buying.* Amsterdam: North Holland.

Ehrenberg, A. S. C. (1992, Jauary). *Theory or Well-Based Results: Which Comes First?* Paper presented at the EIASM Conference on Research Traditions in Marketing, Brussels, Belgium.

Ehrenberg, A. S. C., and Goodhardt, G. J. (1989). *Essays in Understanding Buyer Behavior.* New York: J. Walter Thompson and MRCA.

Eliot, V. (Ed.) (1988). *The Letters of T. S. Eliot,* vol. 1, *1898–1922.* San Diego, CA: Harcourt Brace Jovanovich.

Engel, J. F., Blackwell, R. D., and Miniard, P. W. (1989). *Consumer Behavior.* Hindsdale, IL: Dryden.

Everett, P. B. (1973). The use of the reinforcement procedure to increase bus ridership. *Proceedings of the 81st Annual Convention of the American Psychological Association, 8,* 891–892.

Everett, P. B. (1981). Reinforcement theory strategies for modifying transit ridership. In I. Altman, J. F. Wolwill, and P. B. Everett (Eds.), *Transportation and Behavior* (pp. 63–84). New York: Plenum.

Everett., P. B., Hayward, S. C., and Meyers, A. W. (1974). Effects of a token rein-forcement procedure on bus ridership. *Journal of Applied Behavior Analysis*, 7, 1–9.

Everett, P. B., and Watson, B. G. (1987). Psychological contributions to transporta-tion. In D. Stokols and I. Altman (Eds.), *Handbook of Environmental Psychol-ogy* (pp. 987–1008). New York: Wiley.

Faber, M., and Proops, L. (1991). Evolution in biology, physics and economics: A conceptual analysis. In P. Saviotti and J. S. Metcalfe (Eds.), *Evolutionary Theo-ries of Economic and Technological Change* (pp. 58–87). Chur, Switzerland: Harwood.

Fagerstrom, A., Foxall G. R. and Arntzen, E. (2009). Implications of motivating operations for the functional analysis of consumer behavior. *Journal of Organi-zational Behavior Management*, in press.

Ferster, C., and Skinner, B. F. (1957). *Schedules of Reinforcement*. New York: Appleton-Century.

Feyerabend, P. (1970). Consolations for the specialist. In I. Lakatos and A. Mus-grave (Eds.), *Criticism and the Growth of Knowledge* (pp. 197–230). Cam-bridge: Cambridge University Press.

Feyerabend, P. (1975). *Against Method*. London: NLB.

Finkelstein, P., Wenegrat, B., and Yalom, I. (1982). Large group awareness train-ing. *Annual Review of Psychology*, 33, 515–539.

Fishbein, M., and Ajzen, I. (1975). *Belief, Attitude, Intention, and Behavior: An Introduction to Theory and Research*. Reading, MA: Addison-Wesley.

Fisher, J. D., Silver, R. C., Chinsky, J. M., Goff, B., and Klar, Y. (1990). *Evaluat-ing a Large Group Awareness Training: A Longitudinal Study of Psychosocial Effects*. New York: Springer-Verlag.

Flanagan, O. J. (1991). *The Science of the Mind*. 2nd ed. Cambridge, MA: MIT Press.

Føllesdal, D. (1979). Hermeneutics and the hypothetico-deductive method. *Dialec-tica*, 33, 319–336.

Foxall, G. R. (1979a). On the management of "commons." *Journal of Agricultural Economics*, 30, 55–58.

Foxall, G. R. (1979b). Agricultural improvement of common land. *Journal of Envi-ronmental Management*, 8, 151–161.

Foxall, G. R. (1981). *Strategic marketing management*. London: Routledge; New York: Wiley.

Foxall, G. R. (1983). *Consumer Choice*. London: Macmillan; New York: St. Martin's.

Foxall, G. R. (1984a). Consumers' intentions and behavior: A note on research and a challenge to researchers. *Journal of the Market Research Society*, 26, 231–241.

Foxall, G. R. (1984b). *Corporate Innovation: Marketing and Strategy*. New York: St. Martin's.

Foxall, G. R. (1984c). Marketing's domain. *European Journal of Marketing*, 18, 3–25.

Foxall, G. R. (1986). The role of radical behaviorism in the explanation of con-sumer choice. *Advances in Consumer Research*, 13, 147–151.

Foxall, G. R. (1987). Radical behaviorism and consumer choice: Theoretical prom-ise and empirical problems. *International Journal of Research in Marketing*, 4, 111–129.

Foxall, G. R. (1988a). Consumer innovativeness: Novelty-seeking, creativity, and cognitive style. *Research in Consumer Behavior*, 3, 75–113.

Foxall, G. R. (1988b). Markets, hierarchies and user-initiated innovation. *Manage-rial and Decision Economics*, 9, 237–252.

Foxall, G. R. (1990). *Consumer Psychology in Behavioral Perspective*. London and New York: Routledge.

Foxall, G. R. (1991a). *Environmentally-impacting Consumer Behavior: An Integrative Model for Social Demarketing* (Working Papers in Consumer Research No. 91–10). Consumer Research Unit, University of Birmingham.

Foxall, G. R. (1991b). *Interpreting Consumer Behavior: Evaluation of the Behavioral Perspective Model of Purchase and Consumption* (Working Paper No. CRU/91–04). Research Centre for Consumer Behaviour, Birmingham Business School.

Foxall, G. R. (1992a). A behaviorist perspective on purchase and consumption. *European Advances in Consumer Research, 1*, 501–506.

Foxall, G. R. (1992b). Situated consumer behavior: A behavioral interpretation of purchase and consumption. *Research in Consumer Behavior, 5*, 113–152.

Foxall, G. R. (1992c). The Behavioral Perspective Model of purchase and consumption: From consumer theory to marketing practice. *Journal of the Academy of Marketing Science, 20*, 189–198.

Foxall, G. R. (1992d). *The Behavioral Perspective Model of Purchase and Consumption: Refinement and Extension* (Working Papers in Consumer Research No. 92–06). Consumer Research Unit, University of Birmingham.

Foxall, G. R. (1992e). The consumer situation: An integrative model for research in marketing. *Journal of Marketing Management, 8*, 392–404.

Foxall, G. R. (1993a). Consumer behavior as an evolutionary process. *European Journal of Marketing, 27*(8), 56–68.

Foxall, G. R. (1993b). Situated consumer behavior: A behavioral interpretation of purchase and consumption. *Research in Consumer Behavior, 6*, 113–152.

Foxall, G. R. (1994a). *An Empirical Test of the Behavioral Perspective Model of Purchase and Consumption* (Working Paper). Research Centre for Consumer Behavior, University of Birmingham.

Foxall, G. R. (1994b). Behavior analysis and consumer psychology. *Journal of Economic Psychology, 15*, 5–91.

Foxall, G. R. (1994c). Consumer choice as an evolutionary process: An operant interpretation of adopter behavior. *Advances in Consumer Research, 21*, 312–317.

Foxall, G. R. (1994d). Environment-impacting consumer behavior: A framework for social marketing and demarketing. In M. J. Baker (Ed.), *Perspectives on Marketing Management*, vol. 4 (pp. 27–53). Chichester: Wiley.

Foxall, G. R. (1995a). Environment-impacting consumer behavior: An operant analysis. *Advances in Consumer Research, 22*, 1–7.

Foxall, G. R. (1995b). The psychological basis of marketing. In M. J. Baker (Ed.), *The Encyclopaedia of Marketing*. London and New York: Routledge.

Foxall, G. R. (1996). *Consumers in Context: The BPM Research Program.* London: Routledge.

Foxall, G. R. (1997a). *Marketing Psychology: The paradigm in the wings.* London: Macmillan; New York: St. Martin's.

Foxall, G. R. (1997b). The explanation of consumer behavior: From social cognition to environmental control. In C. Cooper and I. Robertson (Ed.), *The International Review of Industrial and Organizational Psychology*, vol. 12 (pp. 229–287). Chichester: Wiley.

Foxall, G. R. (1998). Radical behaviorist interpretation: Generating and evaluating an account of consumer behavior, *The Behavior Analyst*, 21, 321-354.

Foxall, G. R. (1999). The substitutability of brands, *Managerial and Decision Economics*, 20, 241–57.

Foxall, G. R. (2002). *Consumer Behavior Analysis: Critical Perspectives in Business and Management.* 3 vols. London and New York: Routledge.

Foxall, G. R. (2004). *Context and Cognition: Interpreting Complex Behavior.* Reno, NV: Context Press.

Foxall, G. R. (2005). *Understanding Consumer Choice*. Basingstoke, UK, and New York: Palgrave Macmillan.

Foxall, G. R. (2007). *Explaining Consumer Choice*. Basingstoke, UK: Palgrave Macmillan.

Foxall, G. R. (2008). Reward, Emotion and Consumer Choice: From neuroeconomics to neurophilosophy: towards an integrated consumer psychology, *Journal of Consumer Behaviour*, 7, 368 - 396.

Foxall, G. R., and Goldsmith, R. E. (1994). *Consumer Psychology for Marketing*. London and New York: Routledge.

Foxall, G. R. and Greenley, G. E. (1999). Consumers' emotional responses to service environments, *Journal of Business Research*, 46, 149–58.

Foxall, G. R. and James, V. K. (2009). The style/involvement theory of consumer innovation. In Rickards, T., Runco, M. A. and Moger, S. (Eds) *The Routledge Companion to Creativity* (pp. 71–87). London and New York: Routledge.

Foxall, G. R., James, V. K., Oliveira-Castro, J. M., and Schrezenmaier, T. C. (2007). *The Behavioral Economics of Consumer Brand Choice*. Basingstoke, UK: Palgrave Macmillan.

Foxall, G. R., and Minkes, A. L. (1996). Beyond marketing: The diffusion of entrepreneurship in the modern corporation. *Journal of Strategic Marketing*, 4, 71–94.

Foxall, G. R. and Yani-de-Soriano, M. M. (2005). Situational influences on consumers' attitudes and behavior, *Journal of Business Research*, 58, 518–525.

Foxx, R. M., and Hake, D. F. (1977). Gasoline conservation: A procedure for measuring and reducing the driving of college students. *Journal of Applied Behavior Analysis*, 10, 61–74.

Foxx, R. M., and Schaeffer, M. H. (1981). A company-based lottery to reduce the personal driving of employees. *Journal of Applied Behavior Analysis*, 14, 273–285.

Frank, R. E., Massy, W. F., and Morrison, D. G. (1964). The determinants of innovative behavior with respect to a branded, frequently purchased food product. In L. G. Smith (Ed.), *Proceedings of the American Marketing Association* (pp. 312–323). Chicago: A.M.A.

Freud, S. (1985). *The Complete Letters of Sigmund Freud to Wilhelm Fliess, 1887–1904* (J. Moussaieff Masson, Ed. and Trans.). Cambridge, MA: Belknap Press.

Gadamer, H.-G. (1977). *Philosophical Hermeneutics* (D. Linge, Trans.). Berkeley: University of California Press.

Garcia, J., McGowan, B. K., and Green, K. F. (1972). Biological constraints on conditioning. In A. Black and W. Prokasy (Eds.), *Classical Conditioning II: Current Research and Theory* (pp. 3–27). New York: Appleton-Century-Crofts.

Gatignon, H., and Robertson, T. S. (1985). A propositional inventory for new diffusion research. *Journal of Consumer Research*, 11, 849–867.

Gatignon, H., and Robertson, T. S. (1991). Innovative decision processes. In T. S. Robertson and H. H. Kassarjian (Eds.), *Handbook of Consumer Behavior* (pp. 316–348). Englewood Cliffs, NJ: Prentice-Hall.

Gay, P. (1966). *The Enlightenment: An Interpretation*. New York: Macmillan.

Geertz, C. (1973). *The Interpretation of Cultures*. New York: Basic Books.

Geller, E. S. (1987). Applied behavior analysis and environmental psychology: From strange bedfellows to a productive marriage. In D. Stokols and I. Altman (Eds.), *Handbook of Environmental Psychology* (pp. 361–388). New York: Wiley.

Geller, E. S. (1989). Applied behavior analysis and social marketing: An integration for environmental preservation. *Journal of Social Issues*, 45, 17–36.

Geller, E. S., Farris, J. C., and Post, D. S. (1973). Promoting a consumer behavior for pollution control. *Journal of Applied Behavior Analysis*, 6, 367–376.

Geller, E. S., Mann, M., and Brasted, W. (1977). *Trash can design: A determinant of litter-related behavior.* Paper presented at the American Psychological Association meeting, San Francisco, CA.

Geller, E. S., Winett, R. A., and Everett, P. B. (1982). *Preserving the Environment: New Strategies for Behavior Change.* Elmsford, NY: Pergamon.

Geller, E. S., Wylie, R. C., and Farris, J. C. (1971). An attempt at applying prompting and reinforcement toward pollution control. *Proceedings of the 79th Annual Convention of the American Psychological Association, 6,* 701–702.

Goldsmith, T. H. (1991). *The Biological Roots of Human Nature.* New York: Oxford University Press.

Goodhardt, G. J., Ehrenberg, A. S. C., and Collins, M. (1987). *The Television Audience: Patterns of Viewing.* Aldershot, UK: Gower.

Gordon, W. C. (1989). *Learning and Memory.* Pacific Grove, CA: Brooks/Cole.

Gould, J., and Kolb, W. L. (Eds.). (1964). *A Dictionary of the Social Sciences.* London: Tavistock.

Gould, S. J. (1981). *The Mismeasure of Man.* London: Penguin.

Grant, L., and Evans, A. (1994). *Principles of Behavior Analysis.* New York: HarperCollins.

Greene, A. K. (1977). Bring 'em back, repack, and save. *Proceedings of the 1975 Conference on Waste Reduction.* Washington, DC: U.S. Environmental Protection Agency.

Griffin, D. R. (1976). *The Question of Animal Awareness.* New York: Rockefeller University Press.

Griffin, J., and Parfitt, D. (1987). Hedonism. In J. Eatwell, M. Milgate, and P. Newman (Eds.), *The New Palgrave: A Dictionary of Economics* (pp. 634–635). London: Macmillan.

Gronroos, C. (1994). Quo vadis, marketing? Towards a relationship marketing paradigm. *Journal of Marketing Management, 10,* 347–360.

Guerts, M. D. (1986). The "bottle bill" effect on grocery stores' costs. *International Journal of Retailing, 1,* 12–17.

Habermas, J. (1968). *Knowledge and Human Interests.* London: Heinemann.

Hackenberg, T. D. (2009). Token reinforcement: A review and analysis, *Journal of the Experimental Analysis of Behavior, 91,* 257–86.

Hake, D. F., and Foxx, R. M. (1978). Promoting gasoline conservation: The effects of reinforcement schedules, a leader and self-recording. *Behavior Modification, 2,* 319–369.

Hansen, F. (1976). Psychological theories of consumer choice. *Journal of Consumer Research, 3,* 117–142.

Hardin, G. (1968). The tragedy of the commons. *Science, 162,* 1243–1248.

Hardin, G., and Baden, J. (1977). *Managing the Commons.* San Francisco, CA: Freeman.

Harre', R., and Secord, P. F. (1973). *The Explanation of Social Behavior.* Totowa, NJ: Littlefield Adams.

Harzem, P., Lowe, C. F., and Bagshaw, M. 1978. Verbal control in human operant behavior, *Psychological Record, 28,* 405–423.

Hayes, L. J., and Chase, P. N. (Eds.). (1991). *Dialogues on Verbal Behavior.* Reno, NV: Context Press.

Hayes, S. C. (Ed.). (1989). *Rule-governed Behavior: Cognition, Contingencies, and Instructional Control.* New York: Plenum.

Hayes, S. C., Barnes-Holmes, D. and Roche, B. 2001. *Relational Frame Theory: A Post-Skinnerian Account of Human Language and Cognition.* New York: Kluwer.

Hayes, S. C., Brownstein, A. J., Haas, J. R., and Greenway, D. E. (1986). Instruction, multiple schedules, and extinction: Distinguishing rule-governed from schedule-controlled behavior. *Journal of the Experimental Analysis of Behavior, 46*, 137–147.

Hayes, S. C., and Cone, J. D. (1977). Decelerating environmentally destructive lawnwalking. *Environment and Behavior, 9*, 511–534.

Hayes, S. C., and Cone, J. D. (1981). Reducing residential electricity use: Payments, information, and feedback. *Journal of Applied Behavior Analysis, 10*, 425–435.

Hayes, S. C., and Hayes, L. C. (1989). The verbal action of the listener as a basis for rule-governance. In S. C. Hayes (Ed.), *Rule-governed Behavior: Cognition, Contingencies and Instructional Control* (pp. 153–190). New York: Plenum.

Hayes, S. C., and Hayes, L. J. (Eds.). (1992). *Understanding verbal relations.* Reno, NV: Context Press.

Hayes, S. C., Hayes, L. J., Reese, H. W., and Sarbin, T. R. (1993). *Varieties of scientific contextualism.* Reno, NV: Context Press.

Hayes, S. C., Hayes, L. J., Sato, M., and Ono, K. (1994). *Behavior analysis of language and cognition.* Reno, NV: Context Press.

Heath, T. B. (1992). The reconciliation of humanism and positivism in the practice of consumer research: A view from the trenches. *Journal of the Academy of Marketing Science, 20*, 107–118.

Heberlin, T. A. (1975). Conservation information: The energy cost crisis and electricity consumption in an apartment complex. *Energy Systems and Policy, 1*, 105–117.

Hempel, C. G. (1969). Logical Positivism and the social sciences. In P. Achinstein and S. Barker (Eds.), *The Legacy of Logical Positivism* (pp. 163–194). Baltimore, MD: Johns Hopkins Press.

Hermeneutics (2009, May 3). In *Wikipedia, the free encyclopedia.* Retrieved [June, 10, 2009], from http://en.wikipedia.org/wiki/Hermeneutics

Herrnstein, R. J. (1961). Relative and absolute strength of response as a function of frequency of reinforcement. *Journal of the Experimental Analysis of Behavior, 4*, 267–272.

Herrnstein, R. J. (1988). A behavioral alternative to utility maximization. In S. Maital (Ed.), *Applied Behavioral Economics 1* (pp. 3–60). Brighton, UK: Wheatsheaf.

Herrnstein, R. J. (1990). Rational choice theory: Necessary but not sufficient. *American Psychologist, 45*, 356–367.

Hillner, K. P. (1984). *History and Systems of Modern Psychology: A Conceptual Approach.* New York: Gardner Press.

Hirsch, E. D. (1967). *Validity in Interpretation.* New Haven, CT: Yale University Press.

Hirschman, E. C. (1982). Symbolism and technology as sources for the generation of innovations. *Advances in Consumer Research, 9*, 537–541.

Hirschman, E. C. (1986). Humanistic inquiry in marketing research: Philosophy, method, and criteria. *Journal of Marketing Research, 21*, 237–249.

Hirschman, E. C. (Ed.). (1989). *Interpretive Consumer Research.* Provo, UT: Association for Consumer Research.

Hirschman, E. C., and Holbrook, M. B. (Eds.). (1981). *Symbolic Consumer Behavior.* Ann Arbor, MI: Association for Consumer Research.

Hirschman, E. C., and Holbrook, M. B. (1982). Utilitarian consumption: Emerging concepts, methods and propositions. *Journal of Marketing, 46*, 92–101.

Hirschman, E. C., and Holbrook, M. B. (1986). Expanding the ontology and methodology of research on the consumption experience. In D. Brinberg and R. J. Lutz (Eds.), *Perspectives on Methodology in Consumer Research* (pp. 213–251). New York: Springer-Verlag, New York.

Hirschman, E. C., and Holbrook, M. B. (1992). *Postmodern Consumer Research: The Study of Consumption as Text.* Newbury Park, CA: Sage.

Holbrook, M. B. (1987). What is consumer research? *Journal of Consumer Research, 14*, 128–132.

Holbrook, M. B, Chestnut, R. W., Oliva, T. A., and Greenleaf, E. A. (1984). Play as a consumption experience: The roles of emotions, performance, and personality in the enjoyment of games. *Journal of Consumer Research, 11*, 728–739.

Holbrook, M. B., and Hirschman, E. C. (1982). The experiential aspects of consumption: Consumer feelings, fantasies and fun. *Journal of Consumer Research, 9*, 132–140.

Holbrook, M. B., O'Shaughnessy, J., and Bell, S. (1990). Actions and reactions in the consumption experience: The complementary role of reasons and emotions in consumer behavior. *Research in Consumer Behavior, 4*, 131–164.

Homans, C. G. (1974). *Social behavior.* New York: Harcourt, Brace and Jovanovich.

Horne, P. J., and Lowe, C. F. (1993). Determinants of human performance on concurrent schedules. *Journal of the Experimental Analysis of Behavior, 59*, 29–60.

Howard, J. A. (1989). *Consumer Behavior in Marketing Strategy.* Englewood Cliffs, NJ: Prentice-Hall.

Howard, J. A., and Sheth, J. N. (1969). *The Theory of Buyer Behavior.* New York, Wiley.

Hunt, S. D. (1976). The nature and scope of marketing. *Journal of Marketing, 40*, 17–28.

Hunt, S. D. (1989). Naturalistic, humanistic, and interpretive inquiry: Challenges and ultimate potential. In E. C. Hirschman (Ed.), *Interpretive Consumer Research* (pp. 185–198). Provo, UT: Association for Consumer Research.

Hunt, S. D. (1990). Truth in marketing theory and research. *Journal of Marketing, 54*, 4–10.

Hunt, S. D. (1991). Positivism and paradigm dominance in consumer research: Toward critical pluralism and rapprochement. *Journal of Consumer Research, 18*, 32–40.

Hursh, S. R. (1980). Economic concepts for the analysis of behavior. *Journal of the Experimental Analysis of Behavior, 34*, 219–238.

Hursh, S. R. (1984). Behavioral economics. *Journal of the Experimental Analysis of Behavior, 42*, 435–452.

Ingram, R. E., and Geller, E. S. (1975). A community-integrated, behavior modification approach to facilitating paper recycling. *JSAS Catalog of Selected Documents in Psychology, 5* (MS. No. 1097), 327.

James, W. (1907). *Pragmatism and Four Essays from The Meaning of Truth.* New York: New American Library.

Kagel, J. H. (1988). Economics according to the rats (and pigeons too): What have we learned and what can we hope to learn? In A. E. Roth (Ed.), *Laboratory Experiments in Economics* (pp. 155–192). Cambridge: Cambridge University Press.

Kassarjian, H. H. (1978). Anthropomorphism and parsimony. *Advances in Consumer Research, 5*, xiii–xiv.

Katona, G. (1975). *Psychological Economics.* New York: Elsevier.

Kazdin, A. E. (1977). *The Token Economy: A Review and Evaluation.* New York: Plenum.

Kazdin, A. E. (1981). The token economy. In G. C. L. Davey (Ed.), *Applications of Conditioning Theory* (pp. 59–80). London: Methuen.

Kazdin, A. E. (1983). The token economy: A decade later. *Journal of Applied Behavior Analysis, 15*, 431–445.

Keng, K. A., and Ehrenberg, A. S. C. (1984). Patterns of store choice. *Journal of Marketing Research, 21*, 399–409.

Kline, P. (1989). Objective tests of Freud's theories. In A. M. Colman and J. G. Beaumont (Eds.), *Psychology Survey*, Vol. 7 (pp. 127–145). Leicester: British Psychological Society; London: Routledge.

Kline, P. (1990). Hermeneutics, science and psychoanalysis. *Journal of Psychoanalytic Studies, 45*, 217–220.

Koch, S. (1964). Psychology and emerging conceptions of knowledge as unitary. In T. W. Wann (Ed.), *Behaviorism and Phenomenology* (pp. 1–41). Chicago: University of Chicago Press.

Kohlenberg, R. J., Phillips, T., and Proctor, W. (1976). A behavioral analysis of peaking in residential electricity energy consumption. *Journal of Applied Behavior Analysis, 9*, 13–18.

Kolakowsky, L. (1968). *The Alienation of Reason: A History of Positivist Thought*. New York: Doubleday.

Krasner, L., and Krasner, M. (1973). Token economies and other planned environments. In *National Society for the Study of Education Yearbook, 72*, Part I. (pp. 351–381). New York: NSSE.

Kuhn, T. S. (1962). *The Structure of Scientific Revolutions*. Chicago: University of Chicago Press.

Lacey, H. M. (1974). The scientific study of linguistic behavior: A perspective on the Skinner-Chomsky controversy. *Journal of the Theory of Social Behavior, 4*, 17–51.

Lacey, H. M. (1979). Skinner on the prediction and control of behavior. *Theory and Decision, 10*, 353–385.

Lacey, H. M., and Schwartz, B. (1987). The explanatory power of radical behaviorism. In S. Modgil and C. Modgil (Eds.), *B.F. Skinner: Consensus and Controversy* (pp. 165–176). Philadelphia: Falmer Press.

Lakatos, I. (1970). Falsification and the methodology of scientific research programmes. In I. Lakatos and A. Musgrave (Eds.), *Criticism and the Growth of Knowledge* (pp. 91–196). Cambridge: Cambridge University Press.

Lambkin, M. (1990). Evolutionary models of markets and competitive structure. In G. Day, B. Weitz, and R. Wensley (Eds.), *The Interface of Marketing and Strategy* (pp. 348–362). Greenwich, CT: JAI.

Laudan, L. (1977). *Progress and Its Problems: Toward a Theory of Scientific Growth*. Berkeley: University of California Press.

Laudan, L. (1984). *Science and Values: The Aims of Science and their Role in Scientific Debate*. Berkeley: University of California Press.

Lea, S. E. G. (1978). The psychology and economics of demand. *Psychological Bulletin, 85*, 441–466.

Lea, S. E. G., Tarpy, R. M., and Webley, P. (1987). *The Individual in the Economy*. Cambridge: Cambridge University Press.

Leahey, T. H. (1987). *A History of Psychology*. Englewood Cliffs, NJ: Prentice-Hall.

Lee, A. S. (1991). Integrating positivist and interpretive approaches to organizational research. *Organization Science, 2*, 342–365.

Lee, V. L. (1988). *Beyond Behaviorism*. London: Erlbaum.

Lee, V. L. (1992). Transdermal interpretation of the subject matter of behavior analysis. *American Psychologist, 47*, 1337–1343.

Lieberman, D. A. (1993). *Learning: Behavior and Cognition*. 2nd ed. Pacific Grove, CA: Brooks/Cole.

Lindqvist, A. (1981). *Household Saving—Behavioral Measurement of Household Saving Behavior*. Doctoral dissertation, Stockholm School of Economics.

Lowe, C. F. (1979). Determinants of human operant behavior. *Advances in Analysis of Behavior, 1*, 159–192.

Lowe, C. F. (1983). Radical behaviorism and human choice. In G. C. L. Davey (Ed.), *Animal Models of Human Behavior* (pp. 71–93). Chichester: Wiley.

Lowe, C. F., Beasty, A., and Bentall, R. P. (1983). The role of verbal behavior in human learning: Infant performance on fixed-interval schedules. *Journal of the Experimental Analysis of Behavior, 39*, 157–164.

Lowe, C. F., and Horne, P. J. (1985). On the generality of behavioral principles: Human choice and the matching law. In C. F. Lowe, M. Richelle, D. E. Blackman, and C. M. Bradshaw (Eds.), *Behavior Analysis and Contemporary Psychology* (pp. 97–116). London: Erlbaum.

Lowe, C. F., Horne, P. J., and Higson, P. J. (1987). Operant conditioning: The hiatus between theory and practice in clinical psychology. In Eysenck, H. J. and Martin, J. (Eds.), *Theoretical Foundations of Behavior Therapy* (pp. 153–165). London: Plenum.

Lynch, J. J. (1992). *The Psychology of Customer Care*. London: Macmillan.

MacCorquodale, K. (1969). B. F. Skinner's *Verbal Behavior*: A retrospective appreciation. *Journal of the Experimental Analysis of Behavior, 12*, 831–841.

Macdonald, G., and Pettit, P. (1981). *Semantics and Social Science*. London: Routledge.

Mach, E. ([1893] 1974). *The Science of Mechanics: A Critical and Historical Account of its Development* (T. J. McCormack, Trans.). 6th ed. LaSalle, IL: Open Court.

Mach, E. ([1896] 1959). *The Analysis of Sensations: And the Relation of the Physical to the Psychical* (C. M. Williams, Trans.). New York: Dover.

Mach, E. ([1905] 1976). *Knowledge and Error: Sketches on the Psychology of Enquiry* (T. J. McCormack and P. Foulkes, Trans.). Boston: Reidel.

Mackenzie, B. D. (1977). *Behaviorism and the Limits of Scientific Method*. Atlantic Highlands, NJ: Humanities Press.

Malott, R. W. (1986). Self-management, rule-governed behavior, and everyday life. In H. W. Reese and L. J. Parrott (Eds.), *Behavior Science: Philosophical, Methodological, and Empirical Advances* (pp. 207–228). Hillsdale, NJ: Erlbaum.

Malott, R. W. (1989). The achievement of evasive goals: Control by rules describing contingencies that are not direct acting. In S. C. Hayes (Ed.), *Rule-governed Behavior: Cognition, Contingencies, and Instructional Control* (pp. 269–324). New York: Plenum.

Malott, R. W., and Garcia, M. E. (1991). Role of private events in rule-governed behavior. In L. J. Hayes and P. N. Chase (Eds.), *Dialogues on Verbal Behavior* (pp. 327–356). Reno, NV: Context Press.

Mandler, G. (1985). *Cognitive Psychology: An essay in Cognitive Science*. Hillsdale, NJ: Erlbaum.

Martin, P., and Bateson, P. (1986). *Measuring Behavior*. Cambridge: Cambridge University Press.

Marx, M. H., and Hillix, W. A. (1979). *Systems and Theories in Psychology*. 3rd ed. New York: McGraw-Hill.

Matthews, B. A., Catania, A. C., and Shimoff, E. (1985). Effects of uninstructed verbal behavior on nonverbal responding: Contingency descriptions versus performance descriptions. *Journal of the Experimental Analysis of Behavior, 43*, 155–164.

Maynard Smith, J. (1986). *The Problems of Biology*. Oxford: Oxford University Press.

Mayr, E. (1991). *One Long Argument: Charles Darwin and the Genesis of Modern Evolutionary Thought*. Cambridge, MA: Harvard University Press.

McClelland, L., and Cook, S. W. (1977). *Encouraging energy conservation as a social psychological problem: consumption by tenants with "utilities included."* Paper presented at the meeting of the American Psychological Association, San Francisco, CA.

McFarland, D. (1989). *Problems of Animal Behavior*. NY: Wiley.

Mehrabian, A., and Russell, J. A. (1974). *An Approach to Environmental Psychology.* Cambridge, MA: MIT Press.

Menger, C. (1956). *Principles of Economics* (J. Dingwall and B. F. Hoselitz, Trans.). Glencoe, IL: Free Press.

Midgley, D. F. (1977). *Innovation and New Product Marketing.* London: Croom Helm.

Midgley, D. F., and Dowling, G. R. (1978). Innovativeness: The concept and its measurement. *Journal of Consumer Research, 4,* 229–240.

Miller, G. A. (1962). *Psychology: The Science of Mental Life.* London: Penguin Books.

Moore, J. (1985). Some historical and conceptual relations among logical positivism, operationism, and behaviorism. *The Behavior Analyst, 8,* 53–63.

Morris, E. K. (1991). The contextualism that is behavior analysis: An alternative to cognitive psychology. In A. Still and A. Costall (Eds.), *Against Cognitivism: Alternative Foundations for Cognitive Psychology* (pp. 123–149). London: Harvester Wheatsheaf.

Morse, W. H. (1966). Intermittent reinforcement. In W. K. Honig (Ed.), *Operant Behavior: Areas of Research and Application* (pp. 52–108). New York: Appleton-Century-Crofts.

Newsom, T. J., and Makranczy, V. J. (1978). Reducing electricity consumption of residents living in mass-metered dormitory complexes. *Journal of Environmental Systems, 1,* 215–236.

Nord, W., and Peter, J. P. (1980). A behavior modification perspective on marketing. *Journal of Marketing, 44,* 36–47.

Olson, J. C. (1982). Toward a science of consumer behavior. *Advances in Consumer Research, 11,* v–x.

O'Neill, G. W., Blanck, L. S., and Joyner, M. A. (1980). The use of stimulus control over littering in a natural setting. *Journal of Applied Behavior Analysis, 13,* 379–381.

O'Shaughnessy, J. (1987). *Why People Buy.* New York: Oxford.

O'Shaughnessy, J. (1992). *Explaining Buyer Behavior: Central Concepts and Philosophy of Science Issues.* New York: Oxford University Press.

O'Shaughnessy, J., and Holbrook, M. B. (1988). On the scientific status of consumer research and the need for an interpretive approach to studying consumption behavior. *Journal of Consumer Research, 15,* 398–402.

Osmond, H. (1957, April). Function as the basis of psychiatric ward design. *Mental Hospitals, 8,* 23–29.

Ostlund, L. E. (1974). Perceived innovation attributes as predictors of innovativeness. *Journal of Consumer Research, 1,* 23–29.

Owen, N., Borland, R., and Hill, D. (1991). Regulatory influences on health-related behaviors: The case of workplace smoking bands. *Australian Psychologist, 26,* 188–191.

Ozanne, J. L., and Hudson, L. A. (1989). Exploring diversity in consumer research. In E. C. Hirschman (Ed.), *Interpretive Consumer Research* (pp. 1–9). Provo, UT: Association for Consumer Research.

Page, T. J., and Iwata, B. A. (1986). Interobserver agreement: History, theory and current methods. In A. Poling and R. W. Fuqua (Eds.), *Research Methods in Applied Behavior Analysis* (pp. 99–126). New York: Plenum.

Palmer, M. H., Lloyd, M. E., and Lloyd, K. E. (1978). An experimental analysis of electricity conservation procedures. *Journal of Applied Behavior Analysis, 10,* 665–672.

Perone, M., Galizio, M., and Baron, A. (1988). The relevance of animal-based principles in the laboratory study of human operant behavior. In G. C. L. Davey and C. Cullen (Eds.), *Human Operant Conditioning and Behavior Modification* (pp. 59–85). Chichester: Wiley.

Peter, J. P. (1991). Philosophical tensions in consumer inquiry. In T. S. Robertson and H. H. Kassarjian (Eds.), *Handbook of Consumer Behavior* (pp. 533–547). Englewood Cliffs, NJ: Prentice-Hall.

Peter, J. P. (1992). Realism or relativism for marketing theory and research: A comment on Hunt's "scientific realism." *Journal of Marketing, 56,* 72–79.

Peter, J. P., and Nord, W. (1982). A clarification and extension of operant conditioning principles in marketing. *Journal of Marketing, 46,* 102–107.

Peter, J. P., and Olson, J. (1983). Is science marketing? *Journal of Marketing, 47,* 111–125.

Peters, M. P., and Venkatesan, M. (1973). Exploration of variables inherent in adopting an industrial product. *Journal of Marketing Research, 10,* 312–315.

Phillips, D. C. (1987). *Philosophy, Science and Social Inquiry.* Oxford: Pergamon.

Phillips, D. C. (1992). *The Social Scientist's Bestiary: A Guide to Fabled Threats to, and Defences of, Naturalistic Social Science.* Oxford: Pergamon.

Pierce, W. D., and Epling, W. F. (1983). Choice, matching and human behavior: A review of the literature. *The Behavior Analyst, 6,* 57–76.

Polkinghorne, J. C. (1984). *The Quantum World.* London: Longman.

Poppen, R. L. (1982). The fixed-interval scallop in human affairs. *The Behavior Analyst, 5,* 27–36.

Poppen, R. L. (1989). Some clinical implications of rule-governed behavior. In S. C. Hayes (Ed.), *Rule-Governed Behavior: Cognition, Contingencies and Instructional Control* (pp. 325–357). New York: Plenum.

Popper, K. (1972). *Conjectures and Refutations: The Growth of Scientific Knowledge.* 4th ed. London: Routledge and Kegan Paul.

Proctor, R. W., and Weeks, D. J. (1990). *The Goal of B. F. Skinner and Behavior Analysis.* New York: Springer-Verlag.

Qantas. (n.d.). *Qantas Frequent Flyer. The Program for People Going Places.* ACN: Qantas Airways Limited.

Rabinow, P., and Sullivan, W. (Eds.). (1979). *Interpretive Social Science: A Reader.* Berkeley: University of California Press.

Rachlin, H. (1987). The explanatory power of Skinner's radical behaviorism. In S. Modgil and C. Modgil (Eds.), *B. F. Skinner: Consensus and Controversy* (pp. 155–164). New York: Falmer.

Rachlin, H. (1989). *Judgment, Decision, and Choice: A Cognitive/Behavioral Synthesis.* San Francisco, CA: Freeman.

Rachlin, H. 1994. *Behavior and Mind: The Roots of Modern Psychology.* Oxford University Press, New York.

Rachlin, H. 2000. *The Science of Self Control.* Harvard University Press, Cambridge, MA.

Rajaniemi, P. (1992). Conceptualization of product involvement as a property of a cognitive structure. *Acta Wasensia, 29,* 1–265.

Reese, H. W. (1989). Rules and rule-governance: Cognitive and behavioristic views. In S. C. Hayes (Ed.), *Rule-Governed Behavior: Cognition, Contingencies, and Instructional Control* (pp. 3–84). New York: Plenum.

Reese, H. W., and Parrott, L. J. (Eds.). (1986). *Behavior Science: Philosophical, Methodological and Empirical Advances.* Hillsdale, NJ: Lawrence Erlbaum.

Reid, D. H., Luyben, P. L., Rawers, R. J., and Bailey, J. S. (1979). The effects of prompting and proximity of containers on newspaper recycling behavior. *Environment and Behavior, 8,* 471–483.

Rhinehart, L. (1976). *The Book of est.* London: Sphere.

Richelle, M. N. (1987). Variation and selection: the evolutionary analogy in Skinner's theory. In S. Modgil and C. Modgil (Eds.), *B. F. Skinner: Consensus and Controversy* (pp. 127–137). Philadelphia: Falmer Press.

Richelle, M. N. (1993). *B. F. Skinner: A Reappraisal*. London: Erlbaum.

Robertson, T. S. (1967). The process of innovation and the diffusion of innovation. *Journal of Marketing, 31*, 14–19.

Robertson, T. S. (1971). *Innovative Behavior and Communication*. New York: Holt, Rinehart and Winston.

Robertson, T. S., and Gatignon, H. (1986). Competitive effects on technology diffusion. *Journal of Marketing, 50*, 1–12.

Rogers, E. M. (1983). *Diffusion of Innovations*. New York: Free Press.

Rosenberg, A. (1976). *Microeconomic Laws: A philosophical analysis*. Pittsburgh, PA: Pittsburgh University Press.

Rosenberg, A. (1988). *Philosophy of Social Science*. Oxford: Clarendon.

Roth, T. P. (1988). *The Present State of Consumer Theory*. Lanham, MD: University Press of America.

Rothschild, M. L., and Gaidis, W. C. (1981). Behavioral learning theory: Its relevance to marketing and promotions. *Journal of Marketing, 45*, 70–78.

Runnion, A., Watson, J. D., and McWhorter, J. (1978). Energy savings in interstate transportation through feedback and reinforcement. *Journal of Organizational Behavior Management, 1*, 180–191.

Russell, J. A., and Mehrabian, A. (1976). Environmental variables in consumer research. *Journal of Consumer Research, 3*, 62–63.

Ryle, G. (1968). Thinking and reflecting. In *The Human Agent* (Royal Institute of Philosophy Lectures 1966–1967) (pp. 227–244). London: Macmillan.

Ryle, G. (1971). The thinker of thoughts. In *Collected Papers*, Vol. 2 (pp. 480–496). London: Hutchinson.

Sasser, W. E., Olsen, R. P., and Wyckoff, D. D. (1978). *The Management of Service Operations: Text, Cases, and Readings*. Boston: Allyn and Bacon.

Schafer, R. (1980). Action and narrative in psychoanalysis. *New Literary History, 12*, 18–30.

Schutz, A. (1962). *Collected Papers*. The Hague: Martinus Nijhoff.

Schwartz, B. (1989). *Psychology of Learning and Behavior*. 3rd ed. New York: Norton.

Schwartz, B., and Lacey, H. M. (1982). *Behaviorism, Science and Human Nature*. New York: Norton.

Schwartz, B., and Lacey, H. M. (1988). What applied studies of human operant conditioning tell us about humans and about operant conditioning. In G. C. L. Davey and C. Cullen (Eds.), *Human Operant Conditioning and Behavior Modification* (pp. 27–42). New York: Wiley.

Schwartz, I. S. (1991). The study of consumer behavior and social validity: An essential partnership for applied behavior analysis. *Journal of Applied Behavior Analysis, 24*, 241–244.

Seaver, W. B., and Patterson, A. H. (1976). Decreasing fuel oil consumption through feedback and social commendation. *Journal of Applied Behavior Analysis, 9*, 147–152.

Sharpe, R. (1988). Mirrors, lamps, organisms and texts. In P. Clarke and C. Wright (Eds.), *Mind, Psychoanalysis and Science* (pp. 187–201). Oxford: Blackwell.

Sherry, J. F. (1991). Postmodern alternatives: The interpretive turn in consumer research. In T. S. Robertson and H. H. (Eds.), *Handbook of Consumer Behavior* (pp. 548–591). Englewood Cliffs, NJ: Prentice-Hall.

Siegal, H. (1988). Relativism for consumer research? (Comments on Anderson). *Journal of Consumer Research, 15*, 129–132.

Sigurdsson, V., Saevarsson, H. and Foxall, G. R. 2009. Brand-placement and consumer choice: an in-store experiment, *Journal of Applied Behavior Analysis*, in press.

Skinner, B. F. (1938). *The Behavior of Organisms*. New York: Appleton-Century-Croft.

Skinner, B. F. (1945). The operational analysis of psychological terms. *Psychological Review*, 52, 270–277 and 291–294.

Skinner. B. F. (1947). Experimental psychology. In W. Dennis (Ed.), *Current Trends in Psychology* (pp. 16–49). Pittsburgh, PA: University of Pittsburgh Press.

Skinner, B. F. (1950). Are theories of learning necessary? *Psychological Review*, 57, 193–216.

Skinner, B. F. (1953). *Science and Human Behavior*. New York: Free Press.

Skinner, B. F. (1956). A case history in scientific method. *American Psychologist*, 32, 221–233.

Skinner, B. F. (1957a). The design of cultures. *Daedalus*, 90, 534–546.

Skinner, B. F. (1957b). *Verbal Behavior*. New York: Appleton-Century-Crofts.

Skinner, B. F. (1963, May 31). Behaviorism at fifty. *Science*, 140, 951–959.

Skinner, B. F. (1969). *Contingencies of Reinforcement: A Theoretical Analysis*. Englewood Cliffs, NJ: Prentice-Hall.

Skinner, B. F. (1971). *Beyond Freedom and Dignity*. New York: Knopf.

Skinner, B. F. (1973). Answers for my critics. In H. Wheeler (Ed.), *Beyond the Punitive Society. Operant Conditioning: Social and Political Aspects* (pp. 256–266). London: Wildwood.

Skinner, B. F. (1974). *About Behaviorism*. New York: Knopf.

Skinner, B. F. (1975). The steep and thorny way to a science of behavior. In R. Harré (Ed.), *Problems of Scientific Revolution: Progress and Obstacles to Progress in the Sciences* (pp. 58–71). Oxford: Clarendon Press.

Skinner, B. F. (1976). *Particulars of My Life*. New York: Knopf.

Skinner, B. F. (1977). Why I am not a cognitive psychologist. *Behaviorism, 5*, 1–10.

Skinner, B. F. (1979). *The Shaping of a Behaviorist*. New York: New York University Press.

Skinner, B. F. (1981, July 31). Selection by consequences. *Science, 213*, 501–504.

Skinner, B. F. (1983). Can the experimental analysis of behavior rescue psychology? *The Behavior Analyst, 6*, 9–17.

Skinner, B. F. (1985). Cognitive science and behaviorism. *British Journal of Psychology, 76*, 291–301.

Skinner, B. F (1986). What is wrong with daily life in the modern world? *American Psychologist, 41*, 569–574.

Skinner, B. F. (1988a). Comment on "B. F. Skinner's theorizing." In A. C. Catania and S. Harnad (Eds.), *The Selection of Behavior. The Operant Behaviorism of B. F. Skinner: Comments and Consequences* (pp. 207–208). New York: Cambridge University Press.

Skinner, B. F. (1988b). Comment on "Is Behaviorism Vacuous?" In A. C. Catania and S. Harnad (Eds.), *The Selection of Behavior. The Operant Behaviorism of B. F. Skinner: Comments and Consequences* (pp. 364–365). New York: Cambridge University Press.

Skinner, B. F. (1988c). Methods and theories in the experimental analysis of behavior. In A. C. Catania and S. Harnad (Eds.), *The Selection of Behavior: The Operant Behaviorism of B. F. Skinner. Comments and Consequences* (pp. 77–105). New York: Cambridge University Press.

Smith, L. D. (1986). *Behaviorism and Logical Positivism: A Reassessment of the Alliance*. Stanford, CA: Stanford University Press.

Sober, E. (1993). *Philosophy of Biology*. New York: Oxford University Press.

Sommer, R. (1970). *Tight Spaces: Hard Architecture and How to Harmonize It.* Englewood Cliffs, NJ: Prentice-Hall.

Srivastava, R. K. (1985). A multiattribute diffusion model for adoption of investment alternatives for consumers. *Technological Forecasting and Social Change, 28,* 325–333.

Staats, A. W. (1975). *Social Behaviorism.* Homewood, IL: Dorsey.

Staddon, J. E. R. (1993). *Behaviorism.* London: Duckworth.

Stalker, D., and Ziff, P. (1988). Skinner's theorizing. In A. C. Catania and S. Harnad (Eds.), *The Selection of Behavior: The Operant Behaviorism of B. F. Skinner. Comments and Consequences* (pp. 206–207). New York: Cambridge University Press.

Stevenson, L. (1974). *Seven Theories of Human Nature.* Oxford: Oxford University Press.

Stolorow, R. D., Brandchaft, B., and Atwood, G. E. (1987). *Psychoanalytical Treatment: An Intersubjective Approach.* Hillsdale, NJ: Analytic Press.

Studer, R. G. (1989). Man-environment relations: Discovery or design? In W. F. E. Preiser (Ed.), *Environmental Design Research,* Vol. 2. (pp. 136–151). Stroudsburg, PA: Dowden, Hutchinson and Ross.

Tarr, D. G. (1976). Experiments in token economies: A review of the evidence relating to assumptions and implications of economic theory. *Southern Economic Journal, 43,* 1136–1143.

Taylor, C. (1977). Interpretation and the sciences of man. In F. Dallmayr and T. McCarthy (Eds.), *Understanding and Social Inquiry* (pp. 101–131). South Bend, IN: University of Notre Dame.

Taylor, J. W. (1977). A striking characteristic of innovators. *Journal of Marketing, 14,* 104–107.

Troye, S. V. (1985). Situationist theory and consumer behavior. *Research in Consumer Behavior, 1,* 285–321.

Tunstall, J., and Walker, D. (1981). *Media Made in California.* New York: Oxford University Press.

Valentine, E. R. (1992). *Conceptual Issues in Psychology.* 2nd. ed. London: Routledge.

van Parijs, P. (1981). *Evolutionary Explanation in the Social Sciences: An Emerging Paradigm.* Totowa, NJ: Rowman and Littlefield.

Vargas, J. S. (1990). B. F. Skinner—the last few days. *Journal of Applied Behavior Analysis, 23,* 409–410.

Vaughan, M. (1987). Rule-governed behavior and higher mental processes. In S. Modgil and C. Modgil (Eds.), *B. F. Skinner: Consensus and Controversy* (pp. 257–264). Philadelphia: Falmer.

Vaughn, M. (1989). Rule-governed behavior in behavior analysis: A theoretical and experimental history. In S. C. Hayes (Ed.), *Rule-governed Behavior: Cognition, Contingencies and Instructional Control* (pp. 97–116). New York and London: Plenum.

Viner, J. (1925). The utility concept in value theory and its critics. *Journal of Political Economy, 33,* 369–387.

Wahlund, R., and Wärneryd, K.-E. (1987). Aggregate saving and the saving behavior of saver groups. *Skandinaviska Enskilda Banken Quarterly Review, 3,* 52–64.

Wärneryd, K.-E. (1989a). Improving psychological theory through studies of economic behavior: The case of saving. *Applied Psychology: An International Review, 38,* 213–236.

Wärneryd, K.-E. (1989b). On the psychology of saving: An essay on economic behavior. *Journal of Economic Psychology, 10,* 515–541.

Watson, J. B. (1913). Psychology as the behaviorist views it. *Psychological Review, 20,* 158–177.

Wearden, J. H. (1988). Some neglected problems in the analysis of human operant behavior. In G. Davey and C. Cullen (Eds.), *Human Operant Conditioning and Behavior Modification*. New York: Wiley.

Wearden, J. H., and Shimp, C. P. (1985). Local temporal patterning of operant behavior in humans. *Journal of the Experimental Analysis of Behavior, 44,* 315–324.

Webster, F. E. (1992). The changing role of marketing in the corporation. *Journal of Marketing, 56,* 1–17.

Wessells, M. G. (1981). A critique of Skinner's views on the explanatory adequacy of cognitive theories. *Behaviorism, 9,* 153–170.

Whaley, D. L., and Malott, R. W. (1971). *Elementary Principles of Behavior.* New York: Appleton-Century-Crofts.

Wicker, A. W. (1979). *An Introduction to Ecological Psychology.* Cambridge: Cambridge University Press.

Wicker, A. W. (1987). Behavior settings reconsidered: Temporal stages, resources, internal dynamics, context. In D. Stokols and I. Altman (Eds.), *Handbook of Environmental Psychology* (pp. 613–653). New York: John Wiley and Sons.

Wicker, A. W., and Kirmeyer, S. (1977). From church to laboratory to national park: A program of research on excess and insufficient populations in behavior settings. In D. Stokols ('Ed.), *Perspectives on Environment and Behavior: Theory, Research and Applications* (pp. 69–96). New York: Plenum.

Williamson, O. E. (1975). *Markets and Hierarchies: Analysis and antitrust implications.* New York: Free Press.

Williamson, O. E. (1985). *The economic institutions of capitalism.* New York: Free Press.

Winett, R. A. (1977). Prompting turning off lights in unoccupied rooms. *Journal of Environmental Systems, 6,* 237–241.

Winett, R. A., Neale, M. S., and Grier, H. C. (1979). The effects of self-monitoring and feedback on residential electricity consumption. *Journal of Applied Behavior Analysis, 12,* 73–84.

Winett, R. A., Kaiser, S., and Haberkorn, G. (1977). The effects of monetary rebates and feedback on electricity conservation. *Journal of Environmental Systems, 6,* 329–341.

Winkler, R. C. (1980). Behavioral economics, token economies, and applied behavior analysis. In J. E. R. Staddon (Ed.), *Limits to Action: The Allocation of Individual Behavior* (pp. 269–297). New York: Academic Press.

Winkler, R. C., and Winett, R. A. (1982). Behavioral interventions in resource conservation: A systems approach based on behavioral economics. *American Psychologist, 37,* 421–435.

Witmer, J. F., and Geller, E. S. (1976). Facilitating paper recycling: Effects of prompts, raffles, and contests. *Journal of Applied Behavior Analysis, 9,* 315–322.

Wolpert, L. (1992). *The Unnatural Nature of Science.* London: Faber and Faber.

Zettle, R. D., and Hayes, S. C. (1982). Rule-governed behavior: A potential framework for cognitive-behavioral therapy. In P. C. Kendall (Ed.), *Advances in Cognitive-behavioral Research and Therapy*, Vol. 1 (pp. 73–117). New York: Academic Press.

Ziman, J. M. (1978). *Reliable Knowledge.* Cambridge: Cambridge University Press.

Zuriff, G. E. (1979). Ten inner causes. *Behaviorism, 7,* 1–8.

Zuriff, G. E. (1985). *Behaviorism: A Conceptual Reconstruction.* New York: Columbia University Press.

Index

A

Accomplishment, 11–12, 97–102, 114
  in closed settings, 117–8
  in open settings, 115–7
  private transport as, 139–41
  social de-marketing, 144
accumulation, 12, 97–102, 114
  in closed settings, 122–24
  in open settings, 121–22
  social de-marketing, 146
  waste disposal as 142–44
Ajzen, I., 92, 93, 95
Alhadeff, D. A., 25, 72, 101
Allison, J., 24
Anderson, P. F., 157
applied behavior analysis, 87–90, 91
Archer, D., 137
Arntzen, E., 162
Aronson, E., 137
Attwood, G. E., 46
Ayer, A. J., 39, 58, 158, 159

B

Baars, B. J., 48
Baer, D. M., 105, 106
Bagozzi, R. P., 80, 92
Bagshaw, M., 75
Bandura, A., 35, 48, 70, 131
Barker, R., 71–2
Baron, A., 72, 73
Barnes-Holmes, D., 25
Barry, A., 73
Basman, R. L., 86
Battalio, R. C., 86
Baum, W., 60, 80, 154
behavior analysis, 20–22
  critique of, 33–37
  interpretation in, 28–32,
behavior settings, 71–2

scope of consumer behavior setting,
  77–8, 92, 150–1
Behavioral Perspective Model (BPM)
  passim
and interpretation, 22–28, 92–112
and marketing, 22–23
and radical behaviorism, 22–28
as interpretive model, Chapter 5
basics, 4–5
behavior in, 93
behavior setting, 5–6
classes of consumer behavior, 11–12,
  95–9, 113–5
consumer behavior setting, 5–6
  accessibility of reinforcement, 5–6, 92
    for accomplishment in closed
      settings, 118
    for accomplishment in open set-
      tings, 117
    for accumulation in closed set-
      tings, 123–4
    for accumulation in open set-
      tings, 122
    for hedonism in closed settings,
      121
    for hedonism in open settings, 120
    for maintenance in closed set-
      tings, 126
    for maintenance in open set-
      tings, 124–5
  degree of external control, 5–6, 92
    for accomplishment in closed
      settings, 118
    for accomplishment in open set-
      tings, 117
    for accumulation in closed set-
      tings, 123–4
    for accumulation in open set-
      tings, 122

for hedonism in closed settings, 121
for hedonism in open settings 120
for maintenance in closed settings 126
for maintenance in open settings 124–5
consumer situation 8–9, 91–5, 99–102, 150
specifiable vs unspecifiable, 151
contingency categories 98–102, 113
defined, 10–12
contingency matrix, 10
in saving and financial asset management, 127
contribution to marketing, 22–3
dependent variable, 5
empirical evidence, 84–90
informational reinforcement in, 6–8
model of the consumer situation, 76–83
operational measurement, 84–90
outline, 4–12
rate of consumer behavior, 5
situational analysis, 10
summative depiction, 9
testing hypotheses in, 94–5
three—term contingency, 4–5
utilitarian reinforcement in, 6–8.
See also BPM interpretation of consumer behavior
Bell, S., 79
Berger, P., 44, 46, 113, 148, 157
Bethlehem, D., 30, 62
Betti, E., 43
Betzig, L., 30
Bjork, D. W., 50, 57, 58
Black, R. D., 79
Blackman, D. E., 50, 61
Boden, M., 41
BPM interpretation of consumer behavior
bifurcation of reinforcement, 75–6
consumer situation, 6–8, 150
environmental discontinuity, 68–72
evaluation of, 154–60
in action, 102–112
accomplishment: large group awareness training, 103–6
hedonism: the managed restaurant experience, 106–8
accumulation: frequent flyer programs, 108–110
maintenance: the design o\f airport waiting, 110–112

levels of, 95–102
consumer situation, 99–102
contingency category, 98–112
operant class, 95–8
pattern of reinforcement in, 101
nature of, Chapter 7
pragmatism in, 154–60
problem of discontinuity, 66–7
problem of elusiveness, 68–9
problem of verbal behavior, 73–5
role of behavior setting scope in, 69–72
rule-governed behavior, 80–83
situational analysis, 10
situational discontinuity, 68–72, 101–2
speciational discontinuity, 72–6, 101–2, 150. *See also* operant interpretation of consumer behavior; radical behaviorism, interpretation
BPM research program, 1–3
and radical behaviorism, 13
phases, 2
Brandschaft, B., 46
Bridgman, P., 39, 50, 57
Brownstein, A., 74
Buskist, W. F., 73

C
Catania, A. C., 31, 61, 69, 74, 159
Chalmers, A. F., 41
Chase, P. N., 47, 61
Chinsky, J. M., 104, 105
Chomsky, N., 21, 27
Churchland, P. S., 59
classes of consumer behavior. *See* Behavioral Perspective Model
cognitive psychology, 47–9
communication of innovation, 129–34
adopter categories, 130
categories of later adopters, 133–4
initial versus later adopters, 129–30
learning history, 131–2
pattern of reinforcement, 131
state and setting variables, 132–3
Cone, J. D., 80, 88, 134–45
Connolly, J., 43
consumer behavior, *passim*
ecologically-impacting, 87–90
meaning of, Chapter 4
Consumer Behavior Analysis: Critical Perspectives in Business and Management 3
consumer behavior setting, 150
accomplishment in, 116–8

accumulation in, 122–124
hedonism in, 119–121
maintenance in, 124–126
consumer behavior setting scope, 150–151
defined, 5–6,
Consumer Psychology in Behavioral Perspective, 3, 19, 162
Consumers in Context: The BPM Research Program 3, 161
consumer situation, 8–10, 150
Context and Cognition: The Interpretation of Complex Behavior , 3
contingencies of survival, 31
contingency categories. *See* Behavioral Perspective Model
continuous reinforcement (CRF), 73, 119, 124
Costanzo, M., 137
Crick, F., 41
critical relativism, 38–41
Cullen, C., 72, 73
Currie, G., 45

D
Davey, G., 72, 73
Dawkins, R., 30, 31, 32, 38
Day, W., 60
Delprato, D. J., 52–6
Dennett. D. C., 48, 152
Dewey, J., 46
Dilthey, W., 43, 45
domestic energy consumption, as hedonism, 141–2
domestic water consumption, as maintenance, 144–5
Donovan, R. J., 93
Dosi, G., 32
Dowling, G. R., 132
Dulany, D. E., 92

E
Ehrenberg, A. S. C., 15, 41, 45, 111
Eliott, T. S., 13
environment-impacting consumer behavior, 134–47
applied behavioral research, 134–8
BPM contribution, 138–9
domestic energy consumption as hedonism, 141–2
domestic water consumption as maintenance, 144–5
general propositions, 139
private transport as accomplishment, 139–41
social de-marketing, 145–7

waste disposal as accumulation, 142–44
epistemological anarchy, 38–41
Evans, A., 60
Everett, P. B., 80, 88, 134
evolutionary analog
in behavior analysis, 30–32
experimental analysis of behavior, 50
components, 50–2
Explaining Consumer Choice 3, 15, 161

F
Fagerstrøm, A., 162
feedback, 89–90
Feyerabend, P., 21, 25, 38, 44
Finkelstein, P., 103–6
Fishbein, M., 92, 93
Fisher, E. B., 86
Fisher, J. D., 104, 105
fitness, 31
fixed interval schedule (FI), 11–12, 73, 98, 115, 121, 124, 125, 126
fixed ratio schedule (FR), 11–12, 73, 98, 115, 142
Fliess, W., 91
Føllesdal, D., 45
Foxall, G. R., *passim*
Freud, S., 91
Fulfillment, 10–12
Functional reinforcement, *see* Utilitarian reinforcement

G
Gadamer, H.-G., 43
Galizio, M., 72
Garcia, J., 157
Garcia, M., 74
Gatignon, H., 131–33
Gay, P., 48
Geertz, C., 43, 62, 63, 68, 76, 151–2
Geller, E. S., 80, 88, 134–45
genes, 31
genotype, 31
Goff, B., 104, 105
Goldsmith, T. H., 30
Gould, J., 79
Grant, L., 60
Green, K. F., 157
Greenley, G. E., 161
Greenway, D. E., 74
Griffin, J., 79

H
Haas, J. A., 74
Habermas, J., 45
Hackenberg, T. D., 87

Harnad, S., 31
Harré, R., 44, 46
Harzem, P., 75
Hayes, L. J., 47, 61, 80
Hayes, S. C., 25, 39, 47, 61, 74, 88,
    134–45
hedonic consumption, 81–2
hedonism, 12, 97–102, 114
    domestic energy consumption as,
        141–2
    in closed settings, 120–121
    in open settings, 118–120
    social de-marketing, 146
Hempel, C. G., 42
hermeneutics, 18, 43–4
    and scientific method, 44–47
Herrnstein, R. J., 25
Hirsh, D., 46
Hirschman, E., 79, 81
Holbrook, M., 79, 81
Horne, P. J., 26, 74, 75
Howard, J. A., 116
Hudson, L. A., 47
Hunt, S., 39, 44, 49
Hursh, S., 24
hypothesis testing, 94–5

I
Incentives, 88–90
inescapable entertainment, 10–12
informational (symbolic) reinforcement,
    6–8, 78–80, 93–4, 150
    feedback as, 89–90
intentional behaviorism, 14
interpretation
    in BPM *passim*, 1720
    in radical behaviorism, 1
Iwata, B. A., 94

J
James, V. K., 16,
James, W., 154

K
Kagel, J. H., 86
Katona, G., 126, 128
Kazdin, A. E., 85, 87
Kellner, H., 44, 46, 113, 148, 157
Keutner, T., 43
Klar, Y., 104, 105
Kline, P., 45, 46, 61
Koch, S., 58
Kolakowsky, L., 42
Kolb, W. L., 79

Krasner, L., 85, 86
Krasner, M., 85
Kuhn, T. S., 24, 41

L
Lacey, H., 35, 42, 67, 69, 70, 73, 92
Laudan, L., 38
Lea, S. E. G., 24, 84
Leahey, T. H., 48
learning history, 92–3, 101–2, 151
    operational measurement, 92–3
Lee, V. L., 24 34 35, 42, 70, 76, 100
Lejeune, H., 61
Lieberman, D. A., 61
Lindqvist, A., 127, 128, 129
Lowe, C. F., 26, 74, 75

M
MacDonald, G., 43
Mach, E., 39, 50, 57, 154. *See also*
    Positivism, Machian
maintenance, 12, 97–102, 115,
    domestic water consumption as,
        144–5
    in closed settings, 125–26
    in open settings, 124–25
    social de-marketing, 146–7
Malott, R. W., 70, 72, 74
mandatory purchasing and consump-
    tion, 10–12
Mandler, G., 48
marketing, 1–25 *passim*, 33, 48–50, 75,
    80, 94–5, 123–9,
    BPM interpretations of, 102–12
    contribution of BPM to, 22–23,
        135–6, 149, 154–6
    social, 134–47
    social de-, 145–7
Matthews, B. A., 69, 74
Mayr, E., 30
McGowan, B. K., 157
McKenzie, B., 30, 58, 66
Mehrabian, A., 93
Menger, C., 79
methodological pluralism, 14, 21, 40,
    41–44
Midgley, B. D., 52–6
Midgley, D., 130–33
Miller, G. A., 72
Miller, H. L., 73
Moore, J., 58, 59
Morgan, D., 73
Morris, E. K., 60, 61
Morse, W. H., 72

N

Natural selection, 31–2

O

Olsen, R. P., 106–8
Oliveira-Castro, J. M., 15, 162
operant behaviorism, 51
operant conditioning, 31–2 50–2
operant interpretation of consumer
    behavior *see* BPM interpretation
    of consumer behavior
Orsenigo, L., 32
O'Shaughnessy, J., 41, 79, 84
Osmond, H., 111
Ozanne, J. L., 47

P

Page, T. J., 94
Parfitt, D., 79
Parrott, L. J., 61
pattern of reinforcement 8, 73, 101
    in communication of innovation, 131
Perone, M., 72, 73
Peter, J. P., 156
Pettigrew, T., 137
Pettit, P., 43
Phenotype, 31
Phillips, D. C., 41, 42, 43, 44, 45 46, 59
plausibility
    of radical behaviorist interpretation,
        29–30
Polkinghorne, J. C., 41, 50
popular entertainment, 10–12
positivism
    logical, 38–43, 47–49
    Machian, 27, 49, 57–60, 158–9
    place for, 47–9
Poppen, R. L., 80, 83
Popper, K., 45, 157
post-positivism, 43–4
pragmatism
    of BPM interpretation, 154–6
    radical behaviorism, 60–2
private transport as accomplishment,
    139–41
Proctor, R. W., 30, 66

R

Rabinow, P., 43
Rachlin, H., 25, 69
radical behaviorism, 50–2
    behavior as subject matter, 53
    consequential causality, 56
    determinism, 55

epistemology, 49–56
essence, 51
functional analysis, 54–5
generality of behavioral principles, 56
interpretation *passim*, 61–3, Chapter
    4
locus of behavioral control, 53
methodology, 49–56
ontology, 50–54
operant behavior, 55
organism as locus of biological
    change, 55–6
pragmatism as criterion of truth,
    60–61
reductionism, 56–7
respondent behavior, 55
science and, 49–56
    materialism, 54
    metascience in, 49–56
    purpose of science in, 54
    stimulus control in, 53–4
rate of consumer response, 5
radical behaviorism, 13 14
    and the BPM, 22–28
    explanatory mode, 22–28
reinforcement
    back-up, 84–7
    bifurcation of, 6–8, 75–6
    informational, defined, 6–8
    relative potential strength of, 101
    tokens as generalized conditioned, 85
    utilitarian defined, 6–8
*Reward, Emotion, and Choice: From
    Neuroeconomics to Neurophi-
    losophy* 3
Richelle, M. N., 32, 67
Rhinehart, L., 104
Robertson, T. S., 131–33
Roche, B., 25
Rogers, E. M., 130–33
Rosenberg, A., 41
Rossiter, J. R., 93
routine purchasing, 10–12
rule-governed consumer behavior,
    80–83
    congruent, 83
    contrant, 83
    in token economy, 85–7
    pliance, 82–3, 85
    ply, 82–3
    track, 82–3
    tracking, 82–3
Russell, J. A., 93
Ryle, G., 62, 63, 68, 151, 152

S

Saevarsson, H., 162
Sasser, W. E., 106–8
saving
    and collecting, 10–12
    and financial asset management,
        126–9
schedules of reinforcement
    and classes of consumer behavior,
        11–12,
    and patterns of reinforcement, 73, 98
    defined, 73
Schrezenmaier, T. C., 16, 162
Schutz, A., 43
Schwartz, B., 42, 67, 69, 70, 92, 137
Secord, P. F., 44, 46
selection by consequences, 30, 31, 52
Sharpe, R., 46
Shimoff, E., 69, 74
Shimp, C. P., 75
Sigurdsson, V., 162
Silver, R. C., 104, 105
single-subject research strategy, 50
Skinner, B. F., *passim*
Smith, L. D., 27, 30, 52, 59
Sober, E., 41
social de-marketing, 145–7
    accomplishment, 145
    accumulation, 146
    hedonism, 146
    maintenance, 146–7
Sommer, R., 110–12
St. Augustine, 91
Staats, A., 48
Stalker, D., 34
status consumption, 10–12
Steiner, G., 64
Stevenson, L., 157
Stolorov, R. D., 46
Stolz, S. B., 105, 106
Sullivàn, P., 43
super-personal cognitive psychology,
    14
symbolic reinforcement, *see* Informa-
    tional reinforcement

T

Tarpy, R. M., 84
Tarr, D. G., 86
Taylor, C., 43
*The Behavioral Economics of Con-
    sumer Brand Choice*, 3
The Marketing Firm, 3
thick description, 62–3, 94–5, 100,
    151–153

thin description, 62–3, 94–5, 100,
    151–153
three—term contingency, 51, 65, 76–7,
    150
    basis of BPM, 4–5
token economy, 84–7, 91

U

Understanding Consumer Choice 3, 161
Utilitarian (functional) reinforcement,
    6–8, 78–80, 93–4, 150
    incentives as, 88–90
utility theory, 79

V

Valentine, E. R., 25
van Parijs, P., 32
Vargas, J. S., 48
variable interval schedule (VI), 11–12,
        73, 75, 98, 114, 120, 124, 141
variable person schedue (VP), 141
variable ratio schedule (VR), 11–12, 73,
        75, 98, 114, 115–16, 141
variation, 31
Vaughan, M., 20
Verstehen, 41
Viner. J., 79

W

Warrant of assertibility, 46
waste disposal as accumulation, 142–44
Webley, P., 84
Wyckoff, D. D., 106–8
Wärneryd, K.-E., 126–9
Watson, J. B., 53
Wearden, J. H., 75, 76
Weeks, J. D., 30, 66
Wenegrat, B., 103–6
Wessells, J., 21
Whaley, D. L., 72
Wicker, A. W., 69, 71–2
Wiener, N., 13
Winett, R. A., 80, 88, 134, 137
Winkler, R. C., 85, 86, 137
Wolpert, L., 41, 46, 113

Y

Yalon, I., 103–6
Yani-de-Soriano, M., 161

Z

Ziff, P., 34
Ziman, J. M., 41
Zuriff, E. A., 20, 35, 39, 42, 51, 57,
        60, 61